The Cambridge Shakes

Are you studying Shakespeare a
characters and interpretations? O
essential background on the Shak   ..age? Ideal for
students and theatre enthusiasts al   .. authoritative guide
presents key information, clearly set   ., on all Shakespeare's dramatic and
poetic works, covering plots and people, sources, context, performance
history and major themes. Ordered alphabetically for easy reference, each
play entry features a 'key facts' box providing informative and revealing
statistics, including a breakdown of each play's major roles. The guide is
illustrated with striking performance photographs throughout, and also
provides brief accounts of Shakespeare's life and language, Shakespeare in
print and theatre in Shakespeare's time. This is an indispensable reference
source for all students and theatregoers.

Emma Smith is Fellow and Tutor in English at Hertford College, University of
Oxford. She has published a wide range of books and articles on
Shakespeare and Renaissance drama, including *The Cambridge Introduction
to Shakespeare* (2007).

The Cambridge
Shakespeare Guide

EMMA SMITH

CAMBRIDGE
UNIVERSITY PRESS

CAMBRIDGE UNIVERSITY PRESS
Cambridge, New York, Melbourne, Madrid, Cape Town,
Singapore, São Paulo, Delhi, Tokyo, Mexico City

Cambridge University Press
The Edinburgh Building, Cambridge CB2 8RU, UK

Published in the United States of America by Cambridge University Press, New York

www.cambridge.org
Information on this title: www.cambridge.org/9780521149723

© Cambridge University Press 2012

First published 2012

Printed in the United Kingdom at the University Press, Cambridge

A catalogue record for this publication is available from the British Library

Library of Congress Cataloguing in Publication data
Smith, Emma (Emma Josephine)
The Cambridge Shakespeare guide / Emma Smith.
    p.   cm.
Includes bibliographical references and index.
ISBN 978-0-521-19523-2 – ISBN 978-0-521-14972-3 (pbk.)
1. Shakespeare, William, 1564–1616 – Handbooks, manuals, etc.   2. Shakespeare,
William, 1564–1616 – Stories, plots, etc.   I. Title.
PR2987.S75   2012
822.3′3–dc23   2011035586

ISBN 978 0 521 19523 2 Hardback
ISBN 978 0 521 14972 3 Paperback

Contents

Illustrations

Acknowledgements

I am grateful to Katherine Duncan-Jones, and to Sarah Stanton, Rebecca Taylor and the anonymous reader at Cambridge University Press for their comments and corrections. Thanks are also due to Geraint Lewis for his wonderful production photographs.

All Shakespeare quotations and the spelling of characters' names are taken from the relevant volume of the New Cambridge Shakespeare under the general editorship of Brian Gibbons.

The Key Facts are taken from *The RSC Shakespeare: The Complete Works* edited by Jonathan Bate and Eric Rasmussen (2007), published by Modern Library, an imprint of Random House Publishing Group, a division of Random House, Inc., New York. Reproduced with permission from Palgrave Macmillan.

THE WORKS

All's Well that Ends Well

Key Facts

Date: 1604–5

Length: 3,075 lines

Verse: 55% / Prose: 45%

Major characters' share of lines:

Helena	16%
Parolles	13%
King	13%
Countess	10%
Bertram	9%

Unsettling romantic comedy which poses the question, is all well that ends well?

Plot and characters

Helena (or Helen), daughter of a recently deceased physician, is in love with **Bertram**, Count of Roussillon, whose father has also just died, making him a ward of the **King of France**. While his mother, the **Countess**, is sympathetic to her affections, Bertram is not. Bertram attends the King at court, accompanied by the Countess's friend **Lafew**. In exchanges with the clown, **Lavatch**, the Countess comments on the unfolding plot at a distance. The King has been suffering from a terminal illness that baffles all of his doctors. Helena, armed with her father's prescriptions, persuades him to try her remedy, on condition that she be given the husband of her choice if she is successful. On his recovery, the King agrees to her request to marry Bertram. Bertram himself is horrified by the prospect of marrying so ignobly, but is forced, unwillingly, to accede. He immediately leaves Helena to go off to war with his braggart companion **Parolles**. Bertram's letter to her refuses to recognise the marriage until she has the ring from his finger and a child of his body. Helena is undeterred. Under cover of going to Santiago de Compostela on pilgrimage, she follows Bertram and learns that he is attempting to seduce **Diana**. She arranges with the **Widow**, Diana's mother, that, unbeknownst to Bertram, she will herself substitute for Diana in a bed trick, and Diana arranges the assignation with the ardent Bertram. Meanwhile, Parolles' cowardice is revealed when he is tricked by the **Lords of Dumaine** and other soldiers, speaking a comic nonsense language, into believing he has been captured by the enemy. It is announced that Helena is dead and Lafew and the Countess plan for Bertram to marry Lafew's daughter. Lafew agrees to employ the disgraced Parolles as a fool. Bertram returns and agrees to the new marriage, producing an engagement ring which the King recognises as one he gave to Helena. Bertram cannot explain how he got this ring, and is arrested on suspicion of killing Helena. A letter arrives from Diana claiming that Bertram had seduced her on the promise of marrying her on Helena's death, and the Widow and Diana arrive at court to confront him. Eventually Helena is brought in to explain, and Bertram has to accept that, since she has got his ring and says she is pregnant with his child, he must acknowledge her as his wife.

Context and composition

The play shares linguistic patterns, particularly vocabulary, with *Othello*, *Measure for Measure* and *Troilus and Cressida*, and was probably written around 1604–5. Along with *Measure* and *Troilus* (and, more rarely, *Hamlet*) it is often identified as a so-called 'problem play', and it shares its sexualised plot culminating in a bed trick with *Measure*, its cynicism about war and male camaraderie with *Troilus*, and its defiantly anti-heroic presentation of its characters with both plays. There have also been suggestions of a later composition date of 1607–8, which would place the play between the romantic comedies and the late plays (*Pericles*, *Tempest*, *Winter's Tale*) with which it also shares some of its fairy-tale plot elements. It was first printed in the First Folio of 1623. Shakespeare's source for the play is a story from the Italian collection of novellas, Giovanni Boccaccio's *Decameron* – via a sixteenth-century English translation. His major additions to the source are the comic roles: the clown Lavatch and Parolles, who has something of Falstaff's boastfulness (see *Henry IV* parts 1 and 2).

One notable – and audible – feature of *All's Well* is its frequent use of rhyme – as in Helena's interview with the King in Act 2 – alongside other formal moments such as her letter in the form of a sonnet. This artificiality contrasts effectively with the cynicism of the play-world and its characters, as its attempts at make-believe idealisation – the King's miraculous cure, the winning of a mate through cleverness – are repeatedly undercut by the seedy realities of human motivation.

Performances

We have no details of any early performances – and indeed, there are confusions in the Folio text which have led some scholars to propose it was not actually performed in the early modern period. The play was little revived over the intervening centuries, although the trick played on Parolles was popular during the eighteenth century At the beginning of the twentieth century George Bernard Shaw identified it as a play which had found its time alongside the dark, unflinching work of Ibsen, but it has struggled to establish itself in the repertoire. Subsequent revivals followed Shaw in stressing the play's uncomfortable modernity, often through contemporary dress, such as Barry Jackson's 1927 production with a young Olivier as Parolles. More recently the play has achieved stage success where its combination of artificiality and realism has been acknowledged. Trevor Nunn's 1981 Edwardian production, for example, with Peggy Ashcroft as the Countess, Harriet Walter as Helena and Mike Gwilym as Bertram was praised by one newspaper reviewer for keeping 'the balance between comic hoopla and emotional pain' by 'putting real, suffering people into an unreal situation'. Marianne Elliott's National Theatre production of 2009 stressed the play as fairy tale with a set out of an illustrated

Grimm, complete with ramparts, wolves and magic lanterns and an indeterminate ending with Helena and Bertram caught momentarily in a freeze-frame wedding photograph. The play has not been directed for cinema, but the BBC Shakespeare included a version directed by Elijah Moshinsky (1981), set entirely indoors with elaborate lighting effects and effective performances from Angela Down, Ian Charleson and Celia Johnson as the Countess.

Themes and interpretation

In showing us an interrupted courtship between young people, overlooked by their elders, *All's Well* bears a superficial resemblance to the romantic comedies which precede it in Shakespeare's writing career. But these formal similarities are often seen to be outweighed by tonal discrepancy: that marriage is so ruthlessly divided here into betrothal, consummation and only reluctant acknowledgement perverts the comic plot. Sex, money, disease and casually ignoble warfare undermine that cheerful disposition we like to associate with the genre of comedy. Much criticism of *All's Well* has tended to boil down to an assessment of its central couple. Is Helena Shakespeare's 'loveliest character' (Coleridge) or 'a keen and unswerving huntress of man' (E. K. Chambers)? Is Bertram, as Dr Johnson felt, a 'coward' and 'profligate', or is he to be pitied for Helena's implacable and unsolicited pursuit? Certainly, Shakespeare has here developed the vigorous comic heroine who actively seeks her own romantic fulfilment – Rosalind in *As You Like It*, Julia in *The Two Gentlemen of Verona* – into an often discomforting character who defies expectations from her first soliloquy, revealing that she is not mourning her father but swooning after Bertram. Bantering with Parolles about the value of virginity, cool and unsentimental in making the arrangements with the Widow, Helena does not admit of the vulnerability or insecurity that might make her more likeable. Her credo of self-sufficiency – 'Our remedies oft in ourselves do lie, / Which we ascribe to heaven' (1.1.187–8) – echoes the radical agency of an Iago (in *Othello*) or Edmund (*King Lear*): and these are not happy role models for a comic heroine.

But nor does Bertram garner audience sympathy: at best he is callow, like *Much Ado*'s Claudio; at worst he is deeply selfish, incapable of empathy, resistant to that impulse towards the re-education of young men that is at the heart of much Shakespearean comedy. If *All's Well* complements *The Taming of the Shrew*, this time offering a pattern of male subjection to female will, its ending is no less problematic than that of the earlier play (the plays are printed consecutively in the First Folio). Bertram's final acceptance of his role as husband begins with a conditional 'If', just as the last iteration of the play's title in its closing lines introduces a note of contingency: 'All yet seems well, and if it end so meet, / The bitter past, more welcome is the sweet' (5.3.322–3). The qualifications deny us a 'happy ever after' resolution to the play's unsettling narrative.

Shakespeare takes a fairy tale here and systematically darkens it. Helena's magical healing of the King partakes of a fantasy world, but it is a miracle she exploits for her own agenda, just as her pilgrimage has distinctly earthly aims. Lafew's remark – 'they say miracles are past, and we have our philosophical persons, to make modern and familiar, things supernatural and causeless' (2.3.1–3) – is typical of the play's knowingness as it deploys an idealised folkloric structure in the shrewd service of human selfishness and need. 'All's well that ends well' seems less the conclusion of a fable and more the amorality of the Renaissance pragmatist Machiavelli, advocating ruthless self-interest at the heart of power politics. 'The web of our life is of a mingled yarn, good and ill together' (4.3.60–1) could seem to stand as an epigraph for the play's own tragi-comic structure, but in context – the Dumaine Lords discussing Helena's 'death' – it, too, is ironised. Helena, like Hero in *Much Ado* before her, and Hermione later in *The Winter's Tale*, returns from this 'death' – the conclusion of a tragedy – and instead claims her comedic marriage promise. But the atmosphere of loss and mourning is never fully dispelled in this bracingly uncomic play.

Antony and Cleopatra

Key Facts
Date: 1606
Length: 3,636 lines
Verse: 95% / Prose: 5%

Major characters' share of lines:

Antony	24%
Cleopatra	19%
Octavius	12%
Enobarbus	10%

Epic, cinematic love tragedy between charismatic central protagonists embodying a geopolitical conflict between two great empires

Plot and characters

The Roman general **Mark Antony** is in love with the Egyptian empress **Cleopatra,** and prefers her company in Alexandria to his political and domestic responsibilities in Rome, much to the disapproval of **Octavius Caesar**, his fellow triumvir (joint ruler). **Enobarbus**, a blunt and loyal soldier, recognises the hold that Cleopatra has on his master. On news of the death of his wife Fulvia, and of trouble with a political rival, **Pompey**, Antony returns to Rome. There he agrees to marry Caesar's sister **Octavia**, in an attempt to renew their political alliance, although a **Soothsayer** warns him to stay away from Caesar. Cleopatra expresses her jealousy when a messenger delivers this unwelcome news. Antony and Caesar agree a peace with Pompey and drink together, but the amity does not last: Antony hears that Caesar has attacked Pompey and deposed the third, weaker triumvir **Lepidus**. He returns to Egypt, sending his wife as an envoy to Caesar. Caesar responds to Antony's departure, and to the news that he and Cleopatra have declared themselves monarchs in Egypt, by declaring war. During the sea battle at Actium, the Egyptian fleet is defeated when Antony leaves the fight to follow Cleopatra's ship. He is wracked with despair at his actions, but is victorious in a second battle. On the eve of the third battle, his soldiers are fearful, and Enobarbus deserts. The Egyptian fleet surrenders to Caesar. At

Antony's fury, Cleopatra retreats to her monument and sends her eunuch **Mardian** to tell Antony she has committed suicide. Antony asks his servant **Eros** to kill him, but Eros kills himself and Antony botches his own suicide. He is taken to Cleopatra's monument to die in her arms. **Dolabella**, one of Caesar's followers, warns Cleopatra that she is to be sent away; with her attendants **Iras** and **Charmian**, Cleopatra prepares for her own death. A darkly comic **Clown** (the title suggests a rustic person, rather than a comedian) brings her a basket of figs with hidden snakes. Dressed in her royal robes, Cleopatra allows the asp to bite her breast: Iras and Charmian die too. Caesar announces that the lovers shall be buried together.

Context and composition

In writing the play, around 1606 (first published in 1623), Shakespeare made extensive use of Sir Thomas North's translation of the ancient Greek biographer Plutarch – *Lives of the Noble Grecians and Romans* (1579) – a book he had already drawn on for the writing of *Julius Caesar*, which introduces Antony and Octavius Caesar, and one he would use again for *Coriolanus*. In some parts of the play – as, for example, Enobarbus' lyrical speech of Cleopatra on her barge – Shakespeare is obviously working directly from the open copy of Plutarch; but elsewhere he introduces new elements including the choric figure of Enobarbus himself and a stronger focus on Cleopatra as equal protagonist (Plutarch's biographies are all of male figures). The play is among Shakespeare's longest, at over 3,500 lines.

It is possible to read *Antony and Cleopatra* as a middle-aged version of the earlier story of tragic youth, *Romeo and Juliet*: in both plays, as in the cynical intervening play named for lovers, *Troilus and Cressida*, the central relationship can never be properly private since it is pressurised by, and in some sense epitomises, the struggle between warring families or rival empires. Like Macbeth, Othello and Coriolanus, Antony is a soldier who does not accommodate himself fully to domesticity; like Tamora in *Titus Andronicus* or Margaret of Anjou in the *King Henry VI* plays, Cleopatra represents an exotic, feminised, external threat. As in the other Roman plays, Rome itself and its definitions are being fought over.

Performances

Shakespeare's great dramaturgical innovation in *Antony and Cleopatra* is the use of short, crosscut scenes to represent the escalating emotional and military conflict, particularly in Act 4 (sixteen scenes). But the epic scope of the drama has been difficult to realise in the theatre, and the stage direction '*they heave Antony*

aloft to Cleopatra' registers something of the physical difficulty of raising the fatally wounded hero into Cleopatra's monument (presumably originally represented by the balcony over the stage). After its initial performances in 1606–7, there were none until Garrick's lavishly rearranged version in the mid eighteenth century, and subsequent productions found the scenery required to make this spectacular play palatable to contemporary audiences prohibitively expensive. In the twentieth century the roll call of actors for the two main roles attests to the power of the writing for performers: Vivien Leigh and Laurence Olivier (1951), Janet Suzman and Richard Johnson (1972, filmed for television), Helen Mirren and Michael Gambon (1981), and Judi Dench and Anthony Hopkins (1987) – although in most productions reviewers tend to find one of the protagonists more convincing than the other. Recent productions have tended to use design to stylise the differences between an exotic, passionate Egypt and a colder, more regimented Rome, as in Michael Attenborough's production for the RSC in 2002. Mark Rylance's performance as Cleopatra at the Globe in 1999 was provocative, reminding audiences that the play was written for a pair of male leads: one reviewer found the performance 'true to the spirit of the play, which has to keep battling against farce as it pushes its way towards tragic dignity'.

Themes and interpretation

'No grave upon the earth shall clip in it / A pair so famous' (5.2.353–4). Caesar's final epitaph on the lovers is a striking one, in identifying their predominant characteristic not as passion, pride or grandeur but as that of being famous: Antony and Cleopatra are celebrities, and, as with modern celebrities, what we see is always a performance. In this play the lovers are never alone on stage together: there is never a moment of privacy. Flirtation, tantrum, grandiloquence – and perhaps love too – are all played out for the cameras. We could almost say that these characters know we the audience are there, and they are doing it all for our benefit. In such a culture the question of authenticity – does Cleopatra/Antony really love Antony/Cleopatra? – becomes unanswerable: how would we know? In part the play anticipates the difficulties of understanding public individuals but it does more than this: it acknowledges the inscrutability of the private self. Unlike the heavily soliloquised access to other tragic characters (Macbeth, Hamlet), here we see largely dialogue and performance. Like Caesar, all we really know at the end of the play is that the pair were famous.

Dialogue and self-conscious theatricality ally the play to the structures and tone of comedy, where wit, wordplay and strong female roles are common. Like *Much Ado About Nothing*, for example, it dramatises a female world brought into collision with a male one – and in ending with Cleopatra's triumphant suicide and the words 'Husband, I come' (5.2.281), perhaps the play's formal impulses towards comedy are in fact fulfilled. Cleopatra's choreographed death contrasts markedly with Antony's bungled attempts at suicide, and in her death dressed in her robe and crown, she embodies both Egyptian majesty and Roman fortitude. Act 5, the space of the tragic hero, is hers alone; it is her death, not his, that brings closure to the play. Antony's request to his servant, the significantly named Eros (god of love) to kill him, brings out the ironies of causation in the play. Both lovers suggest that they wish for death as an escape from the ignominy of military defeat and imprisonment, as well as wishing for it as a final consummation of their relationship; for each of them their political and personal honour is as pressing as their passion. Was it indeed, as Dryden's Restoration reworking of the play would have it, *All for Love*?

The conflict between the values of Rome and of Egypt that destroys Antony represents the conflict between duty and desire, between head and heart. The play opens with the disapproval of Antony's decline from stoic soldier to 'dotage' as 'the bellows and the fan to cool a gipsy's lust' (1.1.8–9), but the Cleopatra we meet is much more than the Romans' misogynistic caricature. Her performance – the verbal dexterity, the quicksilver moods, the sexual frankness, the emotional manipulation, the moments of insecurity – epitomises the play's instability, just as the dominant linguistic images of overflowing and liquefaction ('Let Rome in Tiber melt' [1.1.35]) suggest a world at once benignly fertile and dangerously volatile. Although the play's own energies can seem to have been diverted to the seductive luxury of Alexandria rather than the repressive political machinations of Rome, there is no doubt that the conflict will exact final retribution on its sacrificial victim. As Enobarbus witnesses, Antony is torn physically between Rome and Egypt, between Roman wives and Cleopatra, and between fighting and loving. His claim, embracing Cleopatra, that 'The nobleness of life / Is to do thus' (1.1.38–9) attempts to elevate the passions the Romans read as base into a supreme philosophy, but later he recognises 'These strong Egyptian fetters I must break, / Or lose myself in dotage' (1.2.112–13). Enobarbus' own position is one of simultaneous involvement and distance from the events, and as such he may well function as a surrogate for the play's audience. Readers and viewers of the play tend to divide along Roman–Egyptian lines, but, as Marilyn French puts it, 'At the end of *Antony and Cleopatra*, Caesar has the world; Antony and Cleopatra had the living' (*Shakespeare's Division of Experience*).

As You Like It

Key Facts
Date: 1599–1600
Length: 2,796 lines
Verse: 55% / Prose: 45%

Major characters' share of lines:	
Rosalind	25%
Orlando	11%
Celia	10%
Touchstone	10%
Jaques	8%

Romantic pastoral comedy in which a cross-dressed heroine escapes court life to live and woo in the forest

Plot and characters

Since their father's death, **Orlando** has been ill-treated by his envious elder brother **Oliver**, who commissions **Charles** the wrestler to kill Orlando in a competition to be held at court. **Duke Frederick** has taken power from *his* elder brother **Duke Senior** and banished him to the Forest of Arden; he keeps the old duke's daughter **Rosalind** as a companion to his own daughter **Celia**. They watch the wrestling match in which Charles is beaten by Orlando, who gains no reward when Frederick hears that Orlando's father was loyal to the old duke. Rosalind and Orlando fall in love. Frederick banishes Rosalind in a rage, and the cousins agree to escape in disguise to the forest: Rosalind as a man, Ganymede, and Celia as Aliena. They are accompanied by **Touchstone**, a jester. Orlando is warned by an old servant, **Adam**, to flee his brother, and the two go together into the forest, where they meet Duke Senior's lords including **Jaques**, a melancholy and satirical courtier. **Silvius** the shepherd is in love with the haughty **Phoebe**, but she falls in love with Ganymede. In disguise, Ganymede encounters Orlando who is proclaiming his love for Rosalind by pinning up terrible verses on trees, and s/he teaches him the way to woo her, having Celia act as a priest for a mock-wedding. Oliver arrives with news of Orlando's bravery in killing a lioness that was about to eat Oliver as he slept under a tree, and brings a bloody cloth from the wounded Orlando to Ganymede, who almost faints and gives away her disguise. Oliver and Celia fall promptly in love. Touchstone woos the goatherd **Audrey**, dismissing her erstwhile suitor the bumpkin **William**, but is persuaded to postpone their marriage which would have been conducted by **Sir Oliver Martext**. Ganymede manipulates Phoebe into accepting Silvius, she and Celia reveal their true identity, and the four couples are married by **Hymen**, god of marriage. Duke Frederick's arrival in the forest is promised by **Jacques de Bois**, the middle brother of Oliver and Orlando, but this is interrupted: Frederick has met a holy man and become a hermit, and so Duke Senior can return to office. Jaques opts to stay with Duke Frederick and the others prepare to return. Rosalind delivers a teasing epilogue.

Context and composition

As You Like It was written around 1599–1600, probably just after *King Henry V* and *Julius Caesar* and around the time of *Hamlet*. It was first printed in 1623. It shares with *The Two Gentlemen of Verona* and *Twelfth Night*, among others, the device of the woman dressed as a man, and, like those other plays, has fun with the double recognition that the woman is really played by a male actor. Its pastoral mode is picked up again in *The Winter's Tale*, where again it provides a contrast from the harsh world of the court. It has a high proportion of prose – including for important speeches such as Rosalind's epilogue – and a number of contemporary songs.

Shakespeare's main source for the play is the prose romance by Thomas Lodge, *Rosalynde* (1590). His alterations point up the parallel sets of warring brothers – Oliver and Orlando, Dukes Frederick and Senior – and also the unreality of the world of Arden (in Lodge's story the rightful duke is restored by a deadly battle rather than a miraculous conversion). Orlando takes his name, and his lovesick behaviour, from the hero of Ariosto's *Orlando Furioso*, which had been dramatised by Robert Greene early in the 1590s.

Performances

There are no records of the play's early staging, although an eighteenth-century anecdote would have us believe that Shakespeare played the role of the old servant Adam. After nineteenth-century productions  overdosed on pastoral sentiment – epitomised by the real deer brought on stage in 1908 – twentieth-century productions showcased the role of Rosalind and tended to darken the play's subtexts. Christine Edzard's film (1992) turns the forest into a derelict urban underworld of rough sleepers and outcasts, with Orlando's verses sprayed graffiti-style on subway walls. The concept that the forest and the court are mirrors of each other rather than complete opposites has been a fruitful one: at Stratford in 1985 (directed by Adrian Noble) the same actors played the courtiers in the forest and the court, Duke Senior and Duke Frederick were doubled (making the latter's miraculous conversion a matter of stage logistics rather than personal repentance) and the same set, its furniture draped in dust sheets, was used for the entire play. Other theatrical forests have been signalled by minimalist chrome and glass towers, by bare trees and by a colourful palette in contrast to the court's monochromes. Cheek by Jowl's iconic all-male production with Adrian Lester as Rosalind (1991) explored the play's teasing interest in homosexuality and gender inversion.

Themes and interpretation

Shakespeare's theatre is directed at a growing urban metropolis – London grows exponentially during this period, and the establishment of a permanent theatre industry is one consequence of this growth. From its earliest classical practitioners, pastoral is a paradoxically urban genre in which an idealised rural location serves to satirise and symbolise the aspirations of educated city dwellers. *As You Like It* both does and does not follow this model: Arden was the forest in Warwickshire close to Shakespeare's birthplace and from which his mother's family took their name; Ardennes, as the wood is sometimes styled, is a French forest suitable to the French setting Shakespeare found in Lodge's novella, his major source. Even this spelling difference divides the forest into being at once local and literary, familiar and strange.

The forest in the play develops this ambiguity: Orlando believes he will encounter criminal outlaws when he is desperately searching for food, but instead he meets a civilised court-in-exile, complete with meat, musicians and melancholics. The associations of Duke Senior's band with the mythical merry men of Robin Hood makes the forest symbolise a legendary folk history, emphasised in Shakespeare's use of the romance name 'de Bois' – meaning 'of the woods' – for Orlando and Oliver. They belong to a more chivalrous, romantic genre 'under the greenwood tree' (2.5.1), as Amiens sings. But part of Rosalind's coaching of her unwitting lover in her disguise as Ganymede is to nudge him from excessive, unreal gestures of love into something more grounded: 'men have died from time to time – and worms have eaten them – but not for love' (4.1.84–5). Moments of artificiality are undercut by realism: Orlando's overblown syntax 'Run, run, Orlando, carve on every tree / The fair, the chaste and unexpressive she' (3.2.9–10) is immediately followed by a prose conversation between Touchstone and Corin about sheep. Real sheep, not the decorative ones of pastoral: Corin's hands are dirtied with his labours, and the play may allude in passing to contemporary concerns about the enclosure of common land for profitable sheep farming by distant landlords.

By the end of the play the forest has become distinctly inhospitable. When in Act 4 Oliver tells of how he was almost strangled by a 'green and gilded snake' (4.3.103) as he slept, and then endangered by a lioness, it is time to go home. Eden has turned sour. It is striking that both these threats are feminised (in Lodge it is a lion, not, as in Shakespeare, 'a lioness, with udders all drawn dry' [4.3.109]): in this play in which a woman dominates – the only play in which a woman has the last word – perhaps there is an underlying anxiety about their power.

But Rosalind, of course, spends much of the play dressed as Ganymede, a classical name with strong associations of homosexuality for early modern audiences. The frisson of the scene in which Rosalind as Ganymede pretends to be Rosalind for Orlando to practise his wooing is continued in the playfulness of the epilogue, when Rosalind – or the male actor underneath – flirts with men and women in the audience, teasing them with the ambiguity of her/his gender position. From this perspective, *As You Like It*, rather than denoting vapid crowd-pleasing, as George Bernard Shaw opined, takes on a saucy, provocative air: anything goes, any which way, whatever you fancy. As is to be found elsewhere in Shakespeare's comedies, gender can be played with and impersonated, but class distinctions are absolute: Rosalind tells Phoebe 'you are not for all markets' (3.6.60), making it clear that her mistake is less the misprision of Ganymede's sex and more her presumption in loving above her station. Touchstone's cynical couplet, 'come, sweet Audrey, for we must be married or we must live in bawdry' (3.4.73–4), is a frank acknowledgement that the social institutions of marriage are structures to police potentially transgressive desire, just as the swiftness of Oliver and Celia falling in love shows us that these institutions are formal gestures towards comic closure. The 'giddiness' of it (5.2.4), as Oliver acknowledges, is part of the play's make-believe. Ending under Hymen's direction confirms conservative structures – marriages, political restitution, the return to the court – even as the epilogue undercuts this finality.

The traveller Jaques and the clown Touchstone are Shakespeare's most prominent additions to his source material, and their different dispositions set out the range of responses the play includes and can produce. Jaques' world-weary contempt constructs an existential stage-play world in which 'All the world's a stage, / And all the men and women merely players' and life is a series of declining stages to an old age 'sans teeth, sans eyes, sans taste, sans everything' (2.7.139–66). Touchstone has a parallel speech on the seven degrees of quarrelling: more expansive, more verbally witty, and ultimately more optimistic. It is intrinsic to the structure and tone of *As You Like It* that it is both Touchstone's and Jaques' play.

The Comedy of Errors

Key Facts
Date: 1594
Length: 1,918 lines
Verse: 85% / Prose: 15%

Major characters' share of lines:

Antipholus of Syracuse	15%
Adriana	15%
Dromio of Syracuse	14%
Antipholus of Ephesus	12%
Dromio of Ephesus	9%

Early farcical comedy of two sets of long-separated twins careering in bewilderment around Ephesus: confusions abound

Plot and characters

Egeon is under arrest and threat of death in Ephesus as an enemy Syracusian merchant, and has until evening to find a ransom. Thirty-three years ago a shipwreck divided his family so that he was parted from his wife **Emilia** and one twin son, **Antipholus** (called **of Ephesus** to try to minimise confusion), along with a twin servant, **Dromio** (**of Ephesus**). The other twins, **Antipholus** (**of Syracuse**) and **Dromio** (**of Syracuse**), have also left Syracuse and spent their adult life looking for their missing brothers. Egeon has now come to look for them. Antipholus of Ephesus is married to **Adriana**, who, discontented at his lack of attention to her, complains to her unmarried sister, **Luciana**, who later finds herself the object of Antipholus of Syracuse's affections. **Nell**, an unseen kitchen maid of substantial proportions, is the love interest for Dromio of Ephesus, and Dromio of Syracuse inevitably finds himself bewildered at her offstage advances. Antipholus of Ephesus' associates include **Angelo**, a goldsmith from whom he has commissioned a gold chain, **Balthazar** a merchant, and a

Courtesan to whom he promises the gold chain intended for his wife which ends up instead in the hands of Antipholus of Syracuse. A **Duke** rules over the state and appears at the beginning and the end of the play. **Dr Pinch** is a comic schoolteacher-cum-magician brought in to cure the apparent madness of the confused Antipholus of Ephesus, who has been arrested for not paying for goods he believes he has never received because they have gone to his brother in error. In the play's final scene Antipholus of Ephesus is interrogated about these debts and approached for the money for his ransom by Egeon, who mistakes him for his brother and unwittingly recognises him as his long-lost son. The **Abbess** promises to cure Antipholus' madness, and introduces Antipholus of Syracuse who has fled to the abbey for sanctuary. She has her own revelation, too: she is Emilia. The confusions of the day are untangled as she invites all to a belated christening party for her sons.

Context and composition

This tightly structured play conforms to classical ideas of unity of time, space and action since it all takes place, unusually for Shakespeare, in one place on one day (compare *The Tempest*). It is based on the Roman playwright Plautus' *Menaechmi* (c. 200 BC), which was well known to Elizabethan schoolboys. The play is Shakespeare's shortest, with a high incidence of end-rhymed verse, related formally to other early comedies such as *The Two Gentlemen of Verona* and *A Midsummer Night's Dream* and to *Romeo and Juliet* and linguistically to the narrative poem *Venus and Adonis*, suggesting a composition date of around 1593–4. A number of the play's themes and motifs are echoed in other plays. Mistaken identity generated by twins occurs again in *Twelfth Night*; the clever servant motif is common to Plautine comedy (see also Gobbo in *The Merchant of Venice*, Lance in *The Two Gentlemen of Verona* and, more darkly, Iago in *Othello*); shipwrecks and family dissolution and reunion by water are echoed in *Pericles*, part of which also takes place in Ephesus and shares some of the same sources and echoes of St Paul. It was first published in 1623, and probably written close to its first performance in 1594.

Performances

Its first recorded performance was at Gray's Inn (December 1594), and it was performed at court in 1604: the play, with its three locations, the Phoenix (house of Antipholus of

Ephesus and Adriana), Porcupine (Courtesan) and Priory (Abbess), may have been written with indoor, occasional performance in mind, where its five-act structure would have been marked by short intervals. Its brevity may also indicate it was not intended for commercial performance but as an accompaniment to feasting or other entertainment. Ben Jonson, Shakespeare's contemporary, felt unable to adapt another Plautus twin play because he could not find identical actors: different productions of *Errors* have had different solutions, sometimes making the twins look alike (Samuel Phelps was even able to cast Irish identical twins as his Dromios in 1864), sometimes using similar costuming, sometimes absurdly stressing their physical dissimilarity, sometimes, as in the BBC television film (directed by James Jones, 1984), by casting a single actor to play both twins. This is more difficult on stage, although Kathryn Hunter (Globe, 1999) is one of a number of modern directors to attempt it.

The play only found its place in the theatrical canon in the twentieth century. Memorable productions include Theodore Komisarjevsky's zany 1938 production at Stratford, with a stylised street-scene set dominated by a crazy clock to emphasise the importance of time to this time-strapped play; Adrian Noble's RSC version (1983), with absurdist costumes and the Dromios with clowns' red noses; Tim Supple's dark 1996 RSC production focusing on the brutality of the play's beatings and arrests and the eeriness of the magical Ephesus; and David Farr's 2003 interpretation for the Bristol Old Vic referencing Magritte, Escher and Freud. Although the play is unique among Shakespeare's comedies in having no scripted songs or music, its rhythms have been adapted to an opera, *Gli Equivoci* (1786) by Mozart's pupil Stephen Storace, to an updated musical comedy, *The Boys from Syracuse* (1938), by Rodgers and Hart, and to several musical stage versions, including Trevor Nunn's in 1976 (televised in 1978).

Themes and interpretation

Coleridge's view of the play as a 'poetical farce' understands something crucial about this cleverly constructed, plot-driven play, particularly when read alongside the theatre theorist Edward Gordon Craig's comment that 'farce refined becomes high comedy, farce brutalized becomes tragedy' (*Index to the Story of My Days*). *Errors*' accretion of misunderstandings and misrecognitions establishes it as a farce, a form of finely timed physical comedy. Farce's speed has no time for questions about plausibility or motivation, just as *Errors* hurtles around Ephesus almost without pause – although the long opening speech of Egeon is one exception to this pacing – and without troubling its protagonists with too much interior psychology. This dynamic construction is a strength, not a weakness, and in its exploration of identity, confusion and the nightmarish implications of its many errors of perception the play often comes closer to the absurdist theatre of the twentieth century than to Shakespeare's own romantic comedies. In fact, while this play gestures towards comic closure in numerous couples, it never really gets there: Adriana's eloquent complaint about her husband hasn't been resolved; Luciana and Antipholus of Syracuse are not to be married, or at least not yet; the Courtesan continues to be defined by being outside marriage. Egeon and Emilia are the play's romantic veterans, but they are hardly the young couples typical of Shakespearean comedy, and the play ends not with the crowded stage with which the genre usually represents the inclusive social world, but with a private moment of reconciliation between the two Dromios.

Many of the play's characters identify themselves as incomplete, musing on the location of identity as a property of the interior or exterior. Are we who we are because of some inner essence, or because other people recognise us as ourselves, or because we are part of a network of social and family relationships? Amid the comedy of Antipholus of Ephesus locked out from his own house because he – or rather his identical twin – is already within, supping with his wife, there is real fear: errors can easily become terrors. Antipholus and Dromio of Syracuse suspect witchcraft, drawing on Ephesus' reputation for magic and sorcery. (Shakespeare has relocated the action to Ephesus, noted in the Bible for exorcists, evil spirits and confusion [Acts 19:13, 29]; he seems to have used Paul's mission in the Mediterranean as one of the sources for Egeon's journeys; and he also uses Paul's letter to the Ephesians, particularly on marriage and domestic government.) The frequency with which the play deploys a lexicon of magic and the supernatural is striking – more mentions of witches than in *Macbeth*, more mentions of conjuring and magic than in *A Midsummer Night's Dream*, more references to Satan than in any other Shakespeare play. Dr Pinch's attempts at exorcism at the end of the play bring out its preoccupation with possession, madness and other forms of self-loss.

Perhaps the characters are in search less of others than of themselves. Antipholus of Syracuse's first brief soliloquy highlights his loneliness: 'I to the world am like a drop of water / That in the ocean seeks another drop, / Who, failing there to find his fellow forth, / Unseen, inquisitive, confounds himself' (1.2.35–8). The fact that we the audience already have a good idea at this early stage that the other drop, the lost twin, will indeed be found does not diminish the pathos. Antipholus is not himself because he has been separated from his family; later, he encounters Adriana, who thinks she is his wife, and pleads with her errant husband about the inviolability of two made one through marriage in a similar image: 'know, my love, as easy mayst thou fall / A drop of water in the breaking gulf, / And take unmingled thence that drop again / Without addition or diminishing, / As take me from thyself' (2.2.116–20).

Under the surface of the play's hectic and humorous exploration of duplicated names, appearances and identities these watery similes capture the sense that identity is fragile, fluid, always in danger of being lost, a hint of panic the farce encodes visually as well as verbally, as in the indicative stage direction from the Folio: 'exeunt omnes, as fast as may be, frighted' (4.4.140).

Coriolanus

Key Facts

Date: 1608

Length: 3,837 lines

Verse: 80% / Prose: 20%

Major characters' share of lines:	
Coriolanus	23%
Menenius	15%
Volumnia	8%
Sicinius Velutus	8%
Cominius	8%

Brutal military and political tragedy of pride and reversal

Plot and characters

In ancient Rome the people are hungry and discontented, and direct their anger against the patrician general **Caius Martius**. The senator **Menenius** tries to calm them with the fable of the belly, about how the body politic must work together. Martius is sent by the Senate to meet an army of the Volscians, led by his arch-rival **Tullus Aufidius**. At home Martius' wife **Virgilia** fears for his safety but his mother **Volumnia** takes pleasure in his bravery and the danger. **Valeria**, Virgilia's friend, likens Martius' young son to his father when he dismembers a butterfly. Martius leads his men to an impossible victory over the Volscians and single-handedly captures the town of Corioles, being awarded the surname **Coriolanus** in remembrance of this feat. On his return, he is proposed as consul, an office which requires the assent of the people under their representatives, the tribunes **Sicinius** and **Brutus**. Through his pride and outspoken contempt for the Roman crowd, Coriolanus alienates the people, and he refuses to supplicate for their favour in the marketplace. While they give grudging consent to his appointment, the tribunes persuade them to change their minds. Angrily and publicly upbraiding the people for their behaviour, Coriolanus is accused of treason and is banished, to the delight of the tribunes. He leaves Rome, stoically bidding farewell to his family, and goes in disguise to Aufidius. When his identity is revealed, he is received with great honour, and leads his erstwhile enemies against Rome, although the Volscians, including Aufidius, do not fully trust him. First **Cominius**, then Menenius, then his family come as envoys from Rome to ask him to spare the city. Volumnia pleads eloquently and they kneel: wordlessly he takes her hand and agrees to sue for peace. They return triumphant to Rome, but Coriolanus is accused by Aufidius of betraying the Volscians. The people demand his death and murder him: Aufidius promises a noble burial.

Context and composition

Coriolanus is probably Shakespeare's final tragedy, written in 1608 shortly after *Antony and Cleopatra* and *Timon of Athens* and sharing some of their cynicism about tragic glory. It was first published in 1623. In it Shakespeare returns to Thomas North's translation of Plutarch's *Lives of the Noble Grecians and Romans* (1579, his source for *Julius Caesar* and *Antony and Cleopatra*) and to the fifth century BC, close to the events described in his narrative poem *The Rape of Lucrece* (1593). The characterisation of Volumnia is largely Shakespeare's addition to his source. Unusually, there is no subplot and no alternative locus of interest: the play single-mindedly builds up Coriolanus and then destroys him.

For the play's first audiences, its representation of the insurrections and corn riots of urban Rome may have had an added piquancy due to similarities with the Midlands Riot in England during 1607–8, and the play may also have chimed with the Jacobean debate over parliamentary versus royal prerogatives.

Performances

The play was probably performed in 1608–9, perhaps in the new Blackfriars theatre (see '*Shakespeare's Theatre*' below) – the Folio text is divided into acts, which were to allow for the trimming of candles in the indoor theatre. Its stage history from the Restoration onwards has tended to have more or less radically partisan interpretations, from eighteenth-century versions shadowing anti-Jacobite controversy to the

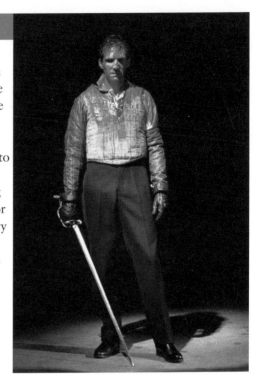

attempt to use the play to provoke a military coup in France in 1934.

With the rise of European fascism in the 1920s the play gained a new relevance on stage. But the history of the play in the twentieth century shows its inherent ambiguity. Laurence Olivier played Coriolanus as a would-be fascist dictator (1937) and sealed the association in a production in 1959, where his death, strung upside down over the stage, recalled the lynching of Mussolini in 1945. On the other hand, it was the preferred Shakespeare play of the Nazis because it was interpreted as a paean to strong leadership, and, as such, was banned in occupied Germany after the war. At other times, too, this ambiguous play has gained a clarity in particular performances: the struggle for democracy against military dictatorship, in Michael Bogdanov's 1990 English Shakespeare Company version; jackboots and blackshirts in Steven Berkoff's 1995

West Yorkshire Playhouse production; Trevor Nunn and Buzz Goodbody (RSC, 1972), stressed the sociological aspects rather than the individual human tragedy; in 1989 Terry Hands and John Barton did the opposite, subduing everything to the personality of Charles Dance as Coriolanus (RSC). David Thacker's 1994 production (RSC) with Toby Stephens was set in the French Revolution and amplified the play's gender dynamic with a prominent reproduction of Delacroix's iconic *Liberty Leading the People*. Ralph Fiennes played the role in 2000 under Jonathan Kent's direction, and directs and stars in a film version scheduled for release in 2012, with Vanessa Redgrave as Volumnia.

Themes and interpretation

With fewer than forty lines of soliloquy – among the smallest number in any Shakespeare play – the absence of introspection and the relative inarticulacy of the play's central protagonist are clearly defined: Coriolanus is no more chummy with the audience than with the plebeians. The adjective most often used of him is 'proud', and Coriolanus' pride is a carapace – a protective outer shell which can be penetrated only with difficulty and at fatal cost. That inhumanity which is a crucial strength in battle as he slashes his way in and out of Corioles cripples him at home. Battle is a kind of baptism, a name-giving through which he can aggressively assert his own identity. Without it he is lost. As 'a thing of blood' (2.2.103) and 'chief enemy to the people' (1.1.5–6) at home or to opponents abroad, his approach to civil politics is coloured by this anatagonistic view of the world.

In fact, the whole play is seduced by brutality and the cult of violence. The image of the child catching a gilded butterfly and tearing it to pieces is a powerful snapshot of its characteristic cruelty. It glories in wounds and blood as marks of Romanness and of masculinity. The formidable Volumnia's terrible catalogue of the additions to her son's wounds shocks us because of its subversion of normal expectations of maternity. Coriolanus cannot separate himself from his mother, and her demands are ultimately destructive: no wonder that some of the most influential critical readings of the play have found their interpretative framework in psychoanalysis. Her love seems overpowering: her son feels he must be emasculated into a 'harlot' or 'eunuch' to please her in politics. She appears to derive a kind of erotic satisfaction from the spectacle of his martial physicality, imagining her son her husband and his fighting a displacement of 'the embracements of his bed' (1.3.4) Her lovingly lingering description of his wounded body contrasts with the chaste and cold marriage of Coriolanus and Virgilia. Elsewhere the homoerotics of militarism are emphasised in Aufidius' description of his meeting with Coriolanus in the imagery of the connubial bed: 'we have been down together in my sleep / Unbuckling helms, fisting each other's throat' (4.5.121–2). This powerfully destructive relationship – the intensely sexualised image of single combat – emerges as momentarily more powerful than the bonds of family and state that form Coriolanus.

As in other Roman plays it is Rome itself and the values it implies which are the prime battleground of this supremely political play: the conflict is between forms of government – republicanism and tyranny – plebeians and patricians. If the play has a message – and that is debatable – it seems to be to show the dangers of both extremes. The idea that power rests either solely with the people or solely with the haughty patricians is shown to be flawed, through the equivocal presentation of all the political factions. Shakespeare emphasises, for example, that the tribunes are motivated not by concern for the people but by pride in their own office, but he also gives voice to the hungry crowd whose physical needs cannot be explained away by Menenius' patronising metaphor of how the belly of the state needs the head, arms and legs. Coriolanus himself is firmly on the side of absolute power, and of absolute autonomy, 'as if a man were author of himself / And knew no other kin' (5.3.36–7). Ultimately, however, this proud soldier is fatally vulnerable to others: to Aufidius, to Volumnia, Virgilia. The glorious and solitary Roman deed of suicide is not allowed to Coriolanus (as to, say, Brutus in *Julius Caesar*): in death, as in life, his attempts at autonomy are ruinously compromised.

The ignoble end of Coriolanus dying of multiple wounds at the hands of conspirators – the stage direction is '*Draw both the*

Conspirators and kill Martius, who falls: Aufidius stands on him' – recalls the trajectory of Julius Caesar in the earlier play. But *Coriolanus'* final mood is ironic, even anticlimactic, more in the spirit of *Troilus and Cressida* than *Julius Caesar*. Its hero dies 'a man by his own alms empoisoned / And with his charity slain' (5.6.10–11). If this is Shakespeare's last tragic play, it is a bathetic, misanthropic and disaffected finale.

Cymbeline, King of Britain

Key Facts
Date: 1610
Length: 3,818 lines
verse: 85% / prose: 15%

Major characters' share of lines:	
Innogen	16%
Posthumus	12%
Iachimo	12%
Belarius	9%
Cymbeline	8%

Fairy tale of lost princes and a wicked stepmother, against a backdrop of the ancient Britons fighting the Romans

Plot and characters

Cymbeline, King of Britain, is in dispute with the Romans about paying tribute. He has a daughter, **Innogen** (sometimes Imogen), and two sons stolen in infancy. His new wife the **Queen** has a doltish son **Cloten,** whom she wishes to marry to Innogen, but Innogen has secretly married a commoner, **Posthumus Leonatus.** When the King discovers the marriage, Posthumus is banished, and while in Rome he enters into a bet with **Iachimo,** who wagers that he can seduce Innogen. When he meets Innogen, Iachimo realises she is not winnable, but, having hidden in a trunk in her bedchamber and stolen her bracelet, a gift from her husband, he is able to describe her private room and a mole on her breast in such detail that Posthumus is convinced that he has indeed slept with her. Cloten presses his suit to Innogen but she is scornful in her rejection, stating that she values even Posthumus' clothing more than him. The jealous Posthumus orders his servant **Pisanio** to kill her at Milford Haven, but, unwilling, Pisanio encourages her to escape in the disguise of a page, Fidele, sending her bloodstained clothing to Posthumus to maintain the illusion that his orders have been carried out. In the wilds of Wales Innogen meets **Belarius,** who confides to the audience that his two young charges Polydore and Cadwal are in fact **Guiderius** and

Arviragus, Cymbeline's sons, whom he abducted from their nursery in revenge for his own banishment. Stung by Innogen's rejection, Cloten follows her dressed in Posthumus' clothes, vowing to kill him and rape her, but when he meets Guiderius they fight and Cloten is decapitated. The young princes are drawn to the mysterious Fidele, and when s/he appears dead having taken a poison of the Queen's – given to Pisario in the guise of a medicine – they lay out her corpse with a solemn rite in the cave, alongside that of the headless Cloten. When Innogen awakes she mistakes the corpse for that of her husband. The Roman commander **Lucius** who has come to exact imperial tribute by force takes her into his service. Belarius, Arviragus and Guiderius join the British army and fight bravely; Posthumus, having come to Britain with the Roman army, changes sides to join the princes and in the battle beats, but spares, Iachimo, who does not recognise him. Sleeping, he is visited by the ghosts of his parents and his brothers, who call on **Jupiter** to aid him; Jupiter descends to deliver a tablet, which when Posthumus awakes he is unable to interpret. In a final scene news of the Queen's death and her confession of her attempts to kill Innogen and the King, the news of Cloten's death and Iachimo's confession of his trick crowd in with the revelation of the princes' identities and Fidele's true character, and the **Soothsayer**'s interpretation of the tablet predicting the reunion of the royal family. Cymbeline finally agrees that, despite having beaten the Romans, they will pay the required tribute after all.

Context and composition

The play was probably written in 1610 as part of a vogue for tragi-comedy often associated with John Fletcher, with whom Shakespeare would collaborate on *The Two Noble Kinsmen* and *King Henry VIII*; there is a rare account, by Simon Forman, of an early performance in April 1611. The spectacular entrance of Jupiter, who '*descends in thunder and lightning, sitting upon an eagle*', may be as much to show off the special effects possible in the private theatre of Blackfriars as to further the plot. *Cymbeline* shares with *The Tempest*, *The Winter's Tale* and *Pericles*, which are often grouped together as 'romances', a melding of realism and fantasy, a journeying plot and an interest in stories spanning two generations, from imperilled infancy to early maturity. It also has a connection with the other Roman plays, *Titus Andronicus, Coriolanus* and *Antony and Cleopatra*: in all these plays Rome is set against an internal or external adversary, but this is the only play to see that conflict from the non-Roman point of view. *Cymbeline* was first printed in 1623, when it was placed at the end of the 'Tragedies', perhaps because its title suggests a closer focus on the king-as-protagonist than the play actually offers. Its complicated plot is matched by an often difficult and contorted syntax: the opening scene is a good example, but things get easier.

Performances

Describing the performance he saw in 1611, Simon Forman was particularly struck by the tense scene in which Iachimo hides in Innogen's bedroom; he has nothing to say about the play's most challenging section, the long series of revelations in the final moments. Productions have found it difficult to present these serial revelations seriously: George Bernard Shaw rewrote the last act (*Cymbeline Refinished*); recent productions have added narrator figures, cut Jupiter, or archly emphasised the Mozartian unreality of the rapidly unspooling plot. Kneehigh's 2007 production modernised the language but affectingly constructed a world overshadowed by national and paternal grief at the loss of the princes. At the Globe in 2001 Mark Rylance and for Cheek by Jowl in 2007 Tom Hiddleston doubled Posthumus and Cloten to draw them into provocative symmetry. No film exists apart from Elijah Moshinsky's BBC television version of 1983, with Richard Johnson, Helen Mirren and

Michael Pennington. Perhaps uniquely in the Shakespearean canon, this is a play still waiting its iconic or revelatory production.

Themes and interpretation

It is somehow appropriate that the most famous lines from *Cymbeline*, the moving dirge 'Fear no more the heat o' the sun' (4.2.257), sung at the death of Fidele, are a sham. Fidele is not even Fidele, still less dead; the mourners do not know themselves. And yet in its lyrical simplicity the moment is wonderfully touching, following the sudden brutality of Cloten's death and the complications of jealousy and anger, bringing a difficult play to a point where emotion, rather than plot, is paramount. As the summary above indicates, plot is the dominant element in this play, as it draws in motifs from fairy tale, court masque, history, tragedy and romantic comedy; but as 'Fear no more' shows us, that plot is often distinct from, or irrelevant to, moments of affecting poignancy. *Cymbeline* is certainly crammed full with plot elements and different genres rubbing unexpectedly up against each other, but modern critics have found more in the play than Dr Johnson's wonderfully caustic refusal to 'waste criticism upon unresisting imbecility, upon faults too evident for detection, and too gross for aggravation' (*The Plays of William Shakespeare*).

One strand of recent discussion has focused on the play's historical position, its melding of ancient British and Roman history, and its apparent relevance to King James, patron of Shakespeare's company. James seems to be glanced at both in the play's Cymbeline, King of Britain (James' preferred name for his adjacent kingdoms of England and Scotland), and as the absent emperor Augustus Caesar – hence, perhaps, that curious fudge in the conclusion on the matter of the tribute Britain owes to Rome. The rest of the play is also a historical palimpsest – Rome in *Cymbeline* is both the ancient empire and the contemporary city – so that it comes as a shock to see the urbane Iachimo among the legionaries; the prominently named Milford Haven would have recalled the founding of the Tudor dynasty in the fifteenth century, as the port where Richmond landed to take the throne from the usurping Richard (see *King Richard III*). Cymbeline was supposed to have been King of Britain at the time of the birth of

Christ, but the world of the play is that of the Renaissance court. *Cymbeline* thus occupies a deliberately non-continuous historical moment, partly because it splices material about the Romans in Britain with a contemporary prose story from the Italian Boccaccio, but more purposively to suggest something about the mythic and idealised identity of Britain.

Another focus of interest has been the presentation of Innogen. The Victorians loved her as the epitome of the chaste, wise heroine, but the frisson of her endangered chastity is troubling: like Iachimo, we seem to be voyeurs in a bedroom decorated in an overdeterminedly sexualised manner. Innogen's bedtime reading is of the rape of Philomel by Tereus in Ovid's *Metamorphoses*, the prototype for the violence of *Titus Andronicus*, and her chamber is decorated with the delicious image of Diana bathing. By prompting both dangerous desire and violent hatred, Innogen makes them look like the same thing, and it is only the folkloric elements of the plot that frustrate Posthumus' murderous intent. The vehemence of his misogyny is hardly countered; even at the play's conclusion he strikes her, albeit mistakenly.

Cymbeline's happy ending is an effortful one, and it is hard not to see Shakespeare experimenting at this late stage in his career with the props of his previous works: poison, discarded daughters, male jealousy, women dressed as men. The play's conclusion gives the bittersweet reminder that its shattered, broken world of loss, war and rejection can only be healed via this self-conscious fantasy.

Hamlet

Key Facts
Date: 1600
Length: 3,904 lines
Verse: 75% / Prose: 25%

Major characters' share of lines:	
Hamlet	37%
Claudius	14%
Polonius	9%
Horatio	7%
Laertes	5%

Iconic revenge tragedy of a brooding hero trapped in a family melodrama and an existential crisis

Plot and characters

The **Ghost** of the old King Hamlet appears on the castle battlements to **Bernardo, Marcellus** and **Horatio**: they vow to report it to his son **Hamlet. Claudius**, the new king, has married his brother's widow **Gertrude**. He dispatches ambassadors to deal with young **Fortinbras**, who wants to regain lands lost by his father during the previous reign. Hamlet is distressed and melancholic at his father's death and his mother's remarriage, but accedes to the request that he stay at court. **Laertes**, son of the councillor **Polonius**, is given permission to go to Paris: taking leave of his sister **Ophelia**, he advises her against her relationship with Hamlet. Polonius secretly sends **Reynaldo** after him to report on his behaviour. Hamlet meets the Ghost and hears that he was murdered by Claudius: he vows revenge and makes Horatio and the others swear an oath of secrecy. He feigns madness to cover his plans. Claudius and Gertrude employ two fellow students, **Rosencrantz** and **Guildenstern**, to spy on Hamlet, but he suspects them. Polonius maintains he is lovesick for Ophelia, and sets her as a bait for the King to watch Hamlet's behaviour. Hamlet rejects Ophelia harshly and denies he ever loved her. A company of **Players** arrive whom Hamlet knows well; he arranges that they will modify a play in their repertoire and that this will make the King reveal himself. The performance of the 'Murder of Gonzago' ends in confusion when Claudius leaves. Hamlet has the opportunity to kill him, but believing he is at prayer and will thus go to heaven, he does not take it. In his mother's chamber he berates her about the death of his father; she says she knows nothing about it. Hamlet kills Polonius, who has been spying on them, thinking he is Claudius. Claudius sends Hamlet to England with Rosencrantz and Guildenstern, where he will be killed. Driven mad by the death of her father, Ophelia drowns. Laertes returns and is persuaded by Claudius to direct his anger towards Hamlet. At Ophelia's funeral, Hamlet returns, having escaped from the ship via some pirates, and sends Rosencrantz and Guildenstern to their deaths. He and Laertes fight in Ophelia's grave. Claudius plans Hamlet's death with Laertes: he will poison the foils in a fencing match. Hamlet accepts the challenge brought by the foppish courtier **Osric**, and in the fight he and Laertes are both mortally poisoned; Gertrude dies from drinking poison intended for Hamlet, and Hamlet kills Claudius before dying in Horatio's arms. Fortinbras enters to take over the battered kingdom.

Context and composition

The date of *Hamlet* is difficult to ascertain: there are two distinct early printings, in 1603 and 1604, which may in part represent different stages of Shakespeare's work on the play. Stylistic evidence tends to place it around 1600, although there are references ten years earlier to a play on the same subject, almost certainly not by Shakespeare but assumed by many to have been one of his sources – the so-called 'Ur-Hamlet'. Other sources for the play are the Norse story of Amleth, available to Shakespeare in a French version, and Thomas Kyd's popular Elizabethan revenge play *The Spanish Tragedy*, which also has a ghost, a character called Horatio and a play-within-a-play. Shakespeare's transformation of this material is thoroughgoing – the depiction of Hamlet's internal state, revealed through soliloquy, is perhaps the most striking change of emphasis from his more plot-driven predecessors. Shakespeare also brings out the parallels and foils in the story – Laertes and Hamlet, Hamlet and

Fortinbras – and compounds the sense of self-loss in his father's death by splitting the name Hamlet.

Close in date to *Hamlet* is another story of the aftermath of regicide, *Julius Caesar*, to which the play alludes when Polonius talks of playing the title role. Together these two plays usher in the political and personal concerns that will dominate the later tragedies.

Performances

The first printed text of the play (1603) boasts it has been performed in the universities of Oxford and Cambridge as well as in London, and one contemporary commentator, Anthony Scolaker, uses it as a touchstone for good writing, which 'should please all, like Prince Hamlet'. From Richard Burbage, the original Prince Hamlet, onwards, the play has always been a star vehicle, offering a roll call of theatrical history:

Thomas Betterton, David Garrick, Sarah Siddons, Edmund Kean, Henry Irving, Sarah Bernhardt, Laurence Olivier, Richard Burton, Kenneth Branagh (the last three available on film). *Hamlet* has been a significant part of the theatrical repertoire outside the anglophone world, particularly in Russia and eastern Europe (see, for example, the film by Grigori Kozintsev of 1964). Its familiarity has prompted recent theatrical interest in the shorter text of 1603 (Q1: see 'Shakespeare in Print' below), a less reflective, more dynamic drama which has had the capacity to refresh a play often found too full of quotations. Sometimes a more intensely psychological focus has been achieved by minimising the play's political narrative (Olivier's film version of 1948, for instance, cuts Fortinbras entirely); in other contexts, and perhaps in its first performances in the uncertainty about the ageing Queen Elizabeth's successor, questions of rule, inheritance and territory have been dominant. If the earlier stage tradition was for idealised Hamlets, more recent incarnations have brought out the less appealing aspects of the play and its central character. A hoodie-wearing Rory Kinnear (National Theatre, directed by Nicholas Hytner, 2010), did not shy away from the brutality of his treatment of Ophelia, for example. More experimental versions of and dramatic supplements to the play include Robert Lepage's *Elsinore* (1995), Heiner Müller's *Die Hamletmaschine* (1977) and Tom Stoppard's *Rosencrantz and Guildenstern are Dead* (1966; filmed in 1990).

Themes and interpretation

Hamlet begins with a question: 'Who's there?' (1.1.1). In context it registers the nerviness of the nightwatch, but it soon expands into a more existential summary of the play's themes, and particularly of its insistent questioning of issues of identity and recognition. It is this inexhaustible interrogation that has given *Hamlet* its unique hold on western culture, and its ability to adapt to speak for new audiences across the centuries. This revenge play steeped in the traditions of the Elizabethan theatre has, in its depiction of psychological trauma and isolation, come to stand as a monument to consciousness itself.

It is appropriate that the most recognisable visual image of the play is from Act 5, Hamlet's encounter with the gravediggers who are displacing old bones as they dig a new grave. Facing the skull of the jester Yorick, Hamlet represents the encounter with human mortality, and with the inevitability of death. For Hamlet himself this fate is sealed once he takes up the ghost's injunction to revenge, since stage revengers had to pay with their own lives, but he is already sickened with grief and weary of life before he hears this terrible summons. The twentieth-century playwright Arthur Miller's observations on tragedy seem particularly appropriate here: 'I believe, for myself, that the lasting appeal of tragedy is due to our need to face the fact of death in order to strengthen ourselves for life' (preface to *Collected Plays*; 1958). What makes this confrontation with death so modern is that there are no comforting pieties about the afterlife. Hamlet embraces death as a sleep but then fears nightmares; the Ghost is an unquiet presence from beyond the grave; Polonius' corpse is so much decomposing lumber. Hamlet comes finally to the realisation that 'the rest is silence', and Horatio's 'flights of angels sing thee to thy rest' (5.2.347–9) seems an overoptimistic gloss from the previously rational student.

Since at least Freud, readings of Hamlet's character have been interested in his inner motivations and in his fractured relationships with women. (A film of 1976 by Celestine Coronado cast Helen Mirren as both Ophelia and Gertrude, to bring out their similarity in Hamlet's jaundiced view.) The play's misogyny is unavoidable and probably reflects attitudes at the end of Elizabeth's long reign, when the play was written: it is striking that Claudius likens his murder of a brother and a king to 'the harlot's cheek, beautied with plastering art' (3.1.53), just as his nephew 'must like a whore unpack[s] my heart with words' (2.2.538). In this context Gertrude's own protestation that she knew nothing of the death of her first husband has rarely been believed. But while scenes of violent intimacy between Hamlet and his mother when he visits her private chamber and discusses her sex life may parody Freudian interpretations (one reviewer of Franco Zeffirelli's 1990 film version with Glenn Close and Mel Gibson as mother and son called that scene 'ghostus interruptus'), the hold of melancholy and unresolved mourning on Hamlet's psyche is abiding. His has often been seen to be a distinctly modern alienation, and although the play does draw extensively on succession anxieties at the end of the Elizabethan period and on the literary heritage of revenge tragedies, it has come to be seen as Shakespeare's most timeless work.

A succession of modern-dress Hamlets from the eighteenth century onwards has asserted the enduring aspects of his situation. *Hamlet* has become Hamlet: less a story than an individual personality in which the specific details of the melodramatic plot are erased by the force of Shakespeare's representation of inner cogitation and distress. Horatio's summary of events in the play's closing lines: 'carnal, bloody, and unnatural acts, / Of accidental judgements, casual slaughters' (5.2.360–1) is laughably inadequate. What really happens in this play is a matter of the interior rather than the exterior; it is psychological rather than physical; and it is structured not around the crime and retaliation of the revenge tragedy genre but by rhetoric, punctuated by soliloquies that decisively displace action into reflection.

Julius Caesar

Key Facts
Date: 1599
Length: 2,730 lines
Verse: 95% / Prose: 5%

Major characters' share of lines:

Brutus	28%
Cassius	20%
Mark Antony	13%
Julius Caesar	5%

Political melodrama centring on the assassination of Julius Caesar

Plot and characters

Flavius and **Murellus**, two tribunes of Rome, discuss a recent victory of **Caesar** in the civil wars, and there is concern in Rome that Caesar is becoming too powerful, aggravated when, off stage, the crowds offer him the crown three times. A **Soothsayer** warns Caesar but is dismissed, while **Mark Antony**, Caesar's friend and ally, runs a festival race. **Cassius** tries to gain support for a conspiracy against Caesar by enlisting **Brutus**, with the help of anonymous letters encouraging him to become involved. Brutus is troubled by the prospect but persuades himself that killing Caesar will prevent future tyranny in a kind of justified pre-emptive strike. He does not agree with Cassius that Antony should also be assassinated. Brutus, Cassius, **Casca, Ligarius, Decius** and others agree to murder Caesar the next day, the Ides of March, in the Capitol. Brutus' wife **Portia** pleads to be kept involved and displays a self-inflicted wound as evidence of her stoicism. Caesar's wife **Calpurnia** has dreamed that her husband's statue spouted blood, and this omen combines with other troubling auguries to persuade him not to attend the Capitol. Decius reinterprets the dream to convince him to reconsider, luring him with the suggestion that the Senate will have him crowned king. Despite last-minute warnings by the Soothsayer and by **Artemidorus**, Caesar is repeatedly stabbed at the Senate, with Brutus inflicting the final wound. Brutus speaks to the plebeians reassuring them that the action has been taken in the best interests of Rome. Against the advice of Cassius he allows Antony to give a further funeral speech, and, alone on stage with Caesar's corpse, Antony vows his revenge. His speech to the crowds wins them over. Brutus and Cassius flee, and amid rioting in the city and the mob murder of an innocent poet, **Cinna**, Antony joins with **Octavius**, Caesar's nephew, and **Lepidus** to command a Roman army against them. News of Portia's suicide reaches Brutus, and he and Cassius are defeated at the Battle of Philippi, as predicted by the ghost of Caesar: they kill themselves rather than be captured, and Brutus is praised by the victors for his nobility.

Context and composition

Julius Caesar was written in 1599 and first published in the First Folio of 1623. It is an example of the transition from the English history plays of the 1590s and their stress on political instability and the characteristics of effective rule, towards the tragedies of the seventeenth century, in which questions of individual motivation and conscience play a major role. The depiction of the consequences of deposition link it to *King Richard II* and *Macbeth*; the contemporary play *Hamlet* makes allusions to its Roman context and also, like *King Richard III*, develops a Ghost role.

Shakespeare makes extensive use of Thomas North's translation of Plutarch's *Lives of the Noble Grecians and Romans* (1579; also the major source for *Coriolanus* and *Antony*), and his cutting of the material and dramatic compression of the timescale is matched by a rhetorical amplification, particularly in the speeches after Caesar's death. The play is highly rhetorical in style, and this rhetoric is also its main theme: the dangerous ability to persuade both characters and audience.

Performances

Comments from the first spectators of Shakespeare's plays are rare, but in September 1599 a Swiss visitor to the newly built Globe theatre in London described seeing 'the tragedy of the first Emperor Julius Caesar, very

pleasingly performed, with approximately fifteen characters [this presumably means fifteen actors, since the play text has more than forty named characters]; at the end of the play they danced together admirably and exceedingly gracefully, according to their custom, two in each group dressed in men's and two in women's apparel'. Perhaps it is not surprising that for a non-native speaker what was most appealing about this intensely verbal play was the concluding dance, but it is salutary to be reminded that, for its first spectators, *Julius Caesar* ended not with the imperial politics of Octavius solemnly arranging the burial of his adversary, but with a paired transvestite jig.

The play's fine balance of sympathies has often been overruled in performance, where directorial decisions have implicitly ratified either Caesar's government or Brutus' conspiracy, often by visual parallels to more recent topical conflicts. An American production in 1770, for instance, presented a modern Brutus as a patriot seeking liberty and independence; Orson Welles subtitled his 1937 production, costumed in contemporary fascist uniforms, *Death of a Dictator*; David Thacker's 1986 RSC production had Caesar as a strong and dignified Charles I beset by his Puritan enemies; the toppling of Caesar's huge statue in a 2004 production (dir. Ben Naylor, Menier Chocolate Factory) clearly recalled media coverage of the fall of Saddam Hussein. It is not known how the Roman plays would have been costumed at the Globe, but the only contemporary illustration of another Roman play, *Titus Andronicus*, suggests that historical costumes were not consistent and that essentially the play, which mentions doublets and handkerchiefs but not togas, may always have been in the 'modern dress' since favoured by modern directors. The atmosphere of rumour, secrecy, plotting and the potential for mob violence makes Joseph Mankiewicz's 1953 film, with tough-guy actors Marlon Brando as Mark Antony and James Mason as Brutus, speak to the conspiratorial atmosphere of Hollywood under McCarthyism; in 1970 Stuart Burge's film version promising 'no grander Caesar, no greater cast' starred John Gielgud in the title role.

Themes and interpretation

'Was Brutus right or wrong in murdering Caesar?' was one of the exemplary debating questions set to train Elizabethan schoolboys in the art of persuasive rhetoric. The object of the exercise was to be able to argue effectively for both sides (the Latin term is *in utramque partem*). It is intriguing to see this education, or something like it, seeding *Julius Caesar*'s political equilibrium, in which it is impossible to make the play conform fully to a yes or no answer. Does Caesar aspire to tyranny? By placing the early scene in which he rejects the crown proffered by the eager crowds tantalisingly out of sight, Shakespeare denies the audience direct access. We are unable to read whether he declines the crown willingly or not, just as we do not know whether Antony invented the generosity of Caesar's will. Like everything in the play, these events are filtered through observers and through rhetoric, and just like the play's own commoners, the audience's sympathies can be manipulated by the persuasive charisma of its characters.

Everything in the play is up for reinterpretation, from Calpurnia's ominous dream of Caesar's statue spouting blood to Brutus' orchard soliloquy, which, in beginning with its conclusion – 'It must be by his death' (2.1.10) – exemplifies the pre-emptive logic of his argument about killing a serpent in its shell lest it prove deadly later. Brutus admits that 'the quarrel / Will bear no colour for the thing he is' (2.1.28–9): the bogey version of Caesar is invented, 'augmented' (2.1.30), and those productions that caricature him as a hateful despot ignore the balance intrinsic to the play's careful construction. Given this intensely argumentative, rhetorical cast, it is no wonder it has been a favourite of politicians: Nelson Mandela, who read it while imprisoned on Robben Island, cited Caesar's staunch 'Cowards die many times before their deaths, / The valiant never taste of death but once' (2.2.32–3) as his favourite quotation. It is striking that, having written more than ten plays on the travails of English monarchical history before *Julius Caesar*, here Shakespeare tussles with the perennial problems of absolute power and of democratic participation in a secular context, untrammelled by the idea of the divine right of kings.

Generations of actors and readers have found Brutus the play's most interiorised and complex character, such that the question of renaming the play 'The Tragedy of Brutus' is often raised, particularly since its actual eponymous figure dies in the middle of the play. Certainly, it is in Brutus that the play's depiction of a conflict between public duty and private desire is most fully played out, as the unwilling conspirator turns away from his wife Portia and towards his political role at the beginning of Act 2. The report of Portia's gruesome death symbolises that unrecoverable domestic, private existence sacrificed to public, political life. But Caesar's ongoing presence – his ghost before the decisive Battle of Philippi, his name on Cassius' and Brutus' dying breaths – means that the play's narrative arc is anchored less to the lifespan of Brutus than to the politics of Rome. In the end this is less a play about individuals than about thwarted and distorted ideals, in which Rome itself, rather than any of its citizens, is the dominant character.

The end of the play sees its reinterpretation by the historical winners. Describing Brutus as 'the noblest Roman of them all' (5.5.68), Antony completes the ironic praise for his adversary that began in his magnificent oration over Caesar's body as the advantage swung away from the conspirators. Antony and Brutus as Caesar's symbolic sons (Shakespeare has suppressed the rumour that Brutus was Caesar's illegitimate child) fight for his legacy: the 'happy day' (5.5.81), though, often seems an anticlimax. Cassius describes Caesar as a 'Colossus' who 'doth bestride the narrow world' (1.2.135–6): his loss, even if it is perceived as deserved or necessary, leaves the play-world diminished and directionless.

King Henry IV Part 1

Key Facts
Date: 1596–7
Length: 3,180 lines
Verse: 55% / Prose: 45 %

Major characters' share of lines:

Falstaff	20%
Prince Henry	18%
Hotspur	18%
King Henry IV	11%

Popular history play combining familial and national political strife

Plot and characters

King Henry IV begins the play 'so shaken' by civil wars (1.1.1) and never really regains his composure. His council includes the loyal **Westmorland** and **Blount**. Henry's two sons **John of Lancaster** and **Henry Prince of Wales** (Harry, or Hal) are polar opposites – the one loyal at his father's side, the other truant from courtly duties and enjoying instead the company of **Sir John Falstaff**, a fat reprobate knight, his followers **Bardolph**, **Peto** and **Ned Poins,** and the tavern landlady or **Hostess, Mistress Quickly**. King Henry wishes that the brave and chivalric **Sir Henry Percy (Hotspur)** were his son instead of Prince Henry, but hot-tempered Hotspur's grievances against the King mean that he joins instead with his father **Northumberland,** uncle **Worcester,** Welsh father-in-law **Owen Glendower** and brother-in-law **Lord Edmund Mortimer,** who has a claim to be the rightful heir to the throne, and **Douglas,** a Scot. They plan to divide up England after their victory against Henry, and later **Scroop, Archbishop of York** joins with the rebels. Percy's wife, **Lady Percy,** chides him for his neglect of her; **Lady Mortimer** speaks only Welsh though her relationship with the English-speaking Mortimer seems a tender one. There are signs that Prince Henry's delinquency is not irreversible and that he may ultimately reject his disreputable friends, but not before an extended joke on Falstaff in which he tells a wildly exaggerated story of a robbery committed against him by the disguised prince. After some abrasive encounters with his disapproving father, Prince Henry ends up fighting alongside him at Shrewsbury. Falstaff's cowardice and venality are made clear in the battle environment, where instead of a weapon he carries a bottle of sack. He fakes his death to avoid injury. Prince Henry defends his father from Douglas, and then fights Hotspur in single combat, killing him. He mourns the dead Falstaff, who, when the coast is clear, rises up to claim the credit for Hotspur's defeat; the Prince does not challenge this version of events. The play ends with the King's party triumphant but with more battles to come in order to defeat the rebels.

Composition and context

The play was written around 1596–7 and first published in 1598 as *The History of Henry the Fourth*: it only becomes 'Part 1' when the two plays are published serially for the first time in the First Folio of 1623. We do not know whether Shakespeare intended to write a serial history all along or whether the popularity of the play generated a sequel. Obviously the play has strong connections with *King Richard II*, where the late mention of King Henry's reprobate son seems a hook for this later play, and with *King Henry IV Part 2* and *King Henry V*, which show the continuing fortunes of the Prince as he enters his inheritance.

The character of Falstaff was originally called 'Oldcastle', a pious historical figure who was idealised by Elizabethan reformers as a proto-Protestant martyr, but this naming was suppressed, probably through the intervention of his influential descendant Lord Cobham, offended by the disrespect shown to his ancestor. The play was particularly popular in print, with eight further editions before 1640, and a large number of references and allusions to Falstaff, and his later appearance in a comedy, *Merry Wives*, suggest his wide appeal. It has a high proportion of prose, and thus has more in common stylistically with comedies such as *As You Like It* and *Twelfth Night* than with its verse history predecessor *King Richard II*. The play's nearest thematic relations among the canon are Shakespeare's other history plays, with which it shares an interest in the character and education of the successful/good king, and in moments of transfer or uncertain political allegiance. In its depiction of father and son relations it anticipates *Hamlet*; in showing the aftermath of regicide it may be connected with *Julius Caesar* and *Macbeth*. Shakespeare's sources for the play are Holinshed's prose history *Chronicles* (2nd edn, 1587), Daniel's verse epic *The First Four Books of the Civil Wars* (1595) and the anonymous play *The Famous Victories of Henry V* (performed 1594).

Performances

Until the twentieth century there was no tradition of performing histories as sequences and so this was experienced as a stand-alone play. The original Falstaff may have been the clown Will Kemp, whose other roles included Dogberry in *Much Ado* and, perhaps, Lance in *The Two Gentlemen of Verona*. The play was popular throughout the seventeenth and eighteenth centuries, often in a version combining parts of *King Henry IV Part 2* as a comic vehicle for its Falstaff. Victorian interest in historical spectacle refocused attention on the play's political plot. The twentieth century popularised cycles of history plays – by Frank Benson (1905–6), Barry Jackson (1921), Anthony Quayle (1951), John Barton and Peter Hall (1964), Michael Bogdanov and Michael Pennington (1987–8) and Michael Boyd (2006–7), among many others – in which the play figures as part of an unfolding narrative of the consequences of Richard II's overthrow (in the BBC television version directed by David Giles in 1979, Jon Finch as King Henry repeatedly washes his hands, reliving his guilt as he attempts to exorcise it), and as a stage in Harry's development to maturity. Pennington played a ruthless Prince who kills Hotspur in a brutish breach of chivalric honour in 1987 (English Shakespeare Company, dir. Michael Bogdanov); a more likeable Michael Maloney in Adrian Noble's 1991 RSC production was caught between Falstaff and the King as alternative father figures. For the BBC Shakespeare, Anthony Quayle's Falstaff was anxious and vulnerable behind his hedonism; Robert Stephens gave the role a darkly introspective cast (dir. Adrian Noble, 1991, RSC); father and son Timothy and Sam West played Falstaff and Harry in 1996

(English Touring Theatre, dir. Stephen Unwin). This relationship between Harry and Falstaff is the theme amplified in two significant film adaptations: Orson Welles' nostalgic *Chimes at Midnight* (1965) and Gus van Sant's queer modern update *My Own Private Idaho* (1991).

Themes and interpretations

Prince Henry's first appearance in this play, bandying wordplay with Falstaff in Eastcheap, comes as an immediate relief to the political tension and seriousness of the opening scene. It establishes a sharp contrast, with a pattern of deference, anxious politics and blank verse set as the defining characteristic of the court, and of self-gratification, staged capers and prose that of the tavern. The question about what time it is (1.2.1) also, subtly, suggests that the clock is already ticking on Prince Henry's carefree lifestyle. Political demands and duty will squeeze out recreation, the progress of history will overtake dalliance – but not entirely. Falstaff, after all, is only pretending to be dead at Shrewsbury – the wonderful resurrective stage direction as he gets to his feet once the fighting has passed is '*Falstaff riseth up*' (5.4.109), giving him a green-man spirit of vitality. When Prince Henry grants his old drinking companion the credit for Hotspur's death, moral closure is deferred.

The Prince's soliloquy at the end of his first scene, beginning 'I know you all' (1.2.155), is both crucial to and ambiguous about his characterisation. His promise of 'redeeming time when men think least I will' (1.2.177) may suggest calculation (he is playing at being the prodigal), resignation (he knows his royal obligations will ultimately claim him), self-delusion (he dignifies his apparently wild lifestyle by suggesting it is part of bigger plan), or merely an insouciant attempt to win over the audience at this early point in the play. The range of meanings of this soliloquy engages one of the play's most significant conflicts: that Prince Henry's morally desirable reformation must be at the cost of the play's most dramatically desirable energies; or to put it another way, Prince Henry is going to have to jettison Falstaff (boo), but not yet (hurrah). This play doesn't quite follow through on the moral reform, but it does gesture strongly towards it, particularly in the sinister conclusion to the scene in which the pair take turns to act out the Prince's interview with his father (2.4). Naming is crucial to this: the Prince of Wales is 'Harry' to his father and 'Hal' to Falstaff: the text of the play is more formal and distant, calling him 'Prince' in its stage directions and speech prefixes.

Conflicting ideas of honour and duty structure this play about conflicted allegiances. Just as the Prince owes filial loyalty to both the King and Falstaff, and his father in turn wishes Hotspur were his natural son instead of Henry, so Hotspur himself seems to represent a chivalric past which the play both mourns and dispatches. In his preference for the masculine values of the battlefield over the effeminate court, and in his association with the poetic Celts among the rebels, Hotspur can seem to belong to a different, more heroic story-world than that of the compromised king and his dissolute son. That his corpse is disputed between the pragmatic Henry and the self-interested Falstaff indicates how Hotspur's values have been eclipsed, and even though Henry's eulogy acknowledges his particular 'spirit' (5.4.88), Falstaff's own humorous disquisition on 'honour' as mere 'air' (5.1.132) shows how radical is his challenge to political martial ethics.

Haunted by memories of the past, King Henry is unable really to impose his authority on his country or his play, where his is only the fourth largest speaking role after Falstaff, the Prince and Hotspur. The deposed Richard sends a long shadow over the events in the play: Henry is planning a repentant Crusade in 1.1; he taxes his son with sharing Richard's fatal lust for popularity (3.2); Mortimer claims he is Richard's heir (3.1). The play looks forwards as well as backwards, and its conclusion is really anything but: it is only after a lull in the battle, a provisional victory, a tentative realignment of father and son.

King Henry IV
Part 2

Key Facts

Date: 1597–8

Length: 3,322 lines

Verse: 50% / Prose: 50%

Major characters' share of lines:

Falstaff	20%
Prince Henry	9%
King Henry IV	9%
Shallow	6%

Sequel to the popular Part 1: more tension between Prince Henry and his real and surrogate fathers, King Henry and Falstaff

Plot and characters

Rumour opens the play with a misleading account of the Battle of Shrewsbury; **Lord Bardolph** echoes this, telling **Northumberland** that the rebels have beaten the **King**, who is seriously wounded, and that his son Hotspur has killed **Prince Henry**. Two other witnesses contradict this. The **Lord Chief Justice** accuses **Falstaff** of highway robbery (the Gad's Hill episode in *1 Henry IV*) and is disapproving of his conduct. Falstaff tries to get expenses out of him. The rebellious lords **Mowbray, Hastings**, the **Archbishop of York** and Bardolph discuss tactics. At the tavern the hostess **Mistress Quickly** accuses Falstaff before the Lord Chief Justice of breach of promise for failing to pay his bills: Falstaff persuades her to relent. Prince Henry is concerned for his father's ill-health, but admits to **Poins** that no one will believe he is really troubled. Northumberland is persuaded against joining the rebellion by **Lady Percy**, widow of Hotspur, and flees instead to Scotland. Disguised, Prince Henry and Poins trick Falstaff who is dining in the tavern with the swaggering soldier **Pistol**, Mistress Quickly and **Doll Tearsheet**, but the Prince is recalled to his father, who is anxious about the political crisis. Falstaff goes to the Warwickshire countryside to recruit soldiers and meets old acquaintances **Justice Shallow** and **Justice Silence**. **Prince John's** forces have a parley with the rebels and agree terms, but then he arrests them for treason. In the battle Falstaff takes **Coleville** prisoner and hands him over to John. The King sleeps on hearing the news of the rebels' capture, and Prince Henry watches over him. Believing his father to have died, he takes up the crown; the King wakes and complains of his ingratitude and riot before the pair are reconciled. King Henry advises his heir on good kingship. The Lord Chief Justice announces the King's death; the Prince takes up his responsibilities. Falstaff boasts to Shallow that he will be elevated by the new king; at the coronation procession, Henry banishes Falstaff and the Lord Chief Justice sends him to prison, but the epilogue promises he will return, along with Henry and Princess Katherine of France.

Context and composition

Shakespeare seems to have written Part 2 of *King Henry IV* during 1597–8, straight after the success of the first play and before *King Henry V*. It was first published in 1600, and not reprinted until the First Folio edition of 1623. Like Part 1, the play draws on historical sources by Holinshed and Hall, and also on an anonymous play, *The Famous Victories of Henry V*: again, Falstaff is a major addition to the source material. Its similarity to its popular predecessor may suggest that *King Henry IV Part 2* is a sequel analogous to the second part of a modern cinematic hit, in which a formula that has proved to be successful is repeated, often as a pale shadow of the original. On the other hand, Shakespeare has held back some crucial dramatic incidents, including the rejection of Falstaff and Hal's coronation as Henry V, which might easily have been compressed into a single play, suggesting that a second part had been intended from an early stage, rather than written in response to commercial demand.

The play is half prose and half verse, and thus connected with the rhythms of contemporary comedies including *Much Ado About Nothing* and *As You Like It*.

Performances

Although *King Henry IV Part 2* was apparently originally staged as an independent play, for much of its stage history it has been inextricably linked with its predecessor. Combined versions of the two plays range from a 1623

manuscript for Sir Edward Dering, perhaps intended for private theatrical performance, to the BBC version of 1995 directed by John Caird, and during the twentieth century it has most often been performed as part of a longer sequence, such as the television *Age of Kings* (1960) or the *Wars of the Roses* (English Shakespeare Company, directed by Michael Bogdanov, 1985). In the theatre the play's melancholy tends to emerge: the sickly king, the cynical rebels, the washed-up merriment. For the RSC, Terry Hands' 1973 production had a single leafless tree and a cannon for a set; in 1982 Trevor Nunn stressed dark shadows and the sense of a wasted past; Michael Boyd's 2008 cycle emphasised parallels between Prince Henry and Richard II, in a set and production that continuously brought the ghosts of the past into the present and used doubling to make connections across time and place.

Themes and interpretation

The long title of the play in its first publication announces 'The Second Part of Henry the Fourth, continuing to his death, and coronation of Henry the fifth. With the humours of Sir John Falstaff and swaggering Pistol'. Like the play itself, the title is in a hurry to get to the end of the story: the coronation of Henry V and the separation of the wild prince from his erstwhile companion Falstaff. The inevitability – perhaps the necessity – of the rejection of Falstaff overshadows the play. While Falstaff is bragging to Shallow about how he will be favoured when his protégé Hal ascends the throne, King Henry V, as he now is, is making his regal pronouncements to the Lord Chief Justice and other dignitaries. When he calls the Lord Chief Justice 'father' (5.2.139), the signal is clear: he has turned for ever from his putative Eastcheap father Falstaff. The Oedipal rivalry is over, and with the crown he assumes an unfamiliar tone of majestic gravitas. Falstaff's eager preparations to meet his 'tender lambkin' (5.3.96) are poignant and pathetic, and even though his interests may be principally selfish, his humiliation by his erstwhile companion is a painful end to the play: 'I know thee not, old man. Fall to thy prayers' (5.5.43). Falstaff continues his delusions, in his repeated belief that 'I shall be sent for soon at night' (5.5.83).

Falstaff – perhaps the most popular stage creation of the age – is, it seems, the sacrifice for Hal's reformation. Perhaps this takes the lustre off King Henry's triumphant coronation in the final scene. It is striking, too, that in Henry's coronation the audience is also distanced from him. We can only wait, like Falstaff, for his train to pass by: the days of easy dramatic intimacy with Prince Hal are gone, and in their place is this formal, spectacular relation of monarch and subject. Now we, too, are those onlookers marvelling at the rarely seen personage, as Henry IV advised in 1 Henry IV. Throughout the play the warmth of the comic relationships in the earlier part has cooled, and the overall tone is much more muted, wistful, even bittersweet. The scene in which Poins and Hal are found wearing leather jerkins and waiting on the old reprobate at table does not have the same esprit as the exuberant Gad's Hill escapade in 1 Henry IV – and it is striking that Prince Henry and Falstaff are hardly together on stage. The energy which motivated those earlier pranks is diverted elsewhere, as the hour of Henry's assumption of the role of king comes ever nearer. It is not just Shallow and Falstaff who look back nostalgically on their youth; Orson Welles took the old men's refrain 'We have heard the chimes at midnight' (3.2.177) as the keynote for his classic cinematic version of the two Henry IV plays, Chimes at Midnight (1965).

The weariness that marked some of Henry IV's speeches in the previous play is here solidified into an atmosphere of exhausted enervation around the sovereign, and the prospect of the King's demise is imminent. His hold on this play is even more tenuous than on Part 1, symbolised by his absence from the play's early scenes before his weakened appearance, 'in his nightgown', in Act 3, Scene 1. All his appearances in this play are marked by his physical debility. Images of sickness and disease are applied both to the monarch and to the realm, and the King's illness represents the wider sickness in the body politic. Henry describes 'the body of our kingdom' as 'foul', infected with 'rank diseases', and Warwick continues the imagery but with a more optimistic prognosis: 'It is but as a body yet distempered / Which to his former strength may be restored / With good advice and little medicine' (3.1.36–42). The language of diagnosis and cure is also used at length by the Archbishop: 'we are all diseased', from which 'Our late King Richard being infected died' (4.1.54–8). This vocabulary of political and royal disease is echoed in references to sickness, particularly venereal disease, in the Falstaff scenes, and the addition of minor characters named Mouldy and Wart helps to produce an overarching theme of infection and corruption – physical, material and political.

Where *King Henry IV Part 1* opened with the King's lengthy oration, *Part 2* begins with the omniscient personification Rumour. The different forms of authority represented by these contrasting openings reveal much about the moods of their respective plays. Here, Rumour sets a tone of suspicion and deceit, of 'surmises, jealousies, conjectures' (Induction, 16) that infuses much of the play. Falsified hopes – of victory, of preferment, of repayment, of defeat – spread like disease, creating a subdued mood. It is not surprising that the Epilogue, a predominantly comic device, tries to cheer us up with the prospect of the next instalment. At the end of this regretful, retrospective play we look resolutely forward: 'If you be not too much cloyed with fat meat, our humble author will continue the story, with Sir John in it, and make you merry with fair Katherine of France' (Epilogue, 20–2). Henry V, the long-awaited sovereign, has ascended his throne: there is now much weight of dramatic and political expectation on him.

King Henry V

Key Facts
Date: 1599
Length: 3,381 lines
Verse: 60% / Prose: 40%

Major characters' share of lines:	
Henry V	32%
Llewellyn	9%
Chorus	7%
Archbishop of Canterbury	7%

Classic underdog play with the English victory over the French at Agincourt

Plot and characters

A **Chorus** figure encourages the audience to participate in the play's imaginative reconstruction of history, and punctuates the acts with descriptions. The Archbishop of **Canterbury** and Bishop of **Ely** plot to distract the new king from plans to tax the Church by encouraging him to war with France. Canterbury delivers a long speech to **King Henry** telling him that under Salic Law he has a right to France, when a scornful dispatch from the French **Dauphin** alluding to Henry's riotous youth confirms the King's mind for war. News of his old friend Falstaff's death, perhaps because of the King's disfavour, is reported as **Pistol**, with **Bardolph**, **Nym** and **Boy**, takes leave of his wife **Mistress Quickly** the tavern hostess. News of a conspiracy by **Scroop**, **Grey** and **Cambridge** is revealed: Henry acts decisively to condemn them, although he is dismayed in particular by his friend Scroop's betrayal. In France Henry's forces besiege the town of Harfleur. The Welsh captain **Llewellyn** (usually Fluellen), the Irish captain **MacMorris**, the Scots captain **Jamy** and the English captain **Gower** argue in their various accents about military tactics. Princess **Katherine** of France begins, with her companion **Alice**, to learn English. The French and English armies prepare to fight near a castle called Agincourt: Henry rejects **Montjoy**, the French herald's offer of ransom. Henry passes disguised among his men and hears their fears and questions about the war. He quarrels with **Williams** and they vow to fight after the battle. Privately, he expresses the strains of leadership and prays that God will not punish him for his father's deposition of King Richard II. The French camp, by contrast, is confident. During the battle the French attack the unguarded English and, enraged, Henry has the prisoners killed. Pistol takes **Le Fer**, a French soldier, prisoner and looks for reward. The English win a decisive victory, with miraculously few casualties compared with a long list of slain French nobility. Henry dedicates the victory to God. He tricks Llewellyn into the confrontation with Williams on his behalf, although it ends in merriment; Pistol's attempts to bully Llewellyn are stopped by Gower, who stands up for the Welshman. **Exeter**, **Bedford**, **Warwick**, **Gloucester** and the other Lords negotiate the terms of the peace with the **French King** and **Queen** and the **Duke of Burgundy**: Henry woos an initially reluctant Katherine in broken French, and the announcement of their marriage marks the conclusion of hostilities. The Epilogue reminds us that their son Henry VI lost France again.

Context and composition

It is possible to date *King Henry V* with an accuracy unusual in the Shakespearean canon, because of a contemporary allusion in the Chorus to Act 5, comparing Henry to the Earl of Essex, who led an expedition to Ireland in the summer of 1599. It thus dates from the same productive year as *Much Ado About Nothing*, *As You Like It* and *Julius Caesar*. It is first printed in 1600 in a shorter version that does not include the choruses, and in a longer text in 1623. As for his other plays on English history, Shakespeare uses the chronicle histories by Holinshed and Hall, as well as the anonymous play *The Famous Victories of Henry V*. Nowhere else, except perhaps with the figure of Gower in *Pericles*, does Shakespeare use the chorus figure so prominently, and this gives the play an epic quality, as well as an abiding consciousness of its own status as theatre.

Performances

In its opening allusion to the 'wooden O', the play refers to its original theatre, and it may be that it was one of the first plays performed at the new Globe theatre on Bankside, which opened in 1599.

Perhaps because of its topicality, it does not seem to have been as popular in its own time as the *Henry IV* plays. Its stage history has been intimately connected with war and national strife, from the Napoleonic Wars to Afghanistan. Laurence Olivier's famous wartime film (1944) is notable for its stylisation and avoidance of violence, and for omitting anything that might tarnish Henry's characterisation, such as the blood-curdling speech before the walls of Harfleur; Kenneth Branagh's film version (1989) is elegiac, with a more interiorised Henry troubled by the ethics and the costs of conflict. In the theatre the play has undergone a substantial shift. Until the second half of the twentieth century it was largely performed as a hymn of praise to its charismatic warrior-king Henry. Changing attitudes to leadership and to militarism in the 1960s, however, uncovered a more sceptical and questioning play: Michael Pennington in the English Shakespeare Company production of 1985 (dir. Michael Bogdanov) played a repellent, brutal Henry, prompting one reviewer to note that it was the first time he had wanted the French to win. Nicholas Hytner directed Adrian Lester in a modern-dress version in 2003 (National Theatre) where the emphasis was on the justification for war in 1.2, in a clear reference to pressing contemporary questions about the legality of the British and American campaign in Iraq.

Themes and interpretation

1599 was a tough year for Londoners: high food prices and shortages were exacerbated by large-scale musters of men, horses and supplies for the ongoing war in Ireland. This play's account of a glorious and decisive triumph in France, when a plucky English army led by a charismatic military king win against extraordinary odds, must have had an immediate appeal. Like glossy extravagant Hollywood musicals in the Depression, *King Henry V* was a distraction, wish-fulfilment – a dramatic experience in which, unlike real life, victory was assured. Shakespeare plays up the miraculous elements of this triumph, reducing the number of English casualties from the sources and suppressing the importance of superior military technology – the longbow – to give the glory to God and his inspirational lieutenant Henry.

There is indeed much tub-thumping patriotism in the play. The French are suitably proud and haughty, the English outnumbered but valiant. 'Cry "God for Harry, England and St George"' (3.1.34) sums up the play's appeal to nationalistic sentiment. But the presentation is not entirely positive: the play activates ironies and allows for a more measured interpretation of Henry. Theatre productions that have wanted to present him as an uncomplicated hero have tended to cut those parts of the play which do not entirely accord with that interpretation: the repeated suggestion that the absent Falstaff has died because of Henry's rejection of him; the reiterated question mark over whether the war is legal or not; a hiccup in the text which has Henry order the execution of the French prisoners – a war crime – *before* the French have raided their camp. Even the Chorus, apparently Henry's PR machine, gives a gap for alternative readings of the King's actions: when, for example Henry goes among his soldiers in disguise he does not hear what the Chorus has been telling us – that Henry's presence cheers the men and they serve him gladly. Instead he encounters a dignified and unanswerable challenge to his warmongering and finds himself unable to convince through argument. Rather than uniting his army against their common foe, he picks a fight with one of his own men.

Henry's character, then, is more complicated than it might seem. He is forced into isolation: betrayed by Scroop, Cambridge and Grey, and separating himself from his former companions. The execution of Bardolph for theft further marks Henry's need as king to distance himself from the prodigal youth that no one – not the Archbishop, nor the Dauphin, nor Falstaff, nor perhaps the audience – can forget. It is as if, as king, he has forgone his private personality. In this play he speaks in speeches: formally, rhetorically, publicly. Only one moment of soliloquy and prayer shows a glimpse of inner struggle. If he is tortured in private, it is in public that he is most assured: stage-managing the confessions of the conspirators, addressing the troops as brothers, wooing Katherine in chauvinistically confident broken French, with an eye to the audience. The play works hard to become a romantic comedy in its last, long scene: the truth is that Katherine is a prize of Henry's victory and thus has no more chance to reject him than does her defeated country, but the fiction of a courtship is maintained. Yet the feel-good tone of the play cannot be entirely sustained: it ends not with this image of military success recast as sexual conquest, but with the Epilogue's regretful knowledge that the victory was only temporary. The plays already available to playgoers – the three parts of *King Henry VI* – show that the conflicts, at home and abroad, soon recur.

The play's main rhetorical mode is that of persuasion – persuading Harfleur to surrender, men to fight, women to marry – and the Chorus extends that persuasion to the audience. We are repeatedly required to participate or excuse: 'piece out our imperfections with your thoughts' (Prologue, 23); 'For 'tis your thoughts that now must deck our kings' (Prologue, 28). It is striking that as these are acts of imagination common to all theatre they are not usually explicitly required of audiences, but here they take on a double aspect, at once reminding us of the limitations of the theatre even as they encourage us to transcend them. It is a microcosm of the play's contradictions as both pro-war and anti-war, sentimental and sceptical, idealising and cynical, realistic and self-consciously theatrical; a play in which although Henry speaks almost four times as much as anyone else, the persistent voices of his challengers – Williams, MacMorris, Pistol – still resound.

King Henry VI Parts 1, 2 and 3

Key Facts

Part 1	Part 2	Part 3
Date: 1592	Date: 1590–1	Date: 1591–2
Length: 2,931 lines	Length: 3,355 lines	Length: 3,217 lines
Verse: 100%	Verse: 85% / Prose: 15%	Verse: 100%
Major characters' share of lines:	**Major characters' share of lines:**	**Major characters' share of lines:**
Talbot — 15%	Richard Plantagenet (Duke of York) — 12%	Edward — 15%
Joan la Pucelle — 9%	Henry VI — 10%	Warwick — 15%
Richard Plantagenet (Duke of York) — 7%	Gloucester — 10%	Gloucester — 14%
Duke of Gloucester — 7%	Suffolk — 10%	Henry VI — 12%
Henry VI — 7%	Margaret — 10%	Margaret — 10%

Wars of the Roses epic of political chaos beginning with the funeral of Henry V and ending with the unstoppable ambition of Richard Duke of Gloucester (later Richard III) for the battered English throne

Plot and characters

Part 1

At the funeral of Henry V news is heard of losses in France and quarrels break out among the nobles, particularly the Duke of **Gloucester** and the Bishop of **Winchester**. Their supporters fight in London and have to be dispersed by the **Lord Mayor**. At the siege of Orleans the French are beaten back by the English and the mysterious holy maid **Joan** la Pucelle defeats the **Dauphin** in a test before taking Orleans from the legendary English warrior **Talbot**, during which battle the Earl of **Salisbury** is killed. Talbot, **Burgundy** and **Bedford** retake Orleans, and Talbot evades the attempts of the **Countess of Auvergne** to capture him. In the Temple Garden in London Richard **Plantagenet** and the Duke of **Somerset** declare their animosity as rivals for the throne, and pick a white and red rose respectively as an emblem of their loyalty. **Edmund Mortimer**, heir of Richard II, dies in prison supporting Plantagenet's claim. The young king **Henry VI** makes Plantagenet Duke of **York**, and goes to France to be crowned. In the battle for Rouen Burgundy is persuaded to swap sides. The King attempts, badly, to mediate a quarrel between **Vernon** (a supporter of York) and **Basset** (Somerset) and angers York. The quarrel between York and Somerset affects supplies to Talbot in Bordeaux: he and his son are both killed. In the peace negotiations Henry is offered the daughter of the Earl of Armagnac; instead, **Suffolk** captures **Margaret of Anjou** and woos her for Henry so that she will be his, Suffolk's, lover, handing over two provinces to her father in return. York captures Joan who is raising demonic spirits: the French have turned against her. She is condemned to death. York and Winchester – now a cardinal – negotiate peace but Suffolk persuades Henry to marry Margaret, despite their objections.

Part 2

Margaret of Anjou is presented at court **by Suffolk**: the match is decried by **Gloucester. Winchester, Buckingham** and other nobles agree that Gloucester must be brought down. **York**, too, has secret ambitions for the crown. Gloucester rebukes his wife **Eleanor** for her ambitions to the crown; Eleanor hires a priest, **Hume**, to bring witches to predict the future: Hume is in the pay of Suffolk. The spirit prophesies the downfall of **Henry**, York and Suffolk, but the seance is ended by Buckingham and York who arrest Eleanor and sentence her to be banished. Gloucester resigns as royal protector. York attempts to build support from **Salisbury** and **Warwick** for his claim to the throne, and when Suffolk returns with news of losses in France the nobles conspire against Gloucester to accuse him of treason. Henry defends him. York reveals to the audience that he has incited a clothier, **Jack Cade**, to rebel in the guise of his dead ancestor John Mortimer, and bring the realm to more confusion. Gloucester is found dead and Suffolk is accused and exiled. Winchester dies. Cade's rebellion advances from Kent to London, arresting and executing **Lord Say. Clifford** and Buckingham greet the rebels with Henry's pardon: the riot disperses and Cade flees. He is caught, hungry, in the garden of Alexander **Iden**, and killed. York returns from Ireland to give battle to Henry and his supporters at St Albans. York kills Clifford; Richard kills **Somerset**. Henry and Margaret flee the victorious Yorkists.

Part 3

At court the Yorkists force King **Henry** to disinherit his son **Prince Edward** in favour of **York** and his heirs, in order to stop the civil war. Queen **Margaret** denounces this and vows to defend her son's rights. **Edward** and **Richard**, York's sons, persuade him to take the crown immediately: in the battle his other son, **Rutland**, is killed by young **Clifford** and York is captured, tormented and killed by Margaret. Edward, York's son, is proclaimed king by his supporters, and the Yorkists are victorious at the Battle of Towton. Henry wishes for the simplicity of a shepherd's life rather than the stresses of kingship, and his lament for the horrors of civil war is illustrated by a grieving son who has mistakenly killed his father, and a father who has unwittingly killed his only son. Margaret, Henry, Prince Edward and **Exeter** flee to Scotland. Clifford is killed and Edward is proclaimed king: he has Henry captured and imprisoned in the Tower. **Lady Elizabeth Grey** pleads for her dead husband's lands before Edward, and deflects his sexual proposition by insisting that he must marry her, which he does. The nobles are outraged, and **Warwick** and the French King – to whose sister Edward was betrothed – turn against the new king. **Richard of Gloucester**, Edward's brother, expresses his own ambition for the throne, and joins Edward's enemies. Warwick and **Clarence** uncrown the King and capture him, releasing Henry from the tower and reinstating him as king. The Yorkists land in England and march on London, proclaiming Edward king again. At the Battle of Barnet Warwick is killed. After much changing of sides, at the final battle at Tewkesbury, Edward defeats Margaret and kills her son Prince Edward: she curses them and is banished to France. Gloucester kills Henry in the Tower. Queen Elizabeth gives birth to a son amid Yorkist rejoicing, but Gloucester's ominous 'Judas' kiss of the baby prince suggests that the peace is not completely secure.

Context and composition

The three parts of the *King Henry VI* plays appear for the first time in the First Folio of 1623, which is also the first time Part 1 was published. Parts 2 and 3 had been previously printed, separately and in a combined edition, under different titles: *The First Part of the*

Contention of the Two Famous Houses of York and Lancaster (Part 2) and *The True Tragedy of Richard Duke of York* (Part 3). Part 1 was probably written after this pair, perhaps as a kind of 'prequel' to capitalise on their popularity. All three parts may have been jointly written, and George Peele and Robert Greene have been suggested as co-authors: the stylistic arguments that Part 1 was collaboratively written with Thomas Nashe are strongest. Part 1 was probably written in 1592, Part 2 in 1590–1 (first published in 1594) and Part 3 in 1591–2 (first published in 1595).

All three parts draw extensively on Edward Halle's historical account of the Wars of the Roses and on Holinshed's *Chonicles* (2nd edn, 1587), but give evidence of a wide range of reading in English and French chronicle history. The torture of York in Part 3 may recall the staging of the passion in the medieval mystery cycle plays. Part of the plays' popularity may have been because the historical battles in France resonated with contemporary conflicts: the Earl of Essex, for example, besieged Rouen in 1591–2, just as Talbot did in Part 1.

Performances

All three plays require a relatively large cast to manage the numerous roles. *Richard Duke of York* (Part 3) states on its title page that it was performed by Pembroke's Men, a company formed in 1591; Part 1 was performed at the Rose theatre in March 1592, according to the diary of its impresario-manager Philip Henslowe, and the recorded takings for that performance are the highest of the season: probably Edward Alleyn, the leading actor famous for his roles in Christopher Marlowe's plays, would have played Talbot. There is no evidence of serial performance in the early modern period, although other multiple-part plays, such as Marlowe's two *Tamburlaine*s, do seem to have sometimes played in repertory at the same time. But most of the stage history combines the plays, either in reworked and condensed version (Peter Hall and John Barton's *Wars of the Roses*, 1963–4; Edward Hall/Propeller's *Rose Rage*, 2001), or as serial history (BBC television, *Age of Kings* [1960]; Michael Boyd's *This England: Histories* season, RSC, 2002), and it is rare now ever to see one of the plays performed independently (Katie Mitchell's 1994 RSC production of Part 3, renamed *Henry VI: The Battle for the Throne*, is an exception).

Serial or reworked production, then, has been the form in which these plays have become more familiar to theatre audiences, allowing for their symmetries and repetitions to be emphasised. Adrian Noble's 1988 production, united by Penny Downie as Margaret, circled around a central prop of the throne, raised up on a prison cage. Michael Boyd made extensive use of doubling and ghosting to unify the sequence and bring past and present together: newspaper reviews boasted that his ensemble of 34 actors played 264 parts across 8 history plays and spilled 15 litres of stage blood. Edward Hall's production *Rose Rage* (Propeller, 2001) also stressed bloodshed: the cast were butchers in bloody overalls, accompanying the lines with the percussive clanging of cleavers.

Themes and interpretation

One of the most famous and influential critical paradigms for understanding Shakespeare's history plays has been E. M. W. Tillyard's view that they present an essentially ordered and morally redemptive cycle in which the crime of regicide – the murder of *King Richard II* – is expiated through the violence of the Wars of the Roses. If that is true, then in the *King Henry VI* plays we are in a dark place in the narrative: it is hard to get any sense of order or redemption or even historical progress in a trilogy of plays marked by circularity and repetition rather than teleology. The most prominent theme of these plays is disorder: the rebellion of Jack Cade in Part 2; the Yorkists' sustained challenge to the throne in Part 3; the role of politically powerful and transgressive women across all three plays. And the most prominent structural device is the echo: in Part 1 as one challenging French woman, Joan la Pucelle, is cut down, another, Margaret of Anjou, rises to take her place; rituals of coronation and decoronation pepper Part 3; fathers from Talbot to York to the unnamed, symbolic Father who has killed his own son (Part 3) mourn their offspring; and sons, from Clifford to Edward to the unnamed Son, mourn fathers and vow vengeance in their names; battles follow battles; fortunes change and change back again.

Certainly the plays can be difficult to follow, and doubling, the early modern practice of actors playing more than one role in a play, must have made this even more confusing: the device of the white and red roses in the Temple Garden would have had a practical, as well as a symbolic, purpose in helping to differentiate the factions on stage. What the theatre director John Barton described, in justifying his substantial rewriting of the sequence as *The Wars of the Roses* (1963–4), as 'a mess of angry and undifferentiated barons, thrashing about in a mass of diffuse narrative' makes more sense if we see the plays enacting the essential stasis of civil war, in which no battle is decisive, and instead a sequence of Edwards and Yorks and Richards and Cliffords – sometimes the same individual, sometimes more than one – are serially enmeshed in forms of action and retaliation.

The crown, the central prop amid the melee, passes back and forth: the paper crown York is forced to wear in Part 3 epitomises its empty fragility. Here is no sacramental idea of kingship, such as we get – even though it is challenged – in *King Richard II*. Power seems in these plays the altogether more modern property of political and military might. Part 3 in particular gives us two kings simultaneously, as Edward and Henry are alternately crowned and dethroned, and the back and forth of battles, negotiations and intrigues does nothing to confer especial legitimacy on either claimant. To be king in these plays is to be called it by sufficient numbers of followers, rather than to be anointed as God's temporal regent. It is striking that Shakespeare's first history plays exemplify his interest in power shifts: Shakespeare's sense of politics here is pragmatic and human rather than ideological, and his sense of causation radically secular rather than divine. Things happen because human agents make them happen, as Richard, Duke of Gloucester menacingly suggests at the plays' ultimate, but rather perilous, conclusion.

If there are heroes in this cast, then they are not the kings, particularly not Henry himself, who is buffeted by events and more forceful personalities. For early audiences it seems that Talbot (Part 1) was a nationalistic favourite, 'the terror of the French' in the words of Thomas Nashe, who may have co-authored the play, 'his bones new embalmed with the tears of ten thousand spectators'. But Jack Cade, the rebel leader of Part 2, is also attractively direct in contrast to the politicking of his social superiors, and the plebeian rabble-rousing of Dick the Butcher's 'The first thing we do, let's kill all the lawyers' (4.2.63) continues to raise a laugh in the theatre. Cade may well have been a champion to early audiences, perhaps echoing contemporary popular uprisings: the image of him, starving hungry in the country park of an aristocrat, is a clear anatomisation of social inequality. Our sympathies across the plays are not consistently employed, but individual moments of pathos or candour cut through their moral bleakness and savagery. In their multiple voices and multiple perspectives, the *King Henry VI* plays offer a portrait less of an individual or even a dynasty and more of a civil nation struggling to shape itself amid, between and despite the personal and political selfishness of its protagonists.

King Henry VIII, or All is True

Key Facts
Date: 1613
Length: 3,463 lines
Verse: 98% / Prose: 2%

Major characters' share of lines:

Henry VIII	14%
Wolsey	14%
Katherine	12%

Spectacular late history play ending with the birth of Queen Elizabeth

Plot and characters

The **Prologue** promises a serious play. The Dukes of **Norfolk**, **Buckingham** and **Abergavenny** discuss Cardinal **Wolsey**'s ambitious rise. Buckingham is arrested for treason just as he reveals he will denounce Wolsey. Queen **Katherine**, backed by Norfolk, pleads successfully with King **Henry** to revoke Wolsey's new taxations, but Wolsey's allegations about Buckingham persuade the King of his treason. At a feast the King and his courtiers are disguised as shepherds: he dances with **Anne Bullen** (Boleyn) and withdraws with her once he is recognised. Buckingham is tried and executed; Wolsey, with Henry's secretary **Gardiner**, begins to plot against Queen Katherine and persuades Henry to initiate divorce proceedings. In a conversation with an old **Lady**, Anne Bullen pities the Queen. At the hearing with Wolsey as judge, Katherine is eloquent in defence of her marriage, and appeals to the Pope; Henry argues the marriage is incestuous since she was previously married to his brother. Henry begins to trust his adviser Thomas **Cranmer** over Wolsey. Wolsey and **Campeius**, the papal legate, urge Katherine to accept the divorce. Norfolk, **Suffolk**, **Surrey** and the **Lord Chamberlain** plot against Wolsey. Wolsey's double-dealing with the Pope is revealed; Henry has already secretly married Anne on Cranmer's advice. Wolsey is arrested for treason and Thomas More replaces him as

Lord Chancellor, with Cranmer installed as Archbishop of Canterbury. Anne Bullen is crowned queen. Katherine hears of Wolsey's death, and has a vision of white-robed figures holding a garland over her head. Gardiner and the Lord Chancellor plot against Cranmer, who is imprisoned in the Tower, but he produces the ring given him by the King as a sign of his protection. Anne Bullen gives birth to a girl, and the King appoints Cranmer godfather. At her ceremonial baptism, Cranmer predicts her reign will be a golden age.

Context and composition

Probably written in 1613, and, from accounts of the Globe fire (see below), originally titled *All is True*, the play was probably a collaboration with John Fletcher, like the contemporaneous *The Two Noble Kinsmen*. Stylistic analysis suggests that the two writers alternated blocks of between one and four scenes, with Shakespeare beginning the play and Fletcher ending it. The sources are, as for Shakespeare's other history plays, the *Chronicles* of Raphael Holinshed (2nd edn, 1587) and in addition Foxe's *Acts and Monuments* (1563). The playwrights' skill is, as in other examples of Tudor mythography, to make the birth of Elizabeth at the end of the play seem like a harmonious resolution to all its difficulties: it is unclear how much the play sardonically anticipates its audiences will be well aware that, for example, Anne Bullen will herself be dispatched from Henry's affections even though this is not depicted here. The authors also compress events for dramatic effect – collapsing events that took place between 1529 and 1533 into simultaneity, for example. The play partakes of a Jacobean nostalgia for the reign of Elizabeth, and also structures its understanding of history along the episodic lines of the late romances – such as *Pericles* or *Cymbeline* – in contrast to the history plays Shakespeare wrote fifteen or so years earlier. Its emphasis on spectacle, described in some exceptionally long stage directions, recalls the elaborate masques popular in James' court.

Performances

At an early performance at the Globe in June 1613 a cannonball used to announce the King's arrival burned down the theatre. The fire took hold in the wooden building because the spectators, 'more attentive to the

show', according to one eye-witness, did not notice. The play's spectacle ensured it continued to be performed during the Stuart period and beyond, including at Blackfriars, the site of the historical Katherine's trial. The historical realism beloved of nineteenth-century directors meant that William Macready and Charles Kean tried to outvie each other in terms of lavish, technically sophisticated and historically researched productions, including one in front of Victoria and Albert in 1848. More recently it has been less frequently performed. Greg Doran's 1996 RSC production had the ironic title 'All is True' painted on to the back wall, 'so as to make you aware of how everyone bends the idea of truth to his own purposes', as one reviewer noted. Ian Judge in 1991 took his visual bearing from the iconic Holbein portrait; by contrast, a 2002 modern-dress version directed by Phil Wilmott (Bridewell Theatre) emphasised its conspiratorial air with film noir lighting and contemporary touches including 'Greensleeves' for Henry's mobile ringtone. Despite the familiarity of Henry VIII to cinema audiences, no film of Shakespeare's play exists except for the BBC television version done as part of the complete works, directed by Kevin Billington in 1979.

Themes and interpretation

Dramatising the events of the English break with Rome over Henry's divorce from Katherine of Aragon would have been unthinkable in Elizabeth's time, since the events it depicted were still too current and controversial for dramatic representation. By 1613 things were clearly different: the establishment of the Stuart dynasty and James' policy of peace with European Catholicism took some, but not all, of the heat out of the sectarian divisions of the mid sixteenth century. Rumours about the religious affiliations of Queen Anne continued to circulate, for example. But what is striking about *Henry VIII* is its even-handedness about religious division. Katherine, the Catholic queen appealing to the Pope in the divorce court, is treated with sympathy, and her deathbed vision of '*personages, clad in white robes, wearing on their heads garlands of bays, and golden vizards on their faces*' (4.2.82) is treated as a miraculous sign of divine grace rather than papist superstition. Thomas More, the new chancellor, well known as a Catholic martyr, is also treated positively, if briefly: the allusion to his doing 'justice / For truth's sake, and his conscience' (3.2.396–7) must have echoed with audiences familiar with his principled opposition to Henry's actions. On the other hand, while Anne Bullen is an underdeveloped figure whose own motives and character are unclear, she is certainly not treated with the kind of calumny on sexual or religious grounds that might be expected in a more partisan narrative. Most prominently, her daughter, far from inheriting any suspicion around the circumstances of her birth, is presented, in Cranmer's extraordinary paean, as 'a pattern to all princes living with her, / And all that shall succeed' (5.4.22–3). It is a measure of the play's disinclination to judge its protagonists, particularly on doctrinal grounds, that the Epilogue's declaration that the play has shown us a 'good' woman (Epilogue, 9) could refer either to Katherine, Anne, or the much vaunted infant Elizabeth.

If the play is not strongly committed to the religious politics of its storyline, it does focus on two aspects. One is the rise and fall of courtiers and the fickleness of favour and ambition. This pattern recalls late medieval moralisation in the tradition known as *de casibus*, after the title of a book of such stories of downfalls by Giovanni Boccaccio. The rhythm of the play is clear: Buckingham falls and Wolsey rises, Anne Bullen rises and Katherine falls,

Wolsey falls and Cranmer rises. Each is given the opportunity to reflect on their predicament and thus to gloss the moralising tradition. The court is a treacherous place, as Buckingham advises: friends 'fall away / Like water from ye' at the 'least rub in your fortunes' (2.1.130–1). But Katherine's fall seems closer to a tragic tradition and her powerful self-defence is moving: the parallel with the wronged Queen Hermione in the contemporaneous *The Winter's Tale* is a revealing one as both women are unjustly accused as a result of male appetites and anxieties. In this play, however, the redemption of that male agent is less clear than Leontes', who has his own wife restored to him rather than, as here, a different one. Critical accounts that have attempted to find the play endorsing a Protestant teleology in which the maturation of Henry, symbolised as he casts off Wolsey, is rewarded with the birth of a Protestant heir, ignore the language which insidiously suggests that Henry is driven more by sexual desire than by ideological commitment.

The other prominent feature is the importance of spectacle to court life. The play opens with the descriptions of the peace conference known as the Field of Cloth of Gold, with the kings of England and France 'equal in lustre' (1.1.29) where the 'dwarfish pages were / As cherubins, all gilt' (1.1.22–3) and Wolsey's ambition is etched in every glistering detail. That the peace with France has already been broken, as Norfolk reports, scarcely matters: for Wolsey, the ceremonial spectacle choreographed by him is sufficient index of his proud aspiration. Having described spectacular political theatre in its opening, the play goes on to enact it, particularly in the coronation of Anne Bullen. The stage direction is unprecedented, dividing the procession into ten numbered ranks, and calling on trumpets and choristers to accompany some seventeen named personages, and a canopy carried over the queen, with a running commentary by two other gentlemen. In terms of theatre personnel, props and costumes, this must have stretched the King's Men's resources to the limit. Sir Henry Wotton described these 'many extraordinary circumstances of pomp and majesty' as 'sufficient in truth within a while to make greatness very familiar, if not ridiculous'. The suggestion seems to be that the play has recreated something of court ceremonials for the theatre audience, and that in doing so it has revealed the dangerous proximity between play-acting and political power, and the shared properties of theatre and court. That recognition makes the play's title, *All is True*, even more provocative.

King John

Key Facts
Date: 1596
Length: 2,729 lines
Verse: 100%

Major characters' share of lines:

Bastard	20%
King John	17%
Constance	10%

Unheroic history play in which kingly
authority is sardonically undermined

Plot and characters

King John's claim to succeed Richard I is challenged by the
supporters of the young prince **Arthur**, his nephew. **King Philip of
France** declares war on John in Arthur's name; even John's
mother **Queen Eleanor** acknowledges the strength of the claim.
The King is called to judge a dispute between **Robert** and **Philip
Falconbridge** about their inheritance; Robert asserts that his older
brother is the illegitimate son of Richard I, and Philip takes up
Eleanor's offer to renounce his Falconbridge name and be
acknowledged Richard's son. John knights him as Sir Richard
Plantagenet, but he is always called **Bastard**. **Lady Falconbridge**
reproaches her sons for publicly denigrating her honour. Before
the besieged Angers, **Constance** and her son Arthur, with the
Duke of **Austria** and King Philip, meet John, his niece **Lady
Blanche**, the Bastard and their army. The citizens refuse to
adjudicate on their claims to the throne, and suggest that they
agree a peace. It is decided that the **Dauphin** should marry
Blanche. Constance feels betrayed that the French king has agreed
to the peace, and curses the alliance. **Pandulph**, a papal legate,
arrives to press the Pope's choice for Archbishop of Canterbury, and
when John refuses to agree, excommunicates him. Pandulph calls on
the King of France to resume hostilities, and in the battle Arthur is

captured and Austria killed by the Bastard. **Hubert** is appointed to kill Arthur, but he is dissuaded by the child's innocence.
He announces Arthur's death, and the nobles desert John, hearing that the French have invaded and that both Eleanor and Constance have died. A prophet tells John the loss of his crown is imminent. Arthur, trying to escape, falls to his death from the walls, and the discovery of his body confirms the lords turning against John. John makes peace with Pandulph, but the Dauphin refuses to end the wars. The English lords are torn between the two sides. King John, holed up in Swineshead Abbey, is poisoned by a monk. At his death it is announced that Pandulph has brokered a peace, and the nobles swear allegiance to their new king, John's son **Henry**.

Context and composition

The play was probably written in 1596, between *King Richard II* and *King Henry IV Part 1*, although it dramatises an earlier historical period (John reigned from 1199). It draws on Holinshed's *Chronicles* (2nd edn, 1587), and here its abridgements and juxtapositions are revealing: in Holinshed, for example, the young prince Arthur dies some years before his uncle John, whereas the play suggests that John's downfall is in some way connected to or caused by his decision to have his young rival assassinated. The most prominent addition to the source is the character of the bastard Falconbridge. The play's relation to the anonymous two-part *Troublesome Reign of King John* (1591) is contested: some scholars see it as a source for Shakespeare, others as a derivation from it, and in the seventeenth century it was claimed as being by Shakespeare. In any case, Shakespeare's play as first published in the First Folio text of 1623 is less stridently anti-Catholic than this other depiction of the story.

Performances

There are no early
records of
performance, and the
play does not come
into theatrical
prominence until the
spectacular
historicising of the
Victorian period,
which abandoned
much of the text in
favour of splendid
medieval pageantry.
Constance was
identified as a
prominent role for
Victorian actresses.
A few seconds of a film
of Herbert Beerbohm
Tree survive from
1899, showing him
shuddering towards

death on his throne; the play has not been filmed subsequently except
for television, with Leonard Rossiter as John (BBC TV, 1984).
Deborah Warner's 1988 production for the RSC depicted John
(Nicholas Woodeson) as inept and greedy, carrying the crown
attached to his money belt throughout; Guy Henry played the King as
comically gawky, bested by the cynicism and pragmatism of the
political melee around him (dir. Gregory Doran, 2001, RSC); Josie
Rourke (2006, RSC) directed Richard McCabe to emphasise the
play's ironies, undercutting sublime holy music with power
politics, and bringing out the shortlived but dramatically effective
female roles.

Themes and interpretation

A. A. Milne wrote that 'King John was not a good man', and indeed, Shakespeare's is not – not even Shakespeare could make much of a play about him if he were. Rather, he operates in a world drained of ethical certainty by the doubts over rightful kinship. John has 'strong possession' more than 'right' (1.1.39) – that contested word 'right' occurs more often in *King John* than in any other Shakespeare play, a verbal equivalent of the warring drumbeats that punctuate the text – and the play stoutly refuses to put its own authority behind any of the contenders for the throne. We probably feel that, like the citizens of Angers, we cannot adjudicate between the claims: the absence at the heart of the body politic is revealed when John's question 'who's your king?' receives the riddling reply 'The King of England, when we know the King' (2.1.362–3). The King is the King: the circularity of the argument replaces patrilinear succession with cyclical obfuscation and substitutes political pragmatism for the mystification of divine right.

John's tenuous grasp of the throne is matched by his tenuous grasp of his own play, which repeatedly sidelines him in favour of more dramatic interactions. The opening scene is a good example. John's first words invite Chatillon to convey the King of France's message, thus immediately deferring to his diplomatic adversary. His mother Eleanor interrupts, bristling on his behalf at the insult 'borrowed majesty' (1.1.5), and hers is the first commentary on events when the envoy leaves them alone on stage. Immediately another story intrudes, and the play introduces its dominant figure, the sardonic Philip Falconbridge, who resembles the charismatic Vice figure of medieval morality drama. The themes of precedence and succession and inheritance between fathers, sons and brothers, intrinsic to John's own troubled claim to the throne, are here displaced into the domestic narrative of the Falconbridge family. By introducing Lady Falconbridge to corroborate the revelation that her son is of royal blood, the play presents the Bastard as a fatherless child shaped by maternal influence, just like John and Arthur. Nobody is talking to John; he is fighting both for dramatic and regal authority.

Shakespeare has conjured the play's dominant voice out of the briefest of historical details. Holinshed's history has no chorus or commentary figure, whereas Shakespeare uses the role of the bastard Falconbridge as a surrogate for a particularly arch kind of spectator: an outside observer wryly disengaged from the machinations of politics, constantly aware of its theatricality and always ready with an intimately sardonic analysis from the sidelines. That Shakespeare's major creative addition to his source material should be the play's paradoxically authoritative bastard seems almost a parable of historical fiction: historically and personally illegitimate, Falconbridge's dramatic centrality remains unchallenged by any of the rivals to the throne. He is the best king the play never had, and quite literally, his is the last word.

In *King John*, then, the point is not to present the moral or legal claims of one monarch over another, but rather to enjoy the psychological pageantry of their competition. The history plays are deeply political, in that they relish the human and social aspects of power, but they are not directly partisan. John's action in accepting papal authority reveals his pragmatism and perhaps damages his character, but Arthur's tears as his grandmother and mother fight over him in 2.1 also establish his extreme youth and unworldliness as inappropriate royal attributes. And while keeping John's heir Prince Henry out of the frame until the play's dying minutes insulates him from its pervading atmosphere of ethical expediency and self-interest, it also means that he is an unknown quantity, an unsettlingly hasty alternative to the powerplay of the preceding acts. Could this be a happy ending?

If the play's characters are ruled by expediency, so too is their participation in the play itself. *King John* has no qualms about dispatching characters when they have served their dramatic purpose. The deaths of Constance and Eleanor, announced in a single breath in 4.2, anticlimactically postdate their effective disappearance from the play they dominated for the first half. Women are unusually prominent at the opening of *King John*, which takes a particular delight in the kind of cat-fight which is always threatening to break out when Eleanor and Constance share the stage. In usurping the authority normatively allocated to men, the women enter the political sphere and thicken the play's interest in forms of compromised or challenged power. But Constance's powerful 'grief fills the room up of my absent child' (3.4.93) also gives real depth and pathos to her character. The women's presence is magnified by the frequent rhetorical device of feminising England itself. As Constance and Eleanor decline in significance, the papal representative Pandulph is introduced in a significantly gendered speech, describing the Catholic Church as 'our holy mother' (3.1.141): after the death of Eleanor, John's submission to a new maternal figure is pointed. Even, that is to say, after the play has eliminated the dangerous female voices it is still in thrall to the feminine, as John's final illness parodies the reproductive power of gestation and succession the play investigates: 'within me is a hell, and there the poison / Is, as a fiend, confined to tyrannise' (5.7.47–8).

King Lear

Key Facts

Date: 1605–6, revised 1610
Length: 3,301 lines
Verse: 75% / Prose: 25%

Major characters' share of lines:	
Lear	22%
Edgar	11%
Kent	11%
Gloucester	10%
Edmund	9%
Fool	7%

Bleak tragedy of political, psychological and familial breakdown

Plot and characters

King Lear plans to divide Britain between his three daughters according to a love test. **Gonerill** and **Regan** profess their love and get their shares; their younger sister **Cordelia**, Lear's favourite, will not flatter her father and thus provokes his wrath. He denies her any dowry, and thus the Duke of **Burgundy** refuses to marry her. Instead, she marries the **King of France** and is exiled. The Earl of **Kent**, the King's loyal lord, speaks up for her and is also banished. The Earl of **Gloucester**'s illegitimate son **Edmund** is jealous of his legitimate son and heir **Edgar**, and plots to turn father against child. Gloucester disinherits Edgar, who, in fear of his life, disguises himself as Poor Tom. Kent, also in disguise, is accepted into Lear's service. Accompanied by Kent and by his sardonic **Fool**, Lear quarrels first with Gonerill and then with Regan about the number of his retinue and his living conditions. Kent is placed in the stocks by the Dake of **Cornwall**, husband to Regan, for insulting their servant **Oswald**. When Gonerill and Regan seem to side together against Lear, he is enraged, and goes out into the storm where he rails against their ingratitude and then meets Edgar in a hovel on the heath. Gloucester tells Edmund that Cordelia is coming with a French army; Edmund relays this to Cornwall, who promises him he will inherit his father's title. Regan and Cornwall torture Gloucester to find out more, and pluck out his eyes; horrified, a servant tries to intervene and is killed by Regan, but not before injuring Cornwall, who later dies of the wounds. Edgar meets his blinded father and, unrecognised, leads him to Dover, where Gloucester wishes to stand at the edge of Dover Cliff. Edgar persuades him he can jump off, and then pretends, to remedy his despair, that he has fallen and miraculously survived. Gonerill and Regan each send love letters to Edmund via Oswald; these are intercepted by Edgar who kills Oswald and discovers that Gonerill wants her husband the Duke of **Albany** killed by her lover. The sisters prepare for war against the French. Cordelia and Lear are reconciled, but in the battle they are captured and imprisoned. Gonerill and Regan fight over Edmund, and Regan's illness is revealed as poisoning by her sister. Edmund and Edgar fight; Edgar wins, and reveals that his father has died. Gonerill's suicide is announced. Too late, a repentant Edmund tries to rescind his order to kill Lear and Cordelia; his own death follows shortly. Lear enters with Cordelia dead in his arms, desperate to find signs of life. Lear dies, Kent says he will follow him: Albany and Edgar are left to rule.

Context and composition

The play was probably written in 1605–6 and first printed in 1608, and again in a substantially different text in 1623: opinions vary about the provenance of these two versions, but many scholars believe that Shakespeare revised his own play around 1610 and that the later text represents this authorial reworking (see *Shakespeare in Print*, pp. 232–4). Shakespeare draws on a number of sources, from contemporary gossip about a nobleman whose family were trying to have him declared mad, and whose daughter Cordell looked after him tenderly, to a play called *The True Chronicle History of King Leir and his Three Daughters* (*c.* 1590, published in 1605). The story of King Lear is in Holinshed's *Chronicles* (2nd edn, 1587), and that of Gloucester and his sons in Sir Philip Sidney's *Arcadia* (1590). There are links to older fairy stories of a Cinderella type (youngest daughter suffers depredations from ugly sisters, marries handsome prince).

Most obviously, what Shakespeare has done to this range of literary and historical precedents is to darken them: the death of Cordelia is his own, desolate invention: if this is *Cinderella*, it's without its happy ending. Given that the unity of the kingdoms of Scotland and England was one of King James' pet projects, it may be that here Shakespeare as the playwright of the King's Men is showing the political dangers of division.

Performances

The 1608 text tells us the play was performed at court on St Stephen's Day (26 December) 1606. In the Restoration period a radically reworked version by Nahum Tate (1681) returned Lear to his throne at the end, and married off Cordelia  and Edgar: this version displaced Shakespeare's original until the mid nineteenth century. Numerous other adaptations, including Edward Bond's angry *Lear* (1971) have reworked the play. In the twentieth century the influences of the Theatre of the Absurd and the Theatre of Cruelty were important: Peter Brook's icy film with Paul Scofield (1971) captures this mood of alienation and desolation. Laurence Olivier's performance directed for television by Michael Elliott (1984) was more affirming and elegiac, capturing Lear's whimsy as well as his fury. Attempts to recuperate the play's misogynistic depiction of its women characters have resulted in productions suggesting incestuous abuse at the heart of the dysfunctional royal household (e.g. Warren Mitchell, dir. Jude Kelly, West Yorkshire Playhouse, 1995). In recent years Ian McKellen (directed by Trevor Nunn and filmed for television, 2007) played a wistful, reflective king without histrionics; in 2010 Derek Jacobi,

directed by Michael Grandage (Donmar Warehouse), drew out
Lear's dementia as a recognisable and domestic problem; and in 1999
Yukio Ninagawa presented a sympathetic and touching Lear (Nigel
Hawthorne at the RSC). Less sympathetic Lears include Ian Holm's
violent and irascible father (RSC, dir. Richard Eyre, 1997; filmed for
television in 1998). Antony Sher played a memorably red-nosed,
white-faced Fool opposite Michael Gambon (Adrian Noble, 1982,
RSC).

Themes and interpretation

Writing in the 1960s, the Polish theatre director Jan Kott, in a
famous book called *Shakespeare our Contemporary*, linked *King
Lear* with the absurdist theatre of Samuel Beckett. Like Beckett, Kott
argued, Shakespeare in *Lear* is concerned 'with the decay and fall of
the world', in which established values have been hollowed out and
the stage is merely the inhospitable earthly lodging of the mad, the
blind and the alienated. Kott's analysis was part of a substantial shift
in readings of the play, away from redemptive or cathartic
interpretations of Lear's increased self-knowledge or the proto-
Christian power of Cordelia's sacrificial love, and instead towards
something darker and more existential. Dr Johnson had professed
himself unable to reread the play's ending because of its manifest
unjustness to Cordelia, whose fate should have been different from
that of her sisters (Johnson felt that Nahum Tate's revised version of
the play was much preferable on these grounds). In the later twentieth
century, however, it was precisely this unflinching denial of final
comforts for which the play was to be valued, as the dramatic
corollary to a post-Holocaust world of unthinkable brutality.
Albany's recognition that 'Humanity must perforce prey upon itself /
Like monsters of the deep' (Quarto text, 4.2.47–8) could stand as the
century's epitaph: *Lear* had come to hold up a mirror to a violent and
broken world.

In fact, Albany's is just one of the many ways in which the play's
characters attempt to make sense of the world in which they find
themselves, and the overall effect is of competing and inadequate
narratives for the presence of suffering. It may be this absence of any

grand narrative of causation, and in particular its scepticism that conventional religion supplies such a narrative, that has made the play so relevant to the shattered ideologies of the modern period. The old man Gloucester is superstitious: 'these late eclipses in the sun and moon portend no good to us' (1.2.88–9); his contemporary King Lear curses by 'the orbs / From whom we do exist and cease to be' (1.1.96–7). Edmund understands events to be controlled by human agency and is scornful of this cosmic framework, satirically pointing out that we blame the stars for the misfortunes caused by 'the surfeit of our own behaviour' (1.2.97), while contradictorily committing himself to the stereotypical character of 'Bastard' and the goddess Nature. Edgar tries to understand the world in the trope of Fortune's wheel: 'the worst is not / So long as we can say "this is the worst"' (4.1.27–8); Gloucester blames the gods: 'as flies to wanton boys are we to th'gods; / They kill us for their sport' (4.1.36–7), but his misfortunes are caused by human, not divine, intervention. In fact part of *Lear*'s comfortlessness is the apparent absence of any other realm than the human, perhaps because of the play's setting in pagan Britain, giving it instead a quality of heroic isolation often associated with ancient Greek drama. Ultimately, it is the audience whose 'sport' or entertainment is the deaths of the play's protagonists: more than any other of Shakespeare's tragedies, this play prompts that disturbing question, 'why does tragedy give pleasure?' Certainly the play does not balk at our appetite for brutality: Gloucester's eyes gouged out before us on stage, for example, makes it clear that, for all our philosophising, tragedy's appeal is savage.

Connected with the play's grotesque violence is its humour. The Fool's curious, cruelly oblique commentary on Lear's folly; Edgar persuading Gloucester to throw himself off Dover Cliff; the terrible slow-motion realisation that the instruction to hang Cordelia is still operative: these aspects of the play show the awful proximity of tragedy and farce, or of tragedy and the grotesque. 'When we are born, we cry that we are come / To this great stage of fools' (4.5.174–5). Stripped of his royal office, his retinue, his clothes, his insulation, Lear comes to realise something essential about humanity, but it is a measure of the play's unremitting cruelty that he has no chance to learn from this new insight. Like the reunion with

Cordelia, it is a false comfort. In a play where grief – Lear's – and joy – Gloucester's – are equally fatal and where the loving daughter ends up just as dead as the nasty ones, moral certainties are hard to find. The two different versions of the play diverge on whether Albany or Edgar should speak the last lines: either way, they are a final shocked attempt to make sense of what has been going on, advising 'speak as we feel, not what we ought to say' (5.3.298). It is a measure of the play's cyclical form that even as this proposes a future of emotional rather than orthodox truthfulness, it returns us, queasily, to the catastrophe of Cordelia's inability or unwillingness to play her part in her father's comedy of marriage in the play's opening scene.

King Richard II

Key Facts
Date: 1595
Length: 2,849 lines
Verse: 100%

Major characters' share of lines:	
Richard II	27%
Bullingbrook	15%
York	10%
Gaunt	7%

King Richard's overthrow: political coup or personal tragedy?

Plot and characters

Before **King Richard II**, **Bullingbrook**, the Duke of Hereford, accuses the Duke of Norfolk, Thomas **Mowbray**, of killing the Duke of Gloucester. Mowbray denies this, and Richard intervenes to postpone their combat. The **Duchess of Gloucester** upbraids her brother, Richard's uncle, **John of Gaunt** for not challenging the murder of her husband. Before the combat between Bullingbrook and Mowbray can occur, Richard banishes them for ten years (reduced to six) and life respectively. Bullingbrook's departure is reported to Richard, who mocks him, encouraged by his followers **Aumerle**, **Green**, **Bagot** and **Bushy**. Dying, Gaunt expresses his disappointment in the King's lavish behaviour and the decline of England: Richard is unrepentant and sequesters Gaunt's estate to pay for a military expedition to Ireland, leaving **York** in command as he sets out. Bullingbrook returns to England with an army, but persuades York that he is only after his rightful inheritance from his father. When Richard returns from Ireland, troops including York are defecting to Bullingbrook, but in a parley between the two adversaries, Bullingbrook agrees to surrender if he is reinstated to his property. Bullingbrook's power grows, however, and he has Green and Bagot executed and arrests Aumerle and others on the charge of murdering Gloucester. The **Queen** hears a **gardener** discussing the inevitability of Richard's overthrow. Richard agrees to abdicate and in Parliament publicly hands over the crown to Bullingbrook, who announces his coronation, much to the disgust of the **Bishop of Carlisle**, who speaks passionately about the divine right of kings and is put in the Tower by **Northumberland** for his pains. Richard bids farewell to the Queen as he is taken into captivity. Carlisle, Aumerle and **Westminster** try a counter-conspiracy against Bullingbrook, but this is discovered by York, who betrays his son Aumerle to Bullingbrook despite his wife the **Duchess of York**'s pleading. Bullingbrook, concerned about his own wild son, pardons Aumerle. Piers **Exton** goes to Richard's prison, where Richard, visited by a former **groom** and the **keeper** of Pomfret Castle, is pondering his fate, and, believing he has Bullingbrook's mandate, kills him: Richard defends himself bravely. Exton bears the body to Bullingbrook, who denies this was his wish. He banishes Exton and vows a pilgrimage to the Holy Land to wash away his guilt.

Context and composition

Written in 1595 and first printed in 1597, *King Richard II* was popular in print, with two further editions in 1598 and an extended version in 1608, the first time the scene in Act 4 when Richard hands over the instruments of office to Bullingbrook was printed, perhaps because of state or self-censorship. As with his other English history plays, Shakespeare makes extensive use of Holinshed's *Chronicles* (2nd edn, 1587), as well as Samuel Daniel's verse history of the Wars of the Roses (1594–5). An anonymous contemporary play, *Thomas of Woodstock*, tells the story of the murder of its title character the Duke of Gloucester; it is unclear whether this play was performed before or after Shakespeare's (see *Shakespearean Apocrypha*, pp. 235–6). Some of Shakespeare's additions to his sources include the character of Richard's Queen and the garden scene, and in general he seems to have suppressed some of the justifications for Bullingbrook's actions that he found in the sources. Like *King Richard III*, this play takes its lead from the precociously talented playwright of the rival Admiral's Men, Christopher Marlowe, and in particular his poetic tragedy of *Edward II* (1592), a king caught between public duty and private passion. The sudden introduction of Bullingbrook's wayward son at the very end of the play seems a hook for the sequel, *1 Henry IV*, but the story of Richard's decline looks beyond the genre of serial history to another tragedy of abdication, *King Lear*, and the play's ethical balance anticipates another *coup d'état* in *Julius Caesar*.

Performances

It is generally assumed that the full text as first printed in 1608 was performed in 1595, and from this point the play was associated with contemporary politics. Most notably, the Chamberlain's Men were paid to revive it on the eve of the Earl of Essex's abortive rebellion against Elizabeth in 1601. By the

twentieth century important performances by John Gielgud (1937) and others established it as a tragic vehicle for a poet-martyr rather than a political commentary. In 1973 John Barton's RSC production challenged the orthodox notion that Richard and Bullingbrook were entirely opposite characters by having Richard Pasco and Ian Richardson alternate the roles; Fiona Shaw took the title role in a Deborah Warner production (National Theatre, 1995; filmed for television) which did not associate her sex with effeminacy but drew out a close emotional bond between Richard and Bullingbrook as kinsmen. At the RSC, Barry Kyle stressed an emblematic 'Book of Hours' medieval setting for his 1986 production with a saintly, effete Jeremy Irons, whereas Steven Pimlott chose modern dress in 2000, directing Sam West as a powerful, passionate king. Derek Jacobi stars in the BBC television film (David Giles, 1979); a combative low-budget version directed by John Farrell (2001) stages a modern coup in camouflage.

Themes and interpretation

Something strange happens in all summaries of the plot of *King Richard II*. There is a gap where something momentous ought to be: the time when Bullingbrook stops simply wanting restitution for his confiscated lands, and becomes instead a challenger for the throne itself. There is no decisive battle in *King Richard II*, no distinct break when loyalties shift from him to his rebellious cousin, rather a series of small but significant reductions in Richard's authority: the refusal of Northumberland to bow to his sovereign at Flint Castle; the decision of York to defect; even the report of Richard's favourite horse proudly bearing the new king on his back. Bullingbrook's rise seems invisible and unstoppable, but we never know his motives. Is he self-interested and power-hungry, or, like his father, a patriot trying to save his country from its decline into extravagance and unchecked royal prerogative?

The answer is that the play does not tell us. Bullingbrook's motives are withheld: we know little more than the public dance of diplomacy, sabre-rattling and negotiation. Similarly, Richard, too, is ambiguous. On the one hand he is weak and selfish and his decision to seize John of Gaunt's estate is a manifest abuse of sovereign power. His sense of his authority is repeatedly bolstered by aggrandising imagery: he is the sun, Christ, God's elected deputy. His instincts are to rhetoric and self-pity rather than to action. 'For God's sake let us sit upon the ground', he bemoans at Scroop's news of military setbacks, 'And tell sad stories of the death of kings' (3.2.155–6). He cannot resist a good scene, or an opportunity to take centre stage. When Bullingbrook is urging him to resign the crown in 4.1, Richard's poetic procrastination is in marked contrast to the laconic political urgency of his rival. On the other hand, Richard's introspection is often sympathetic, as he struggles to understand his changing situation. In Act 5 he has his only soliloquy – a moment of emotional truth before his brutal murder. His language, always highly poetic, may here convey self-knowledge rather than self-dramatisation – or it may be that this is his finest dramatic moment. His last action contrasts with his lassitude earlier in the play, as he defends himself with courage. For some critics, Richard represents the last of the doomed feudal kings, whose outmoded belief in absolute monarchical power is untenable; Bullingbrook's political pragmatism marks a new, modern era. On stage, costuming can suggest that this is not just a transfer between individuals but between epochs: Michael Bogdanov, for instance, depicted Richard II in dandified Regency clothes, with Bullingbrook's solemn black Victorianism an implicit moral and historical reproach (1989; filmed for video).

It is impossible to judge where Shakespeare's own sympathies lay, or how early audiences might have responded. Balance is the keynote of Shakespeare's presentation of the transfer of dramatic and sovereign authority. Richard is not a just king, but against the questionable morality of his sovereignty is the questionable legality of Bullingbrook's. A homily appointed by the Elizabethan authorities to be read in churches preached the terrible consequences of rebellion against a ruler, arguing that 'a rebel is worse than the worst prince, and rebellion worse than the worst government of the worst prince that hitherto hath been'. Yet Bullingbrook's demeanour is not that of such a demonised rebel – Lucifer was often cited as the prototype for rebellion – and his final words express deep regret rather than triumph. Taken as a complete and finished play, *King Richard II* does not punish his action in taking the crown, although of course subsequent (and previous) history plays dramatise its consequences: a rightful king is killed in this play and there is no immediate divine or other retribution. But when the Bishop of Carlisle fiercely denounces Bullingbrook's actions in naming himself king, and stoutly defends the doctrine that kings are anointed by God, there is no word of political philosophy in reply: Carlisle is arrested, not answered. The play, then, is finely poised.

The first editions of the play described it as a tragedy, and this suggests that the play is primarily about the downfall of a significant, noble, flawed individual – Richard is the focus, and Bullingbrook is no more significant than, say, Fortinbras at the end of *Hamlet*. But its incorporation into the genre of history in the Folio text, and performances of the history plays as a sequence give more stress to historical process and continuity. *King Richard II* ends with a new king and a new political order, albeit one overshadowed by the crimes of the past. Tragedy ends. The action is complete – the idea of a sequel to *Hamlet* is unthinkable. History continues so that the consequences of Richard's unkinging – a new word coined here (4.1.219) to register the strangeness of the action – reverberate through subsequent generations and subsequent plays.

King Richard III

Key Facts

Date: 1592–3
Length: 3,887 lines
Verse: 98% / Prose: 2 %

Major characters' share of lines:	
Richard III	32%
Buckingham	10%
Elizabeth	7%
Margaret	6%

The last episode of the Wars of the Roses focuses on the rise and fall of the charismatic Richard

Plot and characters

Richard, Duke of Gloucester, plots against his brother, King Edward IV and his house of York, falsely accusing their brother George, Duke of Clarence of treason. Feigning sympathy, Richard nevertheless sends two assassins to the Tower of London to murder him. Richard meets Lady Anne, who is mourning at the coffin of her father-in-law Henry VI, killed by Richard, and in a bravura display of persuasion gains her hand even as he confesses to the murder of Henry and of her husband, Prince Edward, claiming he was prompted by her beauty. On the death of Edward, Queen Elizabeth and her sons Dorset and Grey are disquieted by the prospect of Richard as Lord Protector to the young (another) Prince Edward and the Duke of York, and the Queen takes sanctuary with her younger son and the Duchess of York. Richard's mother the Duchess and old Queen Margaret, widow of Henry VI, curse him. As Lord Protector, Richard imprisons his opponents Rivers and Grey, and with his chief adviser the Duke of Buckingham lodges the princes in the Tower. Richard executes Rivers, Grey, Vaughan and Hastings as obstacles to his plan. He and Buckingham manipulate the Lord Mayor and the citizens of London into begging Richard to take the throne, putting on a show of piety and pretending to be unwilling for coronation. Dorset leaves England to join the forces of **Richmond** overseas. Richard reneges on his promise of an earldom to Buckingham when Buckingham refuses to countenance the murder of the young princes: Richard sends **Tyrell** to kill them, and Buckingham and the **Bishop of Ely** flee to the opposition. Anne's death allows Richard to propose marriage to Princess Elizabeth (not seen in the play), daughter of Edward IV, and the Queen pretends to agree. Richmond lands at Milford Haven, and Richard holds **Young Stanley** as a hostage for his father's loyalty. Richmond and Elizabeth are to marry. On the eve of the battle, Richard is cursed in a dream by the ghosts of his victims, who then go to Richmond to bless his enterprise. At Bosworth Field Richard is defeated by Richmond in single combat; Richmond is crowned and announces he will unite the houses of York and Lancaster and bring peace.

Context and composition

Written and performed around 1592–3 (Shakespeare did not write his history plays in chronological order, and thus this play predates *King Richard II* and the plays about Henry IV and V), *King Richard III* was first printed in 1598 with a title page describing it as a 'tragedy', and reprinted in five further editions, making it among the most popular of Shakespeare's plays in print. Its narrative follows on from the *Henry VI* plays, and, in its depiction of its exuberant villain shows the influence of rival playwright Christopher Marlowe (e.g. in *The Jew of Malta*). Shakespeare draws on existing accounts of Richard of Gloucester, especially those provided by Edward Halle in his account of the Wars of the Roses (1548), Raphael Holinshed in his large-scale history, the *Chronicles* (Shakespeare consulted the second, expanded edition of 1587), and by Sir Thomas More (published in 1543), his primary source for the prejudicial image of Richard as a hunchbacked villain. Shakespeare's attention is more directly focused on his protagonist, who self-consciously adopts the attractive amoral directness of the Vice figure from medieval morality dramas.

Performances

Richard Burbage, the Chamberlain's Men's star actor, was probably the first Richard, and a number of allusions to the play suggest it was popular during the Elizabethan period. Colley

Cibber's adaptation in 1700 simplified its complex plot and dominated the play for more than one hundred and fifty years: even Olivier's film version (1955) takes elements from Cibber. Significant recent productions include Antony Sher's 'bottled spider' at the RSC in 1984 (dir. Bill Alexander), where crutches and a trailing gown gave him an arachnid quality (discussed in his *The Year of the King*, 1985), and Michael Boyd's direction of Jonathan Slinger, again at the RSC (2007). This modern-dress production was memorably dominated by ghosts of the past, including the skeleton of Henry VI shockingly spilled from a bundle carried by a madly grieving Margaret, and the psychopathic Richard was bested by a sinisterly cold Richmond regime, closing the play by training their automatic weapons on the audience. Al Pacino's documentary *Looking for Richard* (1996) investigates the play's ongoing hold through interviews and rehearsal, and Richard Loncraine's film of the same year places Ian McKellen in a sumptuous 1930s fascistic context (McKellen had played the role on stage in 1990, directed by Richard Eyre).

Themes and interpretations

We know from the play's opening moment that one man will dominate its historical events and our reaction to them. Uniquely for a central protagonist in Shakespeare, Richard opens the play with a soliloquy (tragedies more often start with a sideways glance at the main characters delivered by minor figures), in a well-known speech which does much to remind audiences of the events of Henry VI's reign as told in three plays performed between 1590 and 1592. *King Henry VI Part 3*, the play which immediately precedes *King Richard III* in narrative sequence, ended with Richard, Duke of Gloucester's ambition to become king, and it is this bloody ambition which motivates the first half of Richard's own play. He seems consciously to take up wickedness: ' I am determinèd to prove a villain / And hate the idle pleasures of these days' (1.1.30–1), but this extended early use of soliloquy also makes the audience immediately sympathetic with him: unlike Richard's victims, we are in on the plot from the beginning, and while we may scruple at his methods and his lack of conscience, we cannot help but be attracted by this ironic, intelligent, unscrupulous, self-revelatory villain. In one of the play's most compelling expositions of Richard's seductive charm, he woos Lady Anne over the body of her father-in-law: it is as if she is a proxy for the audience, and her eventual compliance signals that we, too, cannot resist Richard's diabolical charisma. Richard addresses his gleeful victory direct to the audience – 'Was ever woman in this humour wooed? / Was ever woman in this humour won?' (1.2.231–2) – and a constant stream of asides and sardonic remarks implicate us irresistibly in his progress towards the throne.

For much of the play Richard's rise seems unstoppable. One effect of his predominant stage presence – his is one of the largest roles in Shakespeare – is that no other character is able to challenge him – morally or dramatically. Only the women in the play, in their formalised rituals of cursing, memory and prophecy, offer any resistance to his plotting, and in the end their maledictions are fulfilled. They have no means of action save language, and thus the women's roles present some of the most noticeable examples of the play's formal rhetorical style, almost as if the moral chaos around them can be contained through artificial, highly wrought utterance. Queen Margaret, widow of Henry VI – and a figure retained, unhistorically, by Shakespeare to give her this keening role – gives form to her grief through the liturgical rhythms of repetition: 'I had an Edward, till a Richard killed him; / I had a husband, till a Richard killed him. / Thou hadst an Edward, till a Richard killed him; / Thou hadst a Richard, till a Richard killed him' (4.4.39–42).

Richard's energies are considerable. As the king surrounded by his enemies at the decisive Battle of Bosworth, he delivers a powerful address to his soldiers and his country: 'Fight, gentlemen of England! Fight boldly, yeomen!' (5.3.340). The echo of this call to arms will be heard in *Henry V*. Richmond's summary of his adversary, 'a bloody tyrant and a homicide; / One raised in blood, and one in blood established' (5.3.247–8), may tell the facts but it does not convey the character of the man. Richard's soliloquy before the battle articulates a painfully isolated sense of self: 'There is no creature loves me, / And if I die, no soul shall pity me. / Nay, wherefore should they, since that I myself / Find in myself no pity to myself' (5.3.203–6). The procession of ghosts which haunts him can be seen as a representation of an inner, conscience-stricken state rather than the sensational irruption of the supernatural. There is no nod towards conventional morality even at the end, as Richard dies without repentance. Having controlled his own destiny through a supreme effort of will, he surrenders to chance rather than to heaven: 'I will stand the hazard of the die' (5.4.10). And for all that Shakespeare's extreme representation of Richard's character may be attributed to the need, under the Tudor monarch Elizabeth, to present her ancestor Richmond as the saviour of his beleaguered country, Richmond himself is pale and uninteresting compared to the dramatic vigour of his adversary. 'Abate the edge of traitors, gracious Lord', prays the godly Richmond, as he predicts that his descendants will 'Enrich the time to come with smooth-faced peace, / With smiling plenty and fair prosperous days' (5.5.33–5). But while this may be a worthy political aspiration, it is not a very dramatic one. For all his wickedness, Richard's vitality ensures his place as hero and dramatic centre of his play, and for all its disturbance, his bloody reign makes for good drama. No wonder, then, that it is not the cul-de-sac 'smooth-faced peace', but the dramatic highway of 'grim-visaged war' (1.1.9) to which Shakespeare returns in his next history plays, on the reigns of Richard II and Henry IV.

Love's Labour's Lost

Sophisticated comedy of love and language

Key Facts
Date: 1595–6
Length: 2,900 lines
Verse: 65% / Prose: 35%

Major characters' share of lines:	
Berowne	22%
King	11%
Princess	10%
Armado	10%

Plot and characters

Ferdinand, **King** of Navarre and three of his lords – **Berowne**, **Longaville** and **Dumaine** – vow to commit themselves to study and to disavow women for three years. The rustic **Costard** is punished for his dalliance with **Jaquenetta** and handed over to the Spaniard Don **Armado** for guarding; Armado is also in love with her, and writes her poetry. The **Princess** of France and her ladies **Maria**, **Katherine** and **Rosaline** arrive: the lords and ladies begin to pair off – although Berowne is scornful of the absurdity of having fallen in love with Rosaline – while the Princess negotiates wittily with the King about territory on behalf of her father. Costard has two letters to deliver: from Don Armado to Jaquenetta and from Berowne to Rosaline. Causing great amusement, he misdelivers Don Armado's affected letter to Jaquenetta to the Princess. The schoolmaster **Holofernes** and the priest **Nathaniel** joke learnedly at the expense of the constable **Dull**; they are asked by the illiterate Jaquenetta to read out her letter from Don Armado, but due to Costard's confusions, this is the letter from Berowne to Rosaline. Berowne overhears the King reading a love poem to the Princess; the King in turn overhears Longaville reading out a poem for Maria; and all three watch as Dumaine, in turn, sighs poetically over Katherine. They reproach each other for hypocrisy, and

Berowne has to join them when his letter to Rosaline is revealed. Armado is to commission an entertainment for the Princess, and Holofernes decides they will do a pageant of the Nine Worthies. The Princess and her ladies wear masks to trick the King and his lords, who are dressed as Muscovites, into wooing the wrong women; the men are all rebuffed and when they return in their own guise the women continue the pretence, to the chagrin of their suitors. Costard, the page **Moth**, Holofernes and Armado perform the Nine Worthies; Costard claims Jaquenetta is pregnant by him, to the disappointment of Armado. Amid the melee comes **Marcadé**, a messenger, with news that the Princess's father has died. The women put off their lovers for a year and a day, and the play ends with songs of spring and winter.

Context and composition

First printed in 1598, this is the earliest Shakespeare play to have his name on the title page. Because of its stylistic similarities with *Romeo and Juliet* and *A Midsummer Night's Dream*, it is generally dated to about 1595–6. There is no obvious literary source for *Love's Labour's Lost*, and although it must allude to contemporary European religio-politics – the King of Navarre had converted to Catholicism and become King of France in 1594, and Lord Berowne, one of his aides, was an associate of the Earl of Essex – the extent of its political symbolism has been debated. It draws explicitly on the literary fashions of the early 1590s, including sonnets, a heavy use of rhyme and poetic forms, and a tendency towards the elaborate style known – not always as a compliment – after John Lyly's fashionable prose narrative *Euphues, or the Anatomy of Wit* (1579), as 'euphuism'. Although its ending puts off the traditional comic conclusion, the play's depiction of spirited and capable women, particularly compared with their more changeable male counterparts, is in keeping with the gender dynamic of, say, *Twelfth Night* or *As You Like It*.

Performances

Some scholars have seen in the play's self-conscious intellectualism some sort of closet allegory intended for a coterie audience, but a poem of 1598 seems to describe a performance at the public theatre, and the title page of the same year boasts that it was acted before Queen Elizabeth at Christmas. It does not have a very full stage history, but there have been some notable modern productions. Peter Brook's 1946 revival at the Shakespeare Memorial Theatre drew inspiration from the composition of light and shadow in the paintings of Jean-Pierre Watteau and crystallised a mood of tentative optimism of the immediate post-war years, ending with a slow dimming of the lights as the messenger entered at the end. Ian Judge's 1994 RSC production captured the play's studenty wistfulness and male camaraderie by setting it in Edwardian Oxford, complete with rowing blades and college photographs, with the impending First World War giving a tinge of sadness. Far, though, from being the difficult and over-intellectual play imagined by some critics, this production prompted one reviewer to see it as 'Shakespeare's nearest equivalent to pantomime'. In 2001 Stephen Unwin (English Touring Theatre) updated the setting to the modern day, with the young men as sharp-suited yuppies in a tower block; at the RSC Barry Kyle in 1984 imagined a late Victorian setting and John Barton (1978) an autumnal arcadia from which death cannot ultimately be banished. Kenneth Branagh's film of 2000 embraces the artificiality of the play by turning it into a thirties song-and-dance musical, with Cole Porter songs set against newsreels of impending war and a montage epilogue in which the lovers are reunited at VE Day after undertaking improving war work.

Themes and interpretation

The entrance of Marcadé bringing news of the death of the King of France is an arresting moment at the end of *Love's Labour's Lost*. As the Princess greets him, 'thou interruptest our merriment' (5.2.692): coming into the disordered, bantering aftermath of Holofernes' extraordinary pageant of the Nine Worthies, the messenger seems almost to be the irruption of Death itself into Arcadia, in the manner of a pastoral painting such as Poussin's *Et in Arcadia Ego* of 1627. Comedies should not end with death: that is the structural expectation of tragedy, but while the play is not a tragedy, it does frustrate the impulse to comic closure. Instead of the four marriages which have been so heavily anticipated – as soon as the Princess and her entourage enter hard on the heels of the King's promise of chastity, the stage is set – we get a year of mourning. Berowne is dispatched to a hospital to practise his jests on a more challenging audience, but as he acknowledges, this is 'too long for a play' (5.4.846): 'Our wooing doth not end like an old play: / Jack hath not Jill' (5.2.842–3). *Love's Labour's Lost* ends with a consciously discordant movement, the deferral of its marital expectations, just as the songs that conclude the play invert the regenerative order of both calendar and comedy and have winter following spring, and just as Don Armado's final words stress division rather than comic harmony: 'you that way; we this way' (5.2.897).

Critics have been exercised over the question of how seriously to take a play so preoccupied with verbal and romantic games. Don Armado's description of his 'curious-knotted garden' (1.1.233) may stand for its careful, geometric comic plotting and ultimately decorative purpose. The perfectly symmetrical courts of the King and the Princess, the structural play with the letters of Berowne and Don Armado, or the scene (4.3) of serial overhearings as the lords in turn catch each other in breaking their vows, all spied on by the unseen Berowne – these all suggest a formal, highly artificial choreography. Set against this mannered comedy is the more rustic humour of

Costard and Jaquenetta, and the elaborate linguistic humour at the expense of the obscurantist academics Nathaniel and Holofernes, and the Spanish Don Armado.

If love is one game here played out with disguises and tricks, then language is another. The play has a large proportion of rhymed lines – a third of its verse is in couplets – a number of interwoven sonnets and other formal poetic devices, as well as a wholehearted enjoyment of linguistic pretension and absurdity. Holofernes' extempore epitaph on the deer killed by the Princess exemplifies the play's delight in verbal silliness and distorted, triumphantly non-naturalistic speech: 'The preyful Princess pierced and pricked a pretty pleasing pricket' (4.2.51). Don Armado's compulsion for what he calls 'the sweet smoke of rhetoric' (3.1.52) is well put: rhetoric here obscures and makes unclear, rather than persuading. The miscarriage of his letter to Jaquenetta is the physical manifestation of his impotence in communication. Berowne, too, is preoccupied by words: 'taffeta phrases, silken terms precise' (5.2.406). The constable Dull's role in the play seems to be baffled by these linguistic games: 'thou hast spoken no word all this while', Holofernes challenges, and Dull's reply may stand for the audience too: 'nor understood none neither, sir' (5.1.120–2). As much as the language may be rebarbative, it was also apparently enjoyed: more than any other play of Shakespeare's, this one was raided by early anthologists.

Against this insistent playfulness, though, there are darker currents. The play's elegant wit and construction are radically undermined by extended bawdy puns. The historical Henri of Navarre's conversion to Catholicism to take up the French throne was a blow to Protestant England, and there may be something of this famous apostasy in the more playful depiction of the King as an oath-breaker. In this way *Love's Labour's Lost* may be a comic companion piece to Christopher Marlowe's cynical docu-drama on these events, *The Massacre at Paris* (1593): Marlowe also includes Navarre and Dumaine in his play. The Princess begins her embassy to Navarre with a discussion about politics and land, and while the women are won over to the diversions of the King's court, they retain an ability to puncture the scholarly pretensions of their hosts. The scene in which the men dressed as Muscovites are bested by the women is a good example: time and again Rosaline and her cohort undermine high-flown or romantic language with a pointed reality.

Writing of Shakespeare's career in 1598, Francis Meres named a number of his plays, including this one. But he followed it with the mysterious *Love's Labour's Won*, a play we do not have any other record of. That this might be a sequel is tantalising: Berowne back from his hospital jests? The infant born to Costard and Jaquenetta? The King's accession to the throne of France? Perhaps the play's self-consciously deferred ending was initially less a challenge to comic convention and more a bait for audiences to return for the next instalment.

Macbeth

Taut Scottish thriller of guilt and violence

Key Facts	
Date: 1606	
Length: 2,528 lines	
Verse: 95% / Prose: 5%	

Major characters' share of lines:	
Macbeth	29%
Lady Macbeth	11%
Malcolm	9%
Macduff	7%

Plot and characters

Three **witches** plan to meet **Macbeth**. King **Duncan** is updated on his army's battle against the rebel Macdonald: a bleeding **Captain** reports that thanks to the bravery of Macbeth and **Banquo**, victory is theirs. Duncan sends **Ross** and **Angus** to Macbeth with news that, on the execution of Cawdor for treason, he, Macbeth, is to have the title. Macbeth and Banquo meet the three witches, who predict that Macbeth will be thane of Cawdor and king, and that Banquo will be the father of kings; the arrival of the messengers with the news sets Macbeth brooding, and Duncan's declaration that his son **Malcolm** shall be his heir prompts Macbeth to consider their murders. Hearing the news from Macbeth, **Lady Macbeth** invokes the forces of darkness to steel her for what they will need to do. She encourages Macbeth to dissemble, and does so herself when Duncan arrives. Macbeth muses on Duncan's murder; Lady Macbeth overcomes his scruples by taunting him about his manhood. Macbeth enacts their plan and murders Duncan, but Lady Macbeth has to plant the bloody weapons on Duncan's drugged guards. A knocking at the door accompanies Macbeth's guilt. A drunken porter lets **Macduff** and **Lennox** into the castle; there have been ominous storms. Macduff discovers Duncan's murder; Macbeth kills the two guards and Malcolm and his brother **Donaldbain** decide to flee to England.

Macbeth goes to be crowned king. Banquo suspects this turn of events, and Macbeth summons two **murderers** to kill him and his son **Fleance**, but Fleance escapes. At a banquet for the thanes, Macbeth is haunted by the ghost of the absent Banquo. The three witches are scolded by **Hecate**; when Macbeth seeks them out they present three apparitions and reassure him in riddling terms. Macduff goes to England, where Malcolm tests his loyalty. Macbeth arranges the murder of Macduff's wife and children; Macduff vows revenge. Lady Macbeth is beset with guilty sleepwalking. Malcolm's forces march on Dunsinane, where Macbeth is isolated after the death of Lady Macbeth. In the fighting **Young Siward** is killed, and Macduff and Macbeth fight. The witches' equivocal prophecies come true: Macbeth is killed and Malcolm is hailed king.

Context and composition

Macbeth is so intimately involved with the concerns of the company's new patron, King James, that it seems to have been written with him directly in mind. The Scottish James claimed ancestry from Banquo and had written a treatise on witchcraft – and it may be that the line of kings the witches present to Macbeth, the last 'with a glass in his hand', was intended to reflect James himself at an early performance. It was probably written during 1606, and alludes to the trial of the Gunpowder conspirators earlier that year as well as to a ship called *The Tiger* which reached Milford Haven after a lengthy and tempest-tossed journey. The play seems to have been written between *King Lear* and *Antony and Cleopatra*. It was first published in the First Folio of 1623, but many scholars believe that text includes some work by Middleton, perhaps for a later Jacobean revival. In particular the scene in which Hecate appears to the three witches may be an interpolation, and it shares some songs with Middleton's own play *The Witch* (unpublished, dating from around 1616).

Shakespeare's major source was, as for the English history plays, Holinshed's *Chronicles* (2nd edn, 1587). As usual, he has undertaken radical compression and restructuring, as well as sanctifying Duncan as the rightful king and suppressing the long historical period of Macbeth's peaceful reign (in the sources, Scotland is a dog-eat-dog world ruled by might rather than right: Macbeth is hardly aberrant, as he is in the play).

Performances

The earliest recorded performance is at the Globe in 1611: Simon Forman, astrologer and doctor, noted in particular Banquo's ghost sitting in Macbeth's chair and Lady Macbeth's sleepwalking, as well as the 'three women fairies or nymphs' (the witches). In the Restoration Davenant adapted the play to bring out similarities between the usurping Macbeth and Oliver Cromwell. Since then it has been a consistent stage presence – although the popular actors' superstition that the play is unlucky may owe something to its high-profile flops during the eighteenth and nineteenth centuries.

Among recent productions, Max Stafford-Clark's site-specific transposing of the play to a violent Africa complete with child soldiers, voodoo and Idi Amin-inspired tartan recovered the play's capacity to horrify (Out of Joint, 2004). For Harriet Walter and Antony Sher (dir. Greg Doran, 1999, RSC), the couple's childlessness was crucial to their *folie à deux*: grief at a dead child had pushed Macbeth into paranoia and Lady Macbeth into icy ambition. Jude Kelly (West Yorkshire Playhouse, 1999) had a similar conceit, with Lady Macbeth rocking a soft toy as if it were her child; for Philip Franks (Crucible Theatre, 1995) an empty pram dominated the stage. Simon Russell Beale was an unusually introspective and troubled Macbeth (dir. John Caird, 2005, RSC).

The play has been popular in film, from Orson Welles' postwar anatomy of a charismatic dictator (1948) to Akira Kurosawa's samurai *Throne of Blood* (1957), with the witches translated into a single spinning figure of the fates. Roman Polanksi's violent 1971 film also suggests that all is not well in conclusion, ending with Donalbain seeking out the witches and, exactly paralleling Macbeth, dismounting to enter their hut. Judi Dench and Ian McKellen's stage performances (dir. Trevor Nunn, 1979, RSC) were recorded for television; updated television versions include the gritty *Macbeth on the Estate* (Penny Woolcock, 1997), which in some ways is closer to the amoral vision of Scotland Shakespeare found in Holinshed, and the *Shakespeare Retold* (2005) updated version set in a restaurant with meat and cleavers literalising the play's brutality. In 2010 Rupert Goold directed Patrick Stewart for television stressing its violent militarism, with the witches as memorably menacing nurses in the opening scene in a hospital corridor.

Themes and interpretation

Macbeth gives us Shakespeare's most sustained treatment of terror, and its insight is to see that terror is both psychologically human and uncannily supernatural. We have to fear both what is within us as well as what is without.

Although Shakespeare has worked on his source material to make Duncan seem a saintly, anointed king, he does not give us an Edenic world disrupted by Macbeth's deviant violence. Rather, Macbeth is a soldier whose capacity for cold brutality is initially applauded because it is on the king's side. The description of the battle which introduces him suggests that his behaviour is breathtaking in its surgical clarity: he 'ne'er shook hands, nor bade farewell to him, / Till he unseamed him from the nave to th'chaps' (1.2.21–2). Like Shakespeare's other demobbed soldiers – Othello or Coriolanus – Macbeth's violence cannot be turned off. Shakespeare here experiments with a tragic consciousness structured around guilt – Macbeth is a developed version of the hints we see in Claudius (*Hamlet*) or Brutus (*Julius Caesar*) or Henry IV (*King Richard II*). In contrast to the structure of these earlier plays, Duncan is killed within the first third of the play; the rest is dedicated to the unquiet minds of his assassins. Macbeth's guilt is never at issue, and thus the play's triumph is to make us experience his conscience. But the question of culpability hovers over a play particularly interested in narratives of causation and agency. Do the witches merely know, or change, what will happen next? Would Macbeth have gone through with the murder without Lady Macbeth's scornful urgings? Tragedy is often considered the genre in which the question of agency is most prominent – why did this happen? – and here Shakespeare's anatomisation of blame and of action refuses easy answers. Macbeth is a centre of consciousness in which external factors – the witches' prophecies, his wife – interact with internal compulsions.

The play also gives us one of Shakespeare's few portraits of an operative marriage. Macbeth and Lady Macbeth are initially mutually dependent: in the tense scenes around the murder of Duncan, they alternate roles as staunch and wavering. At first it appears that Macbeth's nerve will break first, as in his vision of Banquo's ghost sitting in his own seat at the table. But, having established Lady Macbeth as an unsexed monster who will stop at nothing to see her husband crowned, Shakespeare shows us the cost of her self-sacrifice, revealing her tortured attempts to clean her hands, punctuated by an ever-tolling knocking.

The play is deeply anxious about women's role in men's lives. Berating Macbeth for his cowardice, Lady Macbeth declares: 'I have given suck and know / How tender 'tis to love the babe that milks me' (1.7.54–5), but this child and the brightly chattering son of Macduff are evoked only in order to be murdered, either symbolically by Lady Macbeth who promises herself willing to 'dash ... the brains out' (1.7.58), or actually in the case of young Macduff. As many productions have explored, there is no further mention of any children of the Macbeth line and this absence enforces the unnatural sterility of his quest for power. It is Banquo who will found a dynasty, the witches prophesy, whereas Macbeth's is a 'fruitless crown' and 'barren sceptre' (3.1.62–3). Children play an important symbolic role in the play: the witches produce the apparitions of a 'bloody child' (4.6.75) and a child-king; Macbeth describes his infirmity as 'the baby of a girl' (3.4.106); Hecate describes him as the witches' 'wayward son' (3.5.11), and even Lady Macbeth describes her husband as unweaned from goodness: 'too full o'th'milk of human kindness' (1.5.15). The play's concern with succession and royal dynasties is partly a feature of the circumstances of its original presentation before King James, and its squeamish preoccupation with motherhood may also allude to James' own mother, Mary Queen of Scots, who was executed by Elizabeth I. Given the play's apprehensive representation of women, therefore, it is entirely appropriate that Macbeth's nemeses should take the form of Malcolm, 'yet / Unknown to woman' (4.3.125–6) and Macduff, 'none of woman born' (4.1.79). The final victors at Dunsinane have made themselves immune to women's influence.

Measure for Measure

Key Facts

Date: 1604

Length: 2,938 lines

Verse: 65% / Prose: 35%

Major characters' share of lines:	
Duke	30%
Isabella	15%
Lucio	11%
Angelo	11%

Dark comedy of sex, cynicism and punishment

Plot and characters

The **Duke** is to leave Vienna and place a deputy in charge: he chooses the strict **Angelo**. **Claudio** is arrested on pain of death for having made his fiancée **Juliet** pregnant before they are formally married; **Mistress Overdone**'s brothel in the suburbs is to be pulled down. Claudio asks **Lucio** to tell his sister **Isabella** to plead for him with Angelo. Isabella is a novice nun, who agrees unwillingly to Lucio's request. The Duke explains to **Friar Thomas** that under his rule the government of Vienna has been lax, and that he will observe Angelo's performance in reinforcing the law. A farcical court scene with constable **Elbow** as plaintiff and **Froth** and the pimp **Pompey** as defendants is heard by **Escalus** after Angelo leaves in impatience. Isabella pleads with Angelo for Claudio's life, tentatively at first, and then with passion. After she leaves, Angelo muses on his attraction to her and whether it is because of, or despite, her chastity. The Duke, disguised as a friar, discusses with Juliet her culpability for her situation. A second, highly charged interview between Isabella and Angelo results in his proposition: if she sleeps with him, he will revoke Claudio's death sentence. She refuses. In prison, Claudio is visited by the Friar/Duke and urged to prepare himself for death. Isabella tells Claudio of Angelo's terrible offer, and is distraught when he suggests she ought to submit to it. The Friar/Duke suggests a way out:

Mariana, a woman earlier spurned by Angelo who was betrothed to her, will pretend to be Isabella in the nocturnal assignation with Angelo. Lucio discusses the Duke's character with the 'Friar', suggesting that the Duke's own morality is not above suspicion. Isabella tells Mariana the Friar/Duke's plan, and she agrees. Pompey, imprisoned, becomes the hangman **Abhorson**'s servant. Despite his promise, Angelo orders Claudio's execution: the Friar/Duke persuades the **Provost** to substitute the decapitated head of another prisoner for that of Claudio. **Barnardine**, a murderer, is fingered for this, but he refuses to co-operate, saying he is too drunk and therefore unfit for death. Happily, another prisoner has just died and his head is sent instead. The Friar/Duke tells Isabella her brother is dead. At the Duke's return to Vienna, he manipulates Isabella into pleading for Angelo's life, marries Angelo to Mariana and commutes his death sentence, and then reveals that Claudio is alive. Barnardine is pardoned; Lucio is sentenced to marry Kate Keepdown, a prostitute he has made pregnant, for the slandering of the Duke. Finally, the Duke extends a proposal of marriage to Isabella: she does not reply.

Context and composition

The play was probably written in 1604 and alludes to early Jacobean proclamations about demolishing houses of ill-repute in the suburbs of London. Its trope of the disguised ruler is shared with a number of contemporary plays, probably reflecting James' accession to the English throne in 1603. *Measure for Measure* is closer to the contemporary vogue for 'city comedy', in the hands of playwrights such as Thomas Dekker and Thomas Middleton – a satirical urban prose genre in which everything, including human beings, is cynically commodified – than it is to Shakespeare's earlier romantic comedies. Recent scholarship suggests the text, first printed in the Folio of 1623, may include later revisions by Middleton, particularly in the low-life characters. Since the late nineteenth century the play has often been linked with *All's Well that Ends Well*, *Troilus and Cressida* and perhaps *Hamlet* too, as a pessimistic, interrogative subset of Shakespearean drama known as 'problem plays'.

Measure for Measure takes its story of the so-called 'monstrous ransom' – sex for a pardon – from a number of sources, most immediately from Cinthio's prose *Hecatammithi* (1565, also used for *Othello* at around the same date) and George Whetstone's play *Promos and Cassandra* (1578). Shakespeare has invented the Duke's continued presence as a 'looker-on' in Vienna, has raised the stakes on the bargain by making Isabella not simply a virtuous woman but a novice nun, and has avoided the usual outcome of the story, that the Isabella figure does indeed sleep with the governor and is finally married to him as reparation.

Performances

The play was performed at court at Christmas 1604. It was revived, in an adapted version, in the Restoration, but its cocktail of sex and coercion was strong meat for later audiences, and George

Bernard Shaw's prediction in 1898 that in this play Shakespeare was ready and willing to start at the twentieth century if only the seventeenth would let him' has been accurate. As for so many other plays, Peter Brook's production in 1950 was revelatory: John Gielgud as Angelo and Barbara Jefford (Isabella) were well matched in icy self-righteousness, and Isabella's lengthy pause before kneeling on Angelo's behalf has entered theatrical legend. John Barton (RSC, 1970) directed Sebastian Shaw as a complex Duke marked by inconsistencies, and left Estelle Kohler as Isabella alone on stage after his unanswered proposal. Desmond Davis' 1979 BBC film of the play records a then prevalent view that its awkwardnesses can be brought to a happy ending, but more recent productions have emphasised its unresolved ambiguities. Simon McBurney (Complicité, 2004) turned Angelo's regime into a topically modern police state, and the Duke's final turn to a kingsize bed waiting louchely at the back of the stage suggested that his and Angelo's motives were identical. Michael Boyd (RSC, 1998) had Isabella and Mariana swap costumes at the end, exchanging sexuality for absolution. Declan Donnellan (Cheek by Jowl, 1994) stressed Isabella's repressed passionate nature, and kept the imprisoned Claudio on stage throughout the Duke's machinations.

Themes and interpretation

Measure for Measure has been a difficult play for readers and audiences to enjoy: characters polarised between licence and self-righteousness but united in their individual solipsism; a seamy plot about forced and commercialised sex; a world morally and dramatically vacated by its opening device, the Duke's unexplained abdication. But it is also a play that seems disturbingly modern in its refusal of sentiment, its avoidance of preaching, and its shifting centre of gravity. In the first half of the play the balance seems to be held by Isabella and Angelo, whose two electrifying interviews troublingly take the place of the courtships (Claudio and Juliet, Angelo and Mariana, the Duke and Isabella) that are the dominant subject of Shakespeare's romantic comedies (*Much Ado About Nothing*, *As You Like It*) but absent here. In the second half of the play, however, the Duke's power is again ascendant, as he manipulates his characters rather in the manner of a playwright or stage manager. Part of the Duke's new-found agency here is in suppressing Isabella and Angelo, whose roles are much less prominent and who, in the play's final scene, are reduced to unwillingly mouthing a script prepared for them by the Duke.

Views of the Duke himself have shifted radically over the last decades. This ruler, who watches his people's sins while hidden from them and who returns to deliver a final judgement, does share some of the attributes of God, but modern interpretations have tended to interpret that as the Duke's own delusion rather than Shakespeare's intention. The idea that the Duke is a Machiavel – a political pragmatist loosely based on the radical contemporary writings of Niccolo Machiavelli – has been fruitful for criticism and for performance, making the play, for all its superficial religious motifs, a play about temporal power politics rather than the mysterious operations of grace. For Isabella, however, the nun's habit is not a disguise but a desired discipline: her wish at the outset for firmer regulation in the order links her with Angelo and with the play's general movement towards absolutes. Dialogue in *Measure for Measure* is almost never reciprocal or generous, but uncomprehending or coercive – one of the ways this play employs, but twists, comic tropes.

It is in its ending, perhaps, that the play's queasy relation to the genre of comedy is clearest. Marriages here are enforced rather than chosen: Angelo prefers death to the woman he jilted; Isabella's answer is unknown. Even Claudio and Juliet, the couple who apparently wanted to be together, do not speak, denying us them as an antidote to the pervading atmosphere of punishment. The outspoken Lucio's sentence is the most revealing. His death penalty is commuted to marriage to the absent prostitute Kate Keepdown, and when he complains that this is as bad as torture, the Duke snaps back: 'slandering a prince deserves it' (5.1.516). Lucio is marrying the mother of his illegitimate child not as reparation for a social crime, and his punishment is not for fornication. Rather she is the means by which his tongue is silenced, in a judgement which sees female sexuality as man's penance and in which political power asserts itself in arbitrary retribution.

The Duke's actions at the end of the play make it uncertain that anything has changed. Certainly the emphasis has moved away from structural improvement – there is now no talk of closing the brothels – and is preoccupied with sorting out the complications of the plot. In freeing Barnardine, the drunken murderer who point blank refuses to go along with the Duke's elaborate plan to preserve Claudio, the final scene focuses its thoroughgoing ambiguities. Is Barnardine pardoned because there is hope for all sinners, although he shows no inclination to reform? Or is he pardoned in the same kind of general and capricious amnesty that led to social and moral decline in the first place? Like the treatment of Angelo, the Duke's sinisterly repressed double, this judgement is an assertion of will rather than principle. Tellingly, that title phrase 'measure for measure', from Jesus' Sermon on the Mount, is itself qualified: 'an Angelo for Claudio / . . . Like doth quit like, and measure still for measure' (5.1.402–5). That Claudio is not in fact dead means the system of legal and moral equivalences is fatally undermined: what ethical justice might be in such a context remains elusive.

The Merchant of Venice

Key Facts

Date: 1596–7
Length: 2,737 lines
Verse: 80% / Prose: 20%

Major characters' share of lines:

Portia	22%
Shylock	13%
Bassanio	13%
Gratiano	7%
Lorenzo	7%
Antonio	7%

Romantic comedy overshadowed by the vivid depiction of Shylock, Shakespeare's only Jewish character

Plot and characters

In Venice, the merchant **Antonio** is unaccountably melancholy, despite the efforts of friends **Gratiano, Lorenzo, Salerio** and **Solanio**. He agrees to lend his beloved **Bassanio** money to go to Belmont and woo **Portia**, but because his ships are all at sea, he needs to borrow the money himself: three thousand ducats, from the Jewish usurer **Shylock**. Shylock agrees to lend the money, not before expressing his gleeful surprise that the Christians, who have treated him so harshly, now need his help, and expressing his hatred of them in an aside. They settle on a bond of a pound of Antonio's flesh should he default. In Belmont, Portia endures a series of suitors all attempting to win her hand by means of a casket trick devised by her late father. The Prince of **Morocco** chooses gold, the wrong casket, and is sent away, having promised to remain unmarried should he be unsuccessful; the same happens when her next suitor, the Prince of **Arragon**, chooses silver. Shylock's servant **Lancelot Gobbo** decides to leave his service, and plays a trick on his blind father. **Jessica**, Shylock's daughter, sends Gobbo to Lorenzo with a letter arranging her elopement, and escapes the locked house, dressed as a boy, bringing Shylock's money with her. News of Jessica's elopement and Shylock's anger is recounted by

Salerio and Solanio; news also arrives of the loss of Antonio's ships in a storm, and this misfortune cheers Shylock, who discusses Jessica and Antonio with his friend **Tubal**. In Belmont, Portia is eager for Bassanio to make the correct choice, and he does indeed choose the leaden casket, winning her hand. **Nerissa**, her waiting woman, and Gratiano are also to marry. Immediately, a letter arrives telling them that Antonio is bankrupt and at Shylock's mercy. Portia offers to repay the debt of three thousand ducats, and their marriage is postponed while Bassanio returns to Venice. Portia and Nerissa announce they are going to a convent, but instead they go to Venice in male disguise. In the court, Shylock claims repayment of his bond before the **Duke**, despite being offered twice the sum owed by Bassanio. Antonio faces his death like a martyr. Enter a new young lawyer, Balthazar, and his clerk (Portia and Nerissa). Portia asks Shylock to show mercy, and when he will not, turns the tables, stating that he must not shed any blood in taking his bond since there was no mention of it in the agreement, and reminding him that Jews must not harm Christians, on pain of death. Shylock has his property confiscated and is forced to convert to Christianity; he exits saying he is ill. Still in disguise, Portia asks Bassanio for his ring – her own gift – as a sign of his gratitude: Antonio urges him to accede; Nerissa does the same with Gratiano. Back in Belmont they upbraid their menfolk for losing the rings, but all is resolved, and news arrives that Antonio's ships are come safely home.

Context and composition

Probably written around 1596–7, the play was first printed in 1600, with an extended title (probably not authorial): '*The Most Excellent History of the Merchant of Venice. With the extreme cruelty of Shylock the Jew towards the said Merchant, in cutting a just pound of his flesh: and the obtaining of Portia by the choice of three chests*'. There are a number of contemporary sources for the usury plot, from which Shakespeare draws the bond of a pound of flesh, and also for the caskets plot. Although there were few Jewish characters in drama before this play (and no openly Jewish residents in England, after their banishment in 1290), Shakespeare probably drew on

Christopher Marlowe's popular black comedy *The Jew of Malta* (*c.* 1590). Portia's disguise links her with a number of other Shakespearean heroines, such as Viola in *Twelfth Night* and Innogen in *Cymbeline*, though in her striking performance in the court she transgresses gender roles in a more public sphere than these other characters.

Performances

The play is known to have been revived at court in 1605. It returned to the stage in the eighteenth century as a vehicle for Shylock: the movement from performances by comic actors to

ones by tragic actors is symptomatic of a shift in the play's critical reception. Shylock has continued to dominate on the modern stage, and the play is not uncontroversial: the playwright Arnold Wesker has called for it to be banned for its anti-Semitism, and proposed his own politically combative version *The Merchant* (1976) instead. Most postwar productions have made Shylock a broadly sympathetic figure. On film, Laurence Olivier performed a dignified Edwardian banker whose keening grief following his exit from the court completely overshadowed the play's attempt at a comedic ending (dir. Jonathan Miller, 1980); a more confused, or even-handed, film version by Al Pacino (2004) gave a detailed evocation of the Venetian ghetto and the treatment of Jews, but also cast the Christians, particularly Jeremy Irons as Antonio, as glamorous and charismatic. In the modern theatre, memorable recent Shylocks include Henry Goodman, Antony Sher and Dustin Hoffman. Greg Doran's 1997 RSC production made Philip Voss a tragic hero and the Christians barbaric and prejudiced. It has become commonplace for directors to diagnose Antonio's melancholy as unrequited love for Bassanio (as in Pacino's film).

Themes and interpretation

In *The Merchant of Venice* Shakespeare splices fairy tale with realism. Belmont's feminised world of romance, ruled over by the folkloric caskets device, contrasts sharply with the commercialised masculinity of Venice. But in fact these opposites turn out to be rather similar: Bassanio's interest in Portia is, firstly, that she is an heiress 'richly left' (1.1.160), and the substantial loan he requires Antonio to take from Shylock is presumably to give him the appearance of being a wealthy suitor. Ironically, he picks the casket with least obvious material value – lead – not because he is uninterested in wealth but because he understands the code. Just like Antonio's argosies voyaging to the East to bring back valuable cargoes and sell them on, then, the love quest in the play is speculative, requiring an investment of capital but promising great returns. Romance, too, is mercantile: Belmont is less the opposite of Venice and more its weekend cottage. And Shylock, whose structural role in the play is to be the blocking, anti-comic figure who must be circumvented or won over in order to achieve a comic ending, is, by bankrolling the romance, its enabler rather than its obstacle.

Shylock's characterisation has, inevitably, taken over the play. Present in only five scenes, he nevertheless has dominated its theatrical and critical history. Is he a caricature of the merciless Jewish moneylender, prompted by sectarian hatred into barbaric cruelty? Or is he the play's victim, bent into hatred by his position as an outsider whose final fate shows that the Venetian state was always stacked against him because of his race? Both are true, and this perennially highly charged combination gives Shylock his stage dynamism. Antonio does not deny the charges of ill-treatment that Shylock enumerates before he agrees to lend the money, and nor does Shylock avoid the logic of his own famous 'hath not a Jew eyes' (3.1.46) speech, which promotes religious parity only inasmuch as it gives him equal licence to take revenge. Neither Shylock, as a representative of the Jews, nor the Christians, come out of the courtroom unblemished, and the Victorian idealisation of Portia's wisdom has tended to be replaced with an uncomfortable awareness of the racist superiority with which she dismisses her dark-skinned suitors. Like *Othello*, Shakespeare's other play set, in part, in Venice, the play recognises the energy and anxiety of a cosmopolitan city in which friends, business associates and enemies need to be clearly differentiated: for Elizabethan theatregoers in their own commercial metropolis based on water trade and on retail rather than manufacture, Venice must have seemed an exciting and dangerous prototype.

Like other comic heroines in Shakespeare, Portia seems to have the upper hand in her courtship, perhaps even, in the end rhymes of the song for Bassiano before his choice, indicating which of the caskets he should pick. The charade of the rings at the end of the play can seem trivial after the dramatic tension of the court scene in Act 4, but it serves a serious purpose: Portia needs to educate her green husband into proper loyalty and exclusivity, and to direct his primary affections from Antonio to his wife. This need not mean that for the play's first audiences the relationship between Antonio and Bassanio was seen to be homoerotic but rather that contemporary models of male friendship, in the writings, for example, of the philosopher Montaigne, sanctioned strongly emotional bonds between men. But Antonio is still there to triangulate their marriage at the end of the play, and is still, masochistically, promising his body as surety for Bassanio's promises. The play's refusal to separate out financial arrangements from emotional ones, or physical bonds from material ones, gives it an ethical queasiness often closer to the so-called problem plays of *Measure for Measure* and *All's Well that Ends Well* than the romantic comedies of the mid 1590s.

The Merry Wives of Windsor

Key Facts

Date: 1597–8
Length: 2,891 lines
Verse: 10% / Prose: 90%

Major characters' share of lines:

Falstaff	17%
Mistress Page	12%
Ford	12%
Mistress Quickly	10%

Comedy of provincial life with women on top

Plot and characters

Justice **Shallow** is enraged that Sir John **Falstaff** has been poaching his deer. At **Page**'s house, the Welsh parson Hugh **Evans** tries to make peace between them. Shallow wants to marry his inept nephew **Slender** to Page's daughter **Anne**. Evans writes to **Mistress Quickly**, Anne's friend, for her help on Slender's behalf: when the French Dr **Caius** returns she bundles **Simple**, the messenger, into a closet, but he is discovered. Caius is angry because he too wants to woo Anne, and challenges Evans to a duel. **Fenton** presents himself as another would-be suitor. At the Garter Inn Falstaff tells his followers **Bardolph**, **Nim** and **Pistol** that he intends to woo **Mistress Ford** and **Mistress Page** for their money, but when he sends the women identical letters they get together and plot to string him along and bankrupt him. **Ford** is mad with jealousy, and disguises himself as Brooke to find out Falstaff's intentions. Mistress Quickly, in on the wives' plot, tells Falstaff they are in love with him. Brooke asks Falstaff to seduce Mistress Ford on his behalf. The Garter **Host** prevents the duel by sending Caius and Evans to different places: the two men are reconciled and agree to be revenged on the Host instead. Ford's jealousy grows, and he plans to surprise his wife with Falstaff. The women have lured him to the house, but when Mistress Page warns that Ford is coming with armed men to look for him, they hide him in the laundry basket, which is carried away and dumped in the river by servants as Ford arrives. Falstaff is persuaded to seek another rendezvous, and reveals this to Brooke. Fenton woos Anne, although her father prefers Slender and her mother Caius as a son-in-law. There is comedy when young **William** Page has a Latin lesson from Evans, complete with commentary from Mistress Quickly. Falstaff's seduction of Mistress Ford is interrupted again with news that Ford is on his way: this time the women dress him as an old woman who again escapes the husband's notice. The women agree to tell their husbands what has been happening, and together the couples plan a last trick to get Falstaff to Herne's Oak in Windsor Park at midnight dressed as Herne the Hunter. A hoax about a German duke supposedly staying at the Garter results in some stolen horses. Falstaff is brought to Herne's Oak where he is frightened by fairies (really local children in disguise); amid the confusion Slender and Caius are tricked and Anne and Fenton are married. All is revealed.

Context and composition

Since the eighteenth century it has been asserted that the play was commissioned by Queen Elizabeth because she wanted to see Falstaff in love. Windsor has strong associations with royalty. It may be that the last act of the play invokes the ceremony of the Order of the Garter, to which the Lord Chamberlain – patron of Shakespeare's acting company – was admitted in 1597, and if so, this is the only play specifically commissioned for a state event. It is also – except for the Warwickshire Induction to *The Taming of the Shrew* – his only comedy with an English setting. The play's language is closely linked with the two parts of *Henry IV*, and must date from 1597–8: it obviously draws on the popularity of Falstaff in those plays, whether directly requested by Elizabeth or by more general popular acclaim. It was printed in 1602 and in a lengthier version in the 1623 First Folio.

The play refers to a wide range of folkloric and narrative material, but no single major source has been identified. In its comic treatment of male jealousy it can be linked with *Much Ado About Nothing* and *The Winter's Tale*, as well as with the tragic version of that plot line, *Othello*. It has the highest proportion of prose of any play

Shakespeare wrote, giving it pace, innuendo and something of the texture of everyday speech, even as its plot pirouettes in enjoyable absurdities.

Performances

The play sustained its early popularity into the Restoration, and was one of the first Shakespeare plays to be performed at the reopening of the theatres in 1660. Its playfulness and set-piece scenes

have made it particularly attractive to composers, with significant operatic versions by Salieri, Nicolai, Verdi and Vaughan Williams. More recently Greg Doran, with composer Paul Englishby, produced a musical version in the pantomime slot in Stratford with Simon Callow in a Falstaff fat-suit and an expanded role for Judi Dench as Mistress Quickly (2006).

Many recent productions have added stage business to establish the play's bourgeois setting: at the RSC, choirboys playing conkers in Trevor Nunn and John Caird's 1975 production; mock-Tudor suburbia for Bill Alexander (1985), with the wives plotting under salon hairdriers; market stalls for Terry Hands (1995). Updating the play to the immediate postwar austerity period allowed Rachel Kavanaugh (2002, RSC) to bring out its sense of social strain and dissatisfaction, with Fenton as a black US airman adding to Windsor's thoroughgoing mistrust of outsiders. Penelope Keith's red wig as Mistress Ford (dir. Michael Rudman, 1990, Chichester Festival Theatre) evoked Queen Elizabeth I for some reviewers. The apparently perennial comedy value of English with a foreign accent has made many Dr Caiuses the show-stealers.

Themes and interpretation

Shakespeare's romantic comedies end at the point of marriage, and tragedies such as *King Lear* tend to feature widowers: the state of marriage itself is surprisingly rare in the plays, and when we do see married couples their relationship is usually under strain (e.g. Othello and Desdemona, the Macbeths). In *The Merry Wives of Windsor* Shakespeare shows married women acting with the verve and self-determination of their unmarried comic counterparts in other plays, giving a portrait of marriage in which women's cleverness and their friendships are dominant. Thus it is family life – the laundry basket, the schoolroom – that is most prominent, and it is appropriate that in the domestic world the wives hold sway. If Falstaff's insultingly matching letters of seduction to Mistress Ford and Mistress Page prompt their plot to bring about his comic comeuppance, then they also allow the women to re-educate Ford, whose unreasonable jealousy is as socially threatening as Falstaff's libido. Ford, too, treats his wife as a piece of property: as Falstaff promises to make the women his 'East and West Indies' (1.3.53), so Ford splutters that he cannot trust his wife any more than 'a Fleming with my butter . . . an Irishman with my aquavitae bottle, or a thief to my ambling gelding' (2.2.236–8). The comparison is revealing: the middle-England provincialism courted by the play's title combines the suspicious stereotyping of foreigners with the anxiety about cuckoldry.

In some ways, *Merry Wives* corresponds to the emergent city comedy of Thomas Dekker and Thomas Middleton: sharp, urban plays with recognisable types and a salty linguistic tang. The jealous husband, the marriageable daughter arranging her own love life independent of her protective parents, the foreigner marked by his comically accented speech, the tavern crowd – these are all figures from this kind of contemporary drama. It may be the measure of the small-town Stratford boy that his only drama with a contemporary English setting bucks the fashionable literary trend and locates its action not in London but in Windsor, a provincial satellite town. The play's exploration of Englishness is a feature not of the metropolis but of the market town, and images of confinement, from the closet to the laundry basket, are the physical equivalent of its parochial mindset. Falstaff is an incomer into this world – an incomer both from the generically and temporally distant history plays (Parts 1 and 2 of *Henry IV*) in which he had established his stage popularity, and from a world beyond the respectable confines of Windsor. In his first scene in the play he acknowledges poaching Shallow's deer: and as he amply demonstrates, he is no respecter of property, either personal, marital or material.

In the end it is Falstaff, wearing the horns of Herne the Hunter, who is metaphorically cuckolded, frighted by a schoolroom full of children pretending to be fairies. The ending of the play is actually as mundane as its carefully realised provincial setting might suggest – we are not in the magical world of *A Midsummer Night's Dream*, although the plot makes Falstaff believe it ('I do begin to perceive that I am made an ass' [5.5.110]) – but in drawing on the folklore associated with Herne, it evokes a more mysterious and ancient world than is intended by the pranksters. The fairies' fierce moralising – 'Fie on lust and luxury' (5.5.87) – makes clear that the escapade in Windsor Great Park is a kind of festive chastening, a social corrective to bring Falstaff's behaviour into communal line. But the conclusion marks the return to the domestic: 'let us every one go home', instructs Mistress Page, 'And laugh this sport o'er by a country fire'. And, she adds, 'Sir John and all' (5.5.211–14). Through the manipulations of comedy, the play has absorbed the moral and social interloper Falstaff into its image of small-town community. Whether Falstaff has withstood his transplantation into bourgeois comedy has been the dominant critical question about the play, and lovers of this undomesticated character across the previous history plays will have to decide whether this final incorporation is a victory or a defeat.

A Midsummer Night's Dream

Key Facts
Date: 1595–6
Length: 2,222 lines
Verse: 80% / Prose: 20%

Major characters' share of lines:	
Bottom	12%
Theseus	11%
Helena	11%
Puck	10%
Oberon	10%

Fantastical comedy gently satirising love at first sight

Plot and characters

Duke **Theseus** is to be married to **Hippolyta,** the Amazonian queen he has won in battle, and awaits his nuptials impatiently. **Egeus** and his daughter **Hermia,** with her two suitors **Demetrius** and **Lysander,** come before him. Hermia refuses to marry her father's choice Demetrius (who had previously wooed **Helena**) and prefers Lysander. Theseus supports Egeus: Hermia must marry Demetrius or accept either death or a virgin life. Lysander and Hermia agree secretly to run away to his aunt's house, and they confide in Helena. Dismayed that Demetrius prefers Hermia, Helena tells him of the planned elopement, and follows him following them into the wood. In the wood a group of artisans, led by **Quince,** are preparing a play for the Duke's wedding. **Bottom** the weaver wants to play all the roles, but is cast as Pyramus with **Flute** as his Thisbe. **Puck,** or Robin Goodfellow, servant to King **Oberon** of the Fairies, reveals his master has quarrelled with Queen **Titania** over a changeling boy. The row has had terrible consequences in the natural world, but Titania refuses to submit. Puck is sent to get a magic flower, love-in-idleness, which makes a person fall in love with the next creature they see. Oberon instructs him to use it to punish Demetrius who has been disdainful of Helena, but Puck mistakenly applies it to Lysander. He also uses it on

Titania, sleeping in her bower. Lysander awakes and is enamoured of Helena, who thinks she is being mocked; an application of the potion to Demetrius also backfires, as he too falls in love with Helena, resulting in a quarrel between the two women. As the artisans rehearse their play, Puck turns Bottom's head into an ass's head: the others run away terrified, but the enchanted Titania falls in love with him and takes him to her bower with her fairy attendants **Mustardseed, Peaseblossom, Cobweb** and **Moth**. Oberon reports that Titania has surrendered the changeling, so lifts the spell, and the two are reconciled. Theseus, Hippolyta and Egeus find the four lovers while out hunting: Theseus states that Hermia and Lysander, and Helena and Demetrius, will be married with him. At court, under the direction of the master of the revels **Philostrate**, Quince's troupe play the tragic 'Pyramus and Thisbe', with **Snug** as the lion, **Snout** as Wall, and **Starveling** as Moonshine. The three couples leave; Oberon and Titania bless the human marriages, and Puck likens the play to the audience's 'dream' in an epilogue.

Context and composition

Probably written in 1595–6, this marriage play has long been supposed to have a connection with some aristocratic wedding celebrations, but no firm evidence for this exists. It was first printed in 1600. Like the late play *The Two Noble Kinsmen*, it takes one of Chaucer's *Canterbury Tales*, 'The Knight's Tale', as a major source, juxtaposing the marriage of Theseus and Hippolyta with male rivalry over a woman. Puck, or Robin Goodfellow, is a figure from English folklore; Ovid's *Metamorphoses* provides much of the atmosphere of transmutation as well as the story of Pyramus and Thisbe; Bottom's transformation draws on a second-century Latin prose story, Apuleius' *The Golden Ass*; and in the background there may be allusions to poor agricultural conditions in the description of disturbed weather and a memory of the entertainment at Kenilworth – near to Shakespeare's boyhood home of Stratford – for the Queen in 1575.

The play makes heavy use of end rhyme – 'blank verse', the metre most associated with Shakespeare, is blank because unrhymed – appropriately for its stories of multiple pairings. Each strand of the plot has its own linguistic style, resulting in a play of dazzlingly ingenious rhythms, and perhaps explaining its particular appeal to composers and choreographers. Its exact chronological relation to the contemporaneous *Romeo and Juliet*, whose tragic love plot may be being satirised in the mechanicals' story of 'Pyramus and Thisbe', is unclear.

Performances

Popular in its own time, the play was revived at court in 1604. During the nineteenth century its magical woodland elements were stressed, with Herbert

Beerbohm Tree's real rabbits in the wood a high (low?) point in 1900. More recent productions, particularly since Peter Brook's landmark 'white box' production (1970) which dispensed with realist froufrou and involved the cast on trapezes in a minimalist set, have turned away from whimsy in favour of the inner, psychological landscape and a renewed interest in the play's physical comedy. Greg Doran's 2005 RSC production was dominated by a large moon and contrasted the chilly, formal world of the Athenian court with what one reviewer called the 'hippy, trippy dreamland' of the wood; elsewhere the common doubling of Theseus–Oberon and Hippolyta–Titania draws the two worlds together. Comedians including Mickey Rooney (film directed by William Dieterle and Max Reinhardt, 1935), Dawn French (dir. Matthew Francis, Albery Theatre, 2001) and Russ Abbott (dir. Ian Talbot, Regent's Park, 2004) have taken on the role of Bottom, with the climactic amateur performance of

'Pyramus and Thisbe' usually emerging as one of Shakespeare's few funny scenes to need relatively little updating in the theatre.

Recent films include Michael Hoffman's lavishly costumed 1999 version, with Michelle Pfeiffer and Rupert Everett as Titania and Oberon and a penchant for interposed operatic arias. In 2001 Christine Edzard filmed the play with child-actors; a child is prominent in Adrian Noble's 1996 film based on his RSC stage production, which is framed as a young boy's dream and draws on some of the visual techniques of *The Wizard of Oz*.

Themes and interpretation

A schoolteacher led his party of children out of a 1999 Royal Shakespeare Company production of *A Midsummer Night's Dream* because it was too sexually explicit, causing a small furore about appropriate interpretations of Shakespeare's plays. The trouble seemed to be a mismatch of expectations: the Victorian period annexed the play as a children's story of magical make-believe, turning its fairies into ethereal creatures and its Puck into a benignly mischievous sprite, but more recently the play's interest has been located in its exploration of sexuality and desire. Understanding the governing metaphor of the dream – Bottom, Titania, Lysander, Demetrius, Helena and Hermia all sleep during the play, and Puck suggests in the Epilogue that the audience too has 'but slumbered here' – less as light escapism and more in the psychoanalytical sense, as access to unconscious urges, has revealed a darker, more adult play underneath its popular expurgated self. A sexual *Midsummer Night's Dream* is the unconscious of the childish one, just as, perhaps, the passionate Oberon and Titania are intended as the unconscious of Theseus and Hippolyta, and the wood as the unconscious of the repressive court. There are dangers here as well as freedoms: instructing Lysander to lie further away from her, Hermia's fear may be for her safety as well as her reputation, and we can readily begin to imagine what Dr Freud might make of her dream that 'a serpent ate my heart away', or of Titania's frolicking with her donkey-man in her bower, or of the description of the milk-white flower 'love-in-idleness' now 'purple with love's wound' (2.1.167).

For many critics *A Midsummer Night's Dream* has epitomised the proximity of Shakespeare's comedies to the festive calendar of social rituals, and particularly to the fertility rituals associated with traditional May-games. Its lyrical depiction of rural life, that 'bank where the wild thyme blows' (2.1.249), has more in common with the English countryside of Shakespeare's own youth than its supposedly Athenian setting, and this may bring in a political dimension. For some the play's depiction of female authority has resonated with attitudes and anxieties about Queen Elizabeth, depicted in Edmund Spenser's epic poem of 1590 as *The Faerie Queene*.

The opening scene offers a world in which women are conquered by men. Theseus won Hippolyta's 'love doing thee injuries' (1.1.17), and her silence during the opening scene has been interpreted by some directors as her resistance to this captivity; Egeus expects the Duke to support his paternal authority over his daughter's marriage. Repressed conflict in Athens breaks out as self-assertion in the wood: Titania's open quarrel with Oberon is echoed in the war of words between former schoolfriends Hermia and Helena, and in the potential for violence in the rivalry of Demetrius and Lysander. It is a place dominated with references to the moon, associated with the female, but one where, contrary to popular stereotype, the women are constant and the men fickle. 'Pyramus and Thisbe', the farcical love tragedy with which the multiple marriages are celebrated, takes the undercurrent of violence and parodies it, just as it parodies the moon and the sacrificial constancy of women, preserving the play's comic conclusion by neutralising disruptive generic elements via the inset play.

Shakespeare obviously enjoys 'Pyramus and Thisbe', and it is a testament to the power of his cast that he can so confidently have them play bad actors. What is funny about the inset play is that its actors remain so resolutely themselves. Snout's helpful explanation that he is a wall, Snug's anxieties about being too convincing as a lion, Starveling's description of what he depicts – these flat-footed attempts at theatre paradoxically reinforce the power of dramatic transformations elsewhere in the play. 'The lunatic, the lover and the poet / Are of imagination all compact' (5.1.7–8), states Theseus, grandly bringing together the play's themes of topsy-turvy madness, desire and linguistic magic, but the play's real ending is with Puck, its own embodiment of the fleet, amoral and enchanted energies of the theatre.

Much Ado About Nothing

Key Facts

Date: 1598–9

Length: 2,684 lines

Verse: 30% / Prose: 70%

Major characters' share of lines:	
Benedick	17%
Leonato	13%
Don Pedro	12%
Claudio	11%
Beatrice	10%

Witty, bantering romantic comedy

Plot and characters

Leonato, Governor of Messina, with his niece **Beatrice** and daughter **Hero**, hear that **Don Pedro**'s army is returning having defeated his illegitimate brother **Don John**. Beatrice is concerned about the fate of **Benedick**. On his arrival, with Count **Claudio**, the pair resume an old sparring relationship, each mocking romantic love. Claudio tells Benedick he is in love with Hero, and Don Pedro agrees to court her on his behalf at a masked ball. This is overheard and Don John plots to spoil this by telling Claudio that Don Pedro woos for himself, provoking Claudio's jealousy. He and Hero become engaged, though, and the company agree that they will spend the time before the wedding trying to trick Beatrice and Benedick into falling in love. Benedick, hiding in the orchard, believes he is overhearing Don Pedro, Leonato and Claudio discuss how Beatrice is passionately in love with him but fears his scornful rejection. Benedick promises in a soliloquy that he will requite this love. Then Hero, **Margaret** and **Ursula** arrange a similar trick to persuade Beatrice of Benedick's love. Don John pays his servant **Borachio** to prevent the marriage of Claudio and Hero by a pretence with her waiting-woman Margaret, and leads Claudio and Don Pedro to see evidence of her unfaithfulness. A comic constable **Dogberry**, with his assistant **Verges,** overhears Borachio boasting about the plan to **Conrade,** and they try to inform Leonato, who will not listen because he is too busy with the wedding preparations. At the wedding Claudio denounces Hero as an adulterer; Leonato initially believes him, and Hero falls into a faint. **Friar Francis** agrees with Beatrice and Benedick that pretending Hero is dead will help to restore matters. Beatrice tasks Benedick, who has declared his love, with fighting Claudio to avenge Hero's honour, and, unwillingly, Benedick challenges his former friend. Dogberry arrests Borachio who confesses; Don Pedro and Claudio realise their mistake and make a solemn pilgrimage to Hero's grave. Leonato and his brother **Antonio** arrange a new wedding where Claudio will marry a cousin of Hero: a veiled Hero is presented to Claudio and the couple are reconciled. News of the capture of Don John is brought: his punishment is deferred beyond the celebratory dance which ends the play.

Context and composition

The play was written in 1598–9 and printed in 1600. Shakespeare takes the story of the defamed woman from Ariosto's *Orlando Furioso*, widely translated and reworked in European culture in the late sixteenth century, but the lively repartee of Beatrice and Benedick is his own invention. The original edition shows that Shakespeare originally conceived of a wife for Leonato, Innogen, the mother of Hero, but she was apparently written out since she never speaks, and most editors just cut her ghostly presence from the stage directions. Seemingly, Shakespeare wanted to isolate the young women of the play and, as so often in his comedies, to deny a mother figure who might have intervened. The play's tragic potential is something Shakespeare reworks in both *Othello* and *The Winter's Tale*, just as here he riffs on the friar persuading a troubled young wife to play dead that was so disastrous in *Romeo and Juliet*. Beatrice and Benedick's stormy exchanges recall – and perhaps recuperate – the sparks that fly between Petruchio and Katherine in *The Taming of the Shrew*.

Performances

The comic constable Dogberry was originally played by the popular comedian Will Kemp. The play was performed at court for royal wedding celebrations in 1613. During the

Restoration period Beatrice and Benedick were popular witty characters, and the roles have continued to showcase a central couple: Mr and Mrs Charles Kean in the Victorian period; John Gielgud and Peggy Ashcroft in the 1950s; the then married Kenneth Branagh and Emma Thompson in the lavish and sunny Tuscan film of 1993. Harriet Walter and Nicholas le Prevost played an unusually middle-aged couple in Greg Doran's 2002 production, emphasising their defensive pride and their maturity, set against the youth and two-dimensionality of the other pair; an all-female version at the Globe in 2004 directed by Tamara Harvey struck reviewers as unwelcome tampering with a much loved play; Josie Rourke at the Sheffield Crucible (2005) emphasised the demob atmosphere of the play. Beatrice, in particular, has often been a part for a comedian (Catherine Tate: Wyndham's Theatre, 2011; Josie Lawrence: Royal Exchange Theatre, 1997). A reworked version for the BBC television Shakespeare Retold series effectively updated Beatrice and Benedick as squabbling news anchors on a television show, whose rapport is evident to all around them. Interestingly, the only part of the play that was obviously thought too implausible in a modern context was that Hero would take Claudio back: the adaptation ended with her accepting his apology but not resuming their relationship.

Themes and interpretation

Much Ado's first spectators, in a London wearied by Irish wars and shortages, saw a romantic fantasy in which battle gives way to courtship: a different take on the structure of the contemporaneous *Henry V*. The hardships of conflict – both the war within the play and that surrounding its production and reception – are pushed away. Beatrice's anxious question about 'Signor Mountanto' (1.1.23) in the play's opening lines is less a real concern that loved ones do not always return from battle and more a ruse by which she is able to turn the conversation to Benedick, and Benedick's final promise of 'brave punishments' for Don John is postponed. 'War-thoughts', says Claudio, 'have left their places vacant', and into this lull in the hostilities 'come thronging soft and delicate desires' (1.1.228–30). This recuperation of martial energies into marital ones is summed up in the paradox aptly dubbed by Leonato a 'merry war' (1.1.45–6): the witty, dynamic, sexually charged interplay between Beatrice and Benedick, and the encounter between the male and female worlds that this relationship exemplifies.

Many of Shakespeare's comedies dramatise the developmental movement by which young people forgo primary attachments to their own sex in favour of exclusive romantic attachment to an opposite sex partner, and in this movement there is pain as well as gain. Nowhere is pain more evident than in *Much Ado*. Just as Benedick and Beatrice begin to express their mutual love after the shock of Hero's broken nuptials, just as each makes him- or herself vulnerable to the other, there comes immediately a terrible choice. 'Come bid me do anything for thee', offers Benedick in the heady expansiveness of acknowledged love. Beatrice's reply is deadly: 'Kill Claudio' (4.1.278–9).

That romance and marriage signal an end to certain sorts of male relationship is part of the wistfulness of *Much Ado*. From the beginning of the play, rivalries emerge between the men as they shift their interest from masculine friendship to romance. Under provocation from Don John, Claudio suspects that Don Pedro is wooing Hero for himself; Benedick bemoans Claudio's moonish preference for the effeminate 'tabor and pipe' and 'new doublet' over 'drum and fife' and 'good armour' (2.3.12–15), as their shared male pursuits are displaced by Claudio's engagement in the female sphere; Benedick takes up Beatrice's challenge and names Claudio 'a villain' (5.1.137). But despite these problems, male bonding retains a perverse hold over the men of the play. Although their aspirations and their function in activating sexual jealousy are similar, Don John is no Iago (in *Othello*): far from being the honest broker whose evil succeeds because he is so good at dissembling, Don John – named, throughout, the Bastard – is a self-proclaimed 'plain-dealing villain' (1.3.23–4). But, like *Othello*, this is a play in which men are automatically believed over women. When Claudio accuses Hero before her father at the altar, in terms of sexual disgust which revealingly identify marriage primarily as a relation between men ('Give not this rotten orange to your friend' [4.1.27]), Leonato immediately believes his daughter's accuser, crying out in an ecstasy of shame that is as vehement as it is short-lived: 'Do not live, Hero, do not ope thine eyes' (4.1.116). Only Beatrice believes implicitly in her cousin's honesty.

Although the straightforwardness of relationships between men is irreparably damaged in the play, it could be argued that male camaraderie prevails. *Much Ado* is a play profoundly uneasy about female sexuality and its assumed duplicity. Even after Hero's infidelity has been revealed as a piece of Don John's machiavellian theatre, the jokes about cuckoldry are still the currency of male interchange. 'Prince, thou art sad', Benedick notes of the matchmaker Don Pedro, 'get thee a wife, there is no staff more reverend than one tipped with horn' (5.4.114–16). It is significant that the play's last lines equate marriage with the inevitability of female unfaithfulness, before turning final attention back to Don John, whose own malevolent illegitimacy might be thought a kind of proof that women can – and some do – sleep with men not their husbands.

But however imperfect and fearful a prospect, marriage is, as Benedick ruefully acknowledges, a social inevitability: 'the world must be peopled' (2.3.197). As in a Hollywood screwball comedy such as *Bringing up Baby* (1938) or *His Girl Friday* (1940), the interplay between Beatrice and Benedick fizzes with sexual energy – a kind of verbal foreplay, which contrasts with the conformist, distanced wooing of Claudio and Hero who barely exchange two words. It is striking, however, how much social pressure exists to resolve these two confirmed singletons, these potential misfits, into a couple – something about their refusal to do the conventional thing is an inadmissible challenge. The world of Messina is one in which private actions, individual behaviours, are all closely monitored. Almost everything is overlooked or overheard – making even our presence as audience another level of the surveillance culture that governs social codes and sacrifices privacy to a potentially coercive version of 'community'. And the means by which romantic resolution is achieved are, of course, remarkably similar in type, if not in motive, to those of Don John: both Messina's 'fixers' and 'spoilers' are using the same techniques. Reading the play as a feel-good drama means that we may suspend any misgivings about the overlap between rose-tinted wish-fulfilment and authoritarian social control. But, as with the suspect conduct of Claudio or the reappearance of Don John, there are just enough negatives in the play's conclusion to caution our wilful optimism: Shakespeare's feel-good is always cut with realism.

Othello, the Moor of Venice

Key Facts
Date: 1603–4
Length: 3,685 lines
Verse: 80% / Prose: 20%

Major characters' share of lines:

Iago	31%
Othello	25%
Desdemona	11%
Cassio	8%

Passionate tragedy in which the marriage between Moorish Othello and Venetian Desdemona is destroyed by jealousy

Plot and characters

The play opens with **Iago**, an ensign under **Othello**'s command, rousing the Venetian senator **Brabantio** from his bed with news of his daughter **Desdemona**'s elopement to marry **Othello** the Moor. Iago reveals his hatred for Othello; his associate **Roderigo** wishes to marry Desdemona himself; and Brabantio is incited to seek the pair out. He is unable to gain support for his disapproval, however, when the respected general Othello is called to the **Duke**'s council of war, prompted by a Turkish naval threat, and dispatched to Cyprus to deal with the situation. Desdemona tells the council how Othello wooed her with his exotic stories, and is permitted to accompany her new husband. A storm threatens their separate journeys to Cyprus but they are tenderly reunited: the Turkish fleet has been destroyed. Iago tricks Roderigo into believing Desdemona is in love with Othello's lieutenant **Cassio** and then works to discredit Cassio. Plied with drink, Cassio fights **Montano**, the island governor, as well as Roderigo, disturbing Othello. He is stripped of his office by the general. Advised by Iago and his wife **Emilia**, Desdemona's waiting-woman, Cassio approaches Desdemona to plead his case and she promises to help. Iago builds on this to convince Othello that his wife has been unfaithful to him, in a long scene during which the Moor is persuaded to kill her. Helped by Emilia, Iago gains possession of

Desdemona's embroidered handkerchief, a gift from Othello, and, having planted it there, suggests that he has seen the item in Cassio's possession. The enraged Othello asks Desdemona for the handkerchief, but she prevaricates, concerned at its loss. Iago prepares a scene in which he and Cassio, overlooked by Othello, will discuss Cassio's mistress **Bianca**; but he tells Othello that the subject of their bawdy conversation is Desdemona. Othello believes the scene proves his suspicions, especially when Bianca enters to return the handkerchief to Cassio. Desdemona and Emilia discuss Othello's deteriorating behaviour – he slaps her, shocking the Venetian delegation including **Lodovico** – and prepare her bedchamber. Meanwhile Iago's plan that Roderigo kill Cassio backfires: Cassio is only wounded. Iago kills Roderigo. Alone with his wife, Othello accuses her. She denies any wrongdoing but reiterates her love for him. He smothers her in bed. Emilia breaks into the chamber too late, and is killed by Iago as she reveals his plotting. Iago is arrested; Cassio becomes governor; and Othello kills himself with a dagger.

Composition and context

The play was probably written in 1603–4 and based on an Italian novella by Giraldi Cinthio in *Gli Hecatommithi* (another of the novellas was the source for *Measure for Measure*, written around the same time). Other influences include contemporary works on Venice and Turkey, and it may well have been directed towards the new king James I, whose poem on a naval battle between Christians and Turks in 1571 had been recently republished. *Othello* is sometimes identified as part of a popular contemporary subgenre of 'domestic tragedy', located within the bourgeois household rather than with the high-born characters of classical tragedy, but it also has strong structural affinities with comedy, in which a patriarchal blocking figure – Brabantio, like Egeus in *A Midsummer Night's Dream* or Shylock in *The Merchant of Venice* – is circumvented, foolishness is punished – Roderigo resembles Aguecheek in *Twelfth Night* – and lovers are united. Shakespeare's other mistakenly jealous protagonists – in *The Merry Wives of Windsor*, *Much Ado about Nothing* and *The Winter's Tale* – are all comically rehabilitated. Like

Merchant, the play explores the situation of the outsider, again in the cosmopolitan world of Venice, a city-state often likened to early modern London. The play is first published in quarto in 1622 and again, with some variants, the following year in the First Folio.

Performances

Performed at court in 1604, and at the Globe and Blackfriars (according to the quarto title page), the role of Othello was originally taken by the King's Men's prominent tragedian, Richard Burbage, and there  is some evidence that a comic actor took the part of Iago, anticipating W. H. Auden's discussion of Iago as 'the joker in the pack' (*The Dyer's Hand*). Othello's race was probably indicated by black paint or burnt cork, and a woolly wig or other accoutrements may also have been used. Staging the Moor has been one of the play's most insistent challenges, through centuries of white actors pretending, through makeup or accent or gesture, to be black, the beginnings of a black acting tradition in the nineteenth century, and the dominance of black actors in the twentieth. Later milestones include performances by Paul Robeson in London in 1930 and on tour in America in 1943, Laurence Olivier's blacked-up performance in 1964 (preserved, perhaps unhelpfully, on film, where Olivier's acting seems histrionic), and Patrick Stewart as a white Othello amid a largely black cast in Washington, DC in 1997. In its depiction of race the play has often courted topicality: a television version written by Andrew Davies (2001) had Othello as a contemporary chief of police in London; a South African production directed by Janet Suzman in 1987 (Market Theatre, Johannesburg) drew on the politics of apartheid. On the stage Iago's amoral manipulation of the audience has often upstaged Othello's more distant presentation, and since at least Garrick's performance in the eighteenth century has often attracted star actors. Charismatic Iagos include Kenneth Branagh (film directed by Oliver Parker, 1996) and Simon Russell Beale (dir. Sam Mendes, National Theatre, 1997).

Orson Welles' 1952 film of the play translated its language into visual poetry, in particular with black–white contrasts, webs and traps, and shadows; for the BBC Shakespeare, Jonathan Miller emphasised its interiors in the style of Vermeer. O (dir. Tim Blake Nelson, 2001) updated the story to a largely white American high school, with Odin its star basketball player. Recent stage productions have often stressed its military setting or made sense of the play's gender roles by setting it in late Victorian or Edwardian worlds. The play's rhythms and the contrast between Othello's elevated style (what the critic G. Wilson Knight called 'the Othello music' [The Wheel of Fire]) and the bestial language of Iago has made it attractive for musical adaptation, including Verdi's opera Otello (1887) and the rock musical Catch my Soul (1968).

Themes and interpretation

Seeing Desdemona's lifeless body amid her wedding sheets, Othello wishes his loss were registered in the cosmos: 'Methinks it should be now a huge eclipse / Of sun and moon' (5.2.100–1). No eclipse comes: this is a human story, even while it is set against a geopolitical backdrop of territorial and trading relations between Christendom and the Ottoman empire, and amid the troubling ethnic heterogeneity of the early modern city. That this is a personal, intimate tragedy is the source of its power. A spectator at a performance in Oxford in 1610 made no mention of Othello's blackness but was moved by the spectacle of the murdered innocent Desdemona, who 'lying in her bed, entreated the pity of the spectators by her very countenance': that this loving marriage should so viciously and rapidly degenerate into murder before our eyes is key to the play's ongoing capacity to disturb. That Iago gives no substantive motive for his actions, or, rather, that he proposes so many reasons and so casually that they fail to convince, and that he remains, alive and mutely defiant, at the play's conclusion, adds to the unsettling effect. Unlike the figure Shakespeare inherited from his source material, who admits he acts because he is himself in love with Desdemona, Iago's opacity has prompted one of the play's most insistent questions. While he reveals to us his attitudes right from the opening lines – unlike the characters within the fiction, the audience is under no illusions about the ironically dubbed 'honest Iago' (1.3.290) – he never reveals himself.

Denying us access to the private thoughts of the play's characters is part of Shakespeare's technique here. Desdemona changes from a feisty young woman challenging paternal authority to a submissive victim pleading forgiveness from her insanely jealous husband, and it is not clear whether this is the psychological journey of an abused wife or a misprision between the first, more comedic part of the play and its tragic conclusion: we are not told. There is relatively little soliloquy, and Othello himself prefers grand oratory aimed at an onstage audience to private reflection. His final speech, as he turns the knife on himself, seems to capture the sense of self-division and alienation that haunts him as the anomalous 'Moor of Venice', but even here he achieves understanding of himself only by an elaborate analogy with an encounter between Turk and Venetian in Aleppo, and his self-justification that he was 'not easily jealous' but 'wrought' (5.2.341), or worked on, has not always been found convincing.

That final analogy re-establishes a broader stage for the play's action. From the very beginning, the marriage of Othello and Desdemona has been dramatically intertwined with the threat to Venetian interests from the Turks, such that it is hard to know which, if either, is a metaphor for the other. The wreck of the Turkish fleet turns the energy of the conflict inwards: trapped in

Cyprus, far from Christian Venice and in the jaws of the Ottoman empire, the fault lines of the marriage can no longer be contained. *Othello* has been read as a racist play, but it may be more a study of racism, and of its corrosive effects when its inequalities and injustices are internalised.

Pericles

Key Facts

Date: 1607–8

Length: 2,450 lines

Verse: 80% / Prose: 20%

Major characters' share of lines:	
Pericles	25%
Gower	13%
Marina	8%
Simonides	6%

Late romance of family separation, loss and restoration

Plot and characters

The Chorus, **Gower,** introduces **Antiochs,** King of Antioch, who is in an incestuous relationship with his **daughter. Pericles** of Tyre has travelled to Antioch to woo her, and like all her suitors he has to answer a riddle. Realising that if he reveals the answer – incest – or if he fails, he will die, Pericles flees. He confides in his trusted counsellor **Hellicanus,** who advises him to leave Tyre, and just after his departure **Thaliard,** an assassin sent by the King, arrives. In Tarsus, Pericles distributes corn to relieve the city's famine, and **Cleon** and **Dioniza,** its rulers, swear allegiance to him in gratitude. News of Thaliard's pursuit sends Pericles back to sea, where he is shipwrecked at Pentapolis, where some fishermen retrieve his father's armour from the sea. At court the disguised Pericles in his rusty armour presents himself in a tournament to win the hand of the daughter of King **Simonides, Thaisa.** He beats the other suitors in the joust, and, after some intrigue, gains Thaisa's affection and Simonides' consent. In Tyre the noblemen are restless about Pericles' absence, and he is sent a letter saying that Hellicanus will be crowned if he does not return. With the pregnant Thaisa he sets out for home. During a storm, Thaisa apparently dies in childbirth and is cast overboard in a coffin: Pericles takes his baby daughter **Marina** to Tarsus, where he leaves her with Cleon and Dioniza for safekeeping. **Cerimon** finds Thaisa and manages to revive her: he takes her to the temple of Diana in Ephesus. Time passes, Marina grows up, and Dioniza is jealous of her and plans to have her murdered. **Leonine** is hired to kill Marina, but is interrupted by the arrival of pirates, who abduct her. In Miteline she is sold by the pirates to the brothel man **Boult**, and the **Bawd** tries to induct her into the sex trade. Marina refuses to take part. In Tarsus, Cleon charges Dioniza with the death of Marina and Pericles discovers her death. He vows to spend his days, hair and beard uncut, in mourning his wife and daughter. In Miteline Marina's virtue converts the governor, **Lysimachus**, from his lust, and she manages to maintain her chastity. Pericles arrives, and Lysimachus suggests that Marina will cheer him: she visits him and sings, and they discover their relation. In a dream Pericles is directed to Diana's temple: he arrives to find Thaisa, and the family is reunited.

Context and composition

Probably written in 1607–8, the play was published in 1609. It was not included in the collected edition of Shakespeare's plays of 1623, perhaps because it was known to be collaborative. Most scholars believe it was co-written with George Wilkins, although other collaborators have also been proposed for a play in which the last three acts are generally thought to be by Shakespeare. Wilkins published a prose version of the story drawing on the play in 1608. The story is derived from a Greek romance of Apollonius of Tyre, which had been retold by the medieval poet John Gower in his *Confessio Amantis*: Gower features as chorus/narrator in the play. Shakespeare also drew on Laurence Twine's recently reprinted prose version *The Pattern of Painful Adventures* (1576). In its primary theme of fathers and their daughters, the play echoes with *King Lear*, *The Winter's Tale*, *The Tempest* and *Cymbeline*; its chorus is closest to *Henry V*; its geography and its restored mother recall *The Comedy of Errors*.

Performances

The number of early print editions and contemporary allusions suggest that *Pericles* was extremely popular. An early performance in a recusant (resistant Catholic) household may give an insight into the

religious resonances of its saintly women and myths of resurrection. It was revived in the Restoration with Thomas Betterton as Pericles. It fell from theatrical favour, however, and only began to find its place in the repertoire in the twentieth century. Adrian Noble's 2002 RSC production was praised for its affecting reunion scene, movingly accompanied by the clear tone of handbells playing the music of the spheres. Fairy-tale or Arabian Nights style productions have helped to make sense of the play's narrative style and picaresque exoticism: Phyllida Lloyd (National Theatre, 1994) made it into a visual and musical spectacle, with Gower in constant attendance. Kathryn Hunter at the Globe directed Corin Redgrave as the haunted older Pericles and Robert Lucksay as his more swashbuckling younger self (2005), and in the same year Andrew Hilton's Tobacco Factory production accessed the play's emotional power on a bare stage accompanied only by music and the sound of the sea. Cardboard Citizens, a company working with refugees and the homeless, partnered the Royal Shakespeare Company in Adrian Jackson's 2003 production, where the audience were checked into a vast detention centre and given tags and immigration forms as if asylum-seekers like Pericles.

Themes and interpretation

'Thou that begetst him that did thee beget' (5.1.190). Pericles'
recognition of his daughter pays tribute to her ability to renew him,
just as her purity has renewed the morally suspect brothel client
Lysimachus, governor of Miteline. It confirms the importance of
images of birth, rebirth and death to the play's structure. But it also
echoes the riddle with which the play opens, when King Antiochus'
unnamed daughter is 'mother, wife, and yet his child' (1.1.70). The
resonance is an index of the way suffering, separation and an exile
both geographical and psychological bring about restoration in the
play, and a marker of how the play's depiction of temporal and
spatial distances enables it to revisit and purify its opening
corruption. Perhaps the two daughters would have been doubled in
the early modern theatre, emphasising their connection. The threat of
incest, however, hovers over the play, just as *Pericles* is transfixed by
threats to Marina's chastity, from the pirates to the brothel to her
soon-to-be husband Lysimachus. Formulary mating rituals – the
Antioch riddle, Simonides' joust at which Pericles wins Thaisa – and
their inversion in Marina's dissuasion of Lysimachus, structure this
episodic and wandering play.

Music and magic play a dominant role here, as in the other late
romances (*The Winter's Tale*, *The Tempest*), combining in the
discovery of the apparently dead Thaisa washed ashore in Ephesus.
Cerimon calls for music and for 'napkins and fire' (3.2.84) to revive
her, relying on Aesculapius, the god of healing, as he combines the
roles of priest, physician and magus. Thaisa's resurrection, like the
parallel case of Hermione in *The Winter's Tale*, hangs between
romance and realism: this is a play full of archetypal plot elements
rather than inner psychology or believability, where action is
weighted with symbolic rather than everyday meaning. Gower's
prominent role is crucial to this: he appears more than any other
Chorus figure in Shakespeare's plays, attesting to the generic
importance of narration, of telling rather than showing, to the play.
Bringing forward this medieval narrator 'to sing a song that old
was sung' (Prologue, 1), the play is self-consciously archaic, even

mock-medieval, with its tournaments and armour, but the brothel scenes come straight out of Shakespeare's earlier *Measure for Measure* and the gritty urban world of city comedy. The jealous Dioniza is a figure from fairy tale – the wicked stepmother as jealous beldame – just as Antioch emerges like the beginning of a fairy tale, and the sequence in which a reluctant Leonine talks to the young girl he is supposed to murder is recognisable from *Snow White*. Quite different in tone is the encounter of Pericles, unshaven like a wild man, burdened with guilt and depression, with the simple purity of Marina: one of Shakespeare's most powerfully emotional familial scenes. It is striking, therefore, to see the play moving from the highly stylised and artificial opening scenes, via the tribulations of Pericles' purgatorial progress through the seas, to the moving intensity of its recognition scene.

That Marina, named for the sea, should be the agent of this renewal is apt: elsewhere it is the sea that unifies the story. The play is constantly in motion: moving from Antioch to Ephesus via Tyre, Pentapolis, Tarsus, Miteline, as its itinerary traverses the eastern Mediterranean. From the precise technical vocabulary of the sailors, to Pericles' acknowledgement of 'this great sea of joys rushing upon me' (5.1.187), the language of the sea is pervasive. In swallowing and casting out objects and people – Pericles' father's armour, Pericles himself, emerging, as the stage directions instruct, 'wet' (2.1.0), Thaisa's coffin – the sea separates and reunites characters and things: as elsewhere in Shakespeare's seascape nothing is truly lost in this magical marine world. Storms at sea symbolise Pericles' disordered conscience as he flees from the truth at Antioch, but they are also the means by which he regains himself, symbolised in his family. The music of the spheres and the vision of Diana suggest a divine benediction: Pericles' suffering and peregrination come to stand for the human journey towards grace – a kind of morality play. As with Leontes, in *The Winter's Tale*, or Prospero, in *The Tempest*, Pericles' happiness is more complete because of, not despite, his distress, and of course that happiness is achieved on a finally calm sea: his ship at anchor in Miteline.

The Phoenix and the Turtle

Enigmatic poem we just don't (yet) understand

Synopsis

At a convocation of birds, a swan acts as a priest to celebrate the funeral of the mythical bird the phoenix and the turtle dove, lovers who have committed suicide by immolating themselves in the flames. The birds mourn the lovers in a funeral song.

Context and composition

We do not know much about when this was written, or why. It is published over Shakespeare's name in a collection of poems 'by the best and chiefest modern writers', published in 1601 as *Love's Martyr*. The main work in the volume is Robert Chester's long poem of the title, which shows, through the constancy of the phoenix and the turtle dove, the truth of love. Other writers represented in the volume include Shakespeare's fellow playwrights Ben Jonson, John Marston and George Chapman.

The poem has sixty-seven lines, divided into thirteen four-line stanzas rhyming a-b-b-a c-d-d-c, followed by a 'threnos', or funeral lament, of four stanzas, each with three rhyming lines. The tetrameter metre is recognisably that given to the fairies in *A Midsummer Night's Dream*. It does not bear a title, and is sometimes referred to by its first line, 'Let the bird of loudest lay' (1).

Themes and interpretation

'The Phoenix and the Turtle' is a lyrical poem of affecting simplicity. But what does it mean? Critics have been ingenious in reading into it allegorical meanings: that it has hidden Roman Catholic significance, that it alludes to Queen Elizabeth (often associated with the phoenix, as at the end of Shakespeare and

Fletcher's *Henry VIII*) and her subjects, that it is in some way biographical, that it means something to or about the volume's dedicatee, the newly knighted courtier Sir John Salisbury. The poem seems to court this speculation and to frustrate it: its highly wrought and philosophical paradoxes have reminded some readers of contemporary poems by John Donne, but its vision of unity in love has a kind of linguistic austerity: 'So they loved, as two in twain / Had the essence but in one: / Two distincts, division none; / Number there in love was slain' (25–8).

The Rape of Lucrece

Narrative poem of desire, violation and suicide

Synopsis

While her husband Collatine is away, the virtuous Roman wife Lucrece, innocent of any wrong, welcomes his friend Tarquin to their home. Tarquin, while reflecting on his lust and the dishonour he intends to Collatine, forces himself into her chamber as she is sleeping at night and rapes her at swordpoint. He is immediately ashamed and creeps away, leaving Lucrece, who bemoans her violated state. She resolves to tell Collatine and to commit suicide, and so she writes to him and when he returns, tells him and the other lords what has happened. When they vow to avenge the crime, she stabs herself to death, and her father Lucretius and Collatine weep and apostrophise her bleeding corpse. The poem ends with the agreement of the Romans, seeing Lucrece's body, that Tarquin be banished for his crime.

Context and composition

The Rape of Lucrece was published in summer 1594 and probably composed earlier that year or in late 1593 during the closure of the theatres because of the plague. It shares linguistic features with *Titus Andronicus* and *King Richard III*, and, like *Titus*, its detailed imagery of violence and its unflinching depiction of the victim is designed to discomfort. Like *Venus and Adonis*, it was dedicated to Henry Wriothesley, Earl of Southampton, and in terms which, even by the standards of sycophancy encouraged by the patronage system, strike as warmly intimate: 'what I have done is yours; what I have to do is yours, being part in all I have, devoted yours'. It draws extensively on classical sources: Ovid's *Fasti* and Livy's first-century BC account of Lucrece's story, as well as on Englished versions including Chaucer's *Legend of Good Women* and William Painter's *Palace of Pleasure* (1566), which Shakespeare would also use for *Romeo and Juliet*, *All's Well that Ends Well* and *Timon of Athens*. Lucrece is mentioned in a number of other Shakespeare plays, including *Twelfth Night* and *Macbeth*, and the story of Collatine and his friends wagering on their wives' inviolable chastity, depicted in the argument but not in the poem proper, is taken up in *Cymbeline*, where Iachimo, hidden in Innogen's bedchamber, explicitly compares himself to Tarquin. The banishment of Tarquin means that this poem is located in the period of Roman history just before that depicted in *Coriolanus*, and when Julius Caesar is offered the crown in that play, we see the opposite ideological movement from *The Rape of Lucrece* – this time from republic to monarchy, rather than the other way around.

In the text printed by fellow Stratford emigrant to London, Richard Field, a long prose 'Argument' gives an outline of the poem, although one with more stress on the political consequences of Tarquin's actions than on the conflicted private emotions on which the poem itself focuses. Perhaps this Argument was not by Shakespeare himself. It is highly rhetorical, and at least in part an exercise in skill. For example, it radically amplifies a story that Ovid tells in some seventy lines. *The Rape of Lucrece* consists of 1,900 lines (longer than the shortest play, *The Comedy of Errors*) in rhyme royal, a stanza form with seven lines rhyming a-b-a-b-b-c-c, made famous in Chaucer's *Troilus and Criseyde*. It may therefore have seemed a rather old-fashioned form, perhaps appropriate for the serious subject matter.

Themes and interpretation

Although *The Rape of Lucrece* is not a play, it is tempting to see it as such, as it shifts dramatic focus from the inner state of Tarquin to that of Lucrece herself, giving soliloquies to each protagonist. The first third of the poem details Tarquin's inward debate about the morality of his intentions; the next section is a protracted dialogue between them as he enters her chamber; the final third is a 'complaint' by Lucrece (a complaint, as in the poem appended to Shakespeare's sonnets, 'A Lover's Complaint', was a rich late medieval genre of mourning or lament). Throughout, the poem is constructed through binaries and paradox, and in its final declaration that the royal prince Tarquin is banished from Rome for his action, turns his libidinous victory into political defeat and ignominy, turning tragedy on its perpetrator. In giving voice to Lucrece's shame and anger at her rape, however, the poem itself does not conform to the more politicised narrative of the prose Argument in the 1594 edition. Lucrece is more than just a symbolic sacrifice in the political narrative of Rome's movement from monarchy to republic; a woman whose trust has been violently betrayed, whose response is harrowingly honest, and who resolves to reveal her attacker and then to kill herself to expiate her shame.

Early modern readers, schooled in rhetorical tropes of *imitatio* (imitation) and *copia* (expansiveness), may well have valued *The Rape of Lucrece* for exactly those reasons that have caused modern readers most trouble. For us the rhetorical control is incongruous to the horrific events – rather like an extended version of the difficulties critics have felt when Marcus, uncle of the raped Lavinia in *Titus Andronicus*, offers her no practical help but instead delivers an impromptu poetic oration of some fifty lines on the fountains of blood issuing from her wounded body. For us, rhetoric and emotion are distinct literary qualities; not so for the Elizabethans. Rhetorical amplification in the poem gives it an awful slow-motion quality: time stands still as Tarquin debates with himself, and again as he is on the threshold of Lucrece's chamber. Stanzas and stanzas pass in internal dialogue or poetic digression, giving the narrative an almost unbearably deliberative and dilatory progress. The noticing of details – a draught that snuffs out Tarquin's candle, a needle stuck in the seamstress Lucrece's glove – offer momentary resistance to the inexorable plot, but they, like Lucrece herself, must bow to the inevitable.

Lucrece's innocence is repeatedly acknowledged in the text. She is 'guiltless' (89), 'feared no hooks' (103): 'unstained thought do seldom dream on evil' (87). But it is a part of the poem's compelling narrative progression that it constructs her as an object of voyeuristic desire: like Tarquin, we look lingeringly on her sleeping body for five luxuriant stanzas, taking in her 'lily hand', 'rosy cheek' (386), 'hair like golden threads' (400), 'breasts like ivory globes circled with blue' (407), 'azure veins', 'alabaster skin', 'coral lips', 'snow-white dimpled chin' (419–20). The blazon (a rhetorical device of anatomising the beloved's physical beauty) is always fraught with possessiveness in Renaissance literature: here we can see that the disempowering description is itself a form of violation. The poem begins with Tarquin as thinking, desiring subject, and Lucrece as its eroticised object. Her purity, like that of Isabella in her interviews with the lustful Angelo in *Measure for Measure*, is what makes her so desirable; her resistance is aphrodisiac; like Angelo, Tarquin persuades her that her version of events will never be believed.

The rape narrative, then, is a deeply disturbing one, and graphically rendered. By implicating the reader in the slow burn of Tarquin's desire, the poem simultaneously idealises Lucrece's chastity and destroys it; it both deplores what is done to Lucrece and is titillated by it. *The Rape of Lucrece* has a pornographic aspect, therefore, that links it with other Ovidian poems of erotic conquest popular at the time, including Shakespeare's own *Venus and Adonis* and Marlowe's *Hero and Leander*, even though its tone is ostensibly less playfully erotic than these other works.

Lucrece, like other of Shakespeare's badly treated women (Ophelia in *Hamlet* comes to mind), only really gains her voice when she has been violated: it is only after the rape that she possesses the narrative and the spent Tarquin creeps away into the shadows. The irony of her eloquence in the final section of the poem is that it comes only when she is most disempowered. Her concern is about posterity and honour, but in giving up her life she loses control over the meanings of her body, violated anew when it is hawked around Rome to stir up feelings against the ruling Tarquins. Although Collatine acknowledges her innocence, he also says he 'owed [owned] her, and 'tis mine she hath killed' (1803): the cries 'my daughter' and 'my wife'

(1804) mean that mourning Lucrece is structured in the same language of possession as raping her. Although she uses her rhetorical power to fight against it, Lucrece – intended for male readership and presented to a male patron as part of an economy of exchange – is always constructed and constrained by male authorities – including Shakespeare.

Romeo and Juliet

Key Facts
Date: 1595–6
Length: 3,185 lines
Verse: 90% / Prose: 10%

Major characters' share of lines:	
Romeo	20%
Juliet	18%
Friar Lawrence	11%
Nurse	9%
Capulet	9%
Mercutio	8%

Iconic tragedy of doomed young love

Plot and characters

The **Chorus** delivers a prologue telling the plot of the star-crossed lovers in outline. Encouraged by **Tybalt,** the Capulet servants provoke a fight with their Montague counterparts; **Benvolio** attempts to stop the disturbance, but Escales the **Prince** threatens dire punishments if the feud is not stopped. **Montague** and **Lady Montague** are concerned about their son **Romeo,** who is sick with unrequited love for Rosaline. **Capulet** tells **Paris** that if his daughter **Juliet** will accept it, he can marry her. Romeo and Benvolio discover the Capulets' guest list for a feast from the servant **Peter,** and decide to attend, uninvited. Juliet's mother, **Lady Capulet,** and the garrulous **Nurse,** tell her of Paris' suit. Romeo has foreboding dreams, but **Mercutio** ridicules him. Trouble at the feast is averted when Capulet tells Tybalt not to challenge Romeo. Romeo and Juliet meet, belatedly learning each other's identity, and fall in love. Romeo goes back to the Capulet house to see Juliet, and they exchange love vows when she appears on her balcony: Romeo is to arrange their marriage. **Friar Lawrence** agrees to it in the hope it will reunite the families. Romeo sends a message to Juliet via the Nurse. Tybalt challenges Romeo to a fight, but Mercutio becomes involved in a fracas and is killed by Tybalt. Romeo kills Tybalt in fury, then flees. The Prince sentences him to immediate banishment. Juliet hears of events from the Nurse, who finds Romeo in despair with Friar Lawrence; the pair are married. Capulet agrees with his wife that Juliet and Paris will be married. Romeo and Juliet spend the night together; after he has left, the Capulets put pressure on Juliet to accept Paris' suit. The Nurse urges her to agree, but she goes instead to Friar Lawrence, who gives her a sleeping drug which will make her appear dead. As the household prepares for the wedding she takes the drug, and is found 'dead'. News reaches Romeo, exiled in Mantua: he buys poison from an **apothecary** and returns to Verona, where Friar Lawrence discovers his letter explaining the plan has not reached the young man. Romeo kills Paris at the Capulet tomb, lies next to Juliet and takes his poison. He dies. Juliet awakes, and kills herself with his dagger. The Prince suggests these deaths are all punishment for the feud, and Montague and Capulet shake hands, agreeing to build a monument to their dead children.

Context and composition

The play shares certain stylistic features with *Love's Labour's Lost* and *A Midsummer Night's Dream*, particularly their formal linguistic devices – and probably dates from the same period, 1595 or 1596. Its proximity to the comedies which dominate Shakespeare's early writing career is also visible in its plot and early tone. It was first printed in 1597, and then in a fuller version in 1599. It seems to have been immediately popular in print and in an unexpected variety of contexts: it was quoted in an Oxford sermon in 1620, and the copy of the First Folio held in the university's library was worn through on only one page – the play's balcony scene.

The story of the star-crossed lovers was well known in myth and story. The most direct source for the play is Arthur Brooke's long narrative poem *The Tragical History of Romeus and Juliet* (1562), which is itself a translation from the French from the Italian. Shakespeare compresses the action and does away with Brooke's moralising preface, which sets up the story as a cautionary tale for young people not to follow 'dishonest desire' nor to trust to gossips and Catholic friars rather than respecting their own parents. The play's perspective is shifted away from the parents towards the lovers (but cannot go so far as to reward them for their determined autonomy). The play follows the outline of Brooke's poem closely, but the character of Mercutio is Shakespeare's own invention.

Performances

No early records of performance survive. For much of the play's stage history its mingling of comedy and tragedy has been problematic: in the eighteenth century it was performed on alternate nights

with a happy and a sad ending. More recent productions have tended to follow the influential Broadway musical *West Side Story* (1957, filmed 1961), in emphasising the play's perennial relevance through updating the setting: a 2000 version in Edinburgh directed by Kenny Ireland drew on conflict in contemporary Beirut, with the Prince a blue-bereted UN general trying to keep the peace; in the same year Tim Supple implied a racial motive for the feud (Shakespeare himself offers no real explanation for the antipathy between the Montagues and the Capulets) by casting the Capulets as a white family and the Montagues as black. Franco Zeffirelli's 1968 film, set in the Renaissance and shot in Italy, captured the freshness of its lovers by casting unknowns Leonard Whiting (aged 17) and Olivia Hussey (15). Baz Luhrmann's 1996 film *Romeo + Juliet* was the most successful film of Shakespeare of all time, advertised under the tagline: 'Shakespeare has never been this sexy'. Its rock soundtrack, vividly rapid editing and insistent, often witty updating – guns, snooker halls, warring family business empires and the Friar's message misdelivered by Post Haste couriers – established the lovers trapped in a youthful world spinning rapidly out of control and shaped by the solipsistic culture of late adolescence. More experimental versions include Joe Calarco's compelling 1999 adaptation for four actors, set in a repressive Catholic boarding school where immersion in this forbidden text of the play enables the boys to explore their adolescent sexuality and emotions. The play has been translated into ballet, with music by Prokofiev; Tchaikovsky and Berlioz have also composed musical adaptations. The play's recognisability, in particular the familiarity of the balcony scene, means that it has been much parodied, for example in an animated version starring garden gnomes (*Gnomeo and Juliet*, 2011), and even performed by cats (*Romeo.Juliet*, 1990).

Themes and interpretation

Romeo and Juliet is a play so apparently familiar that it hardly needs much gloss. Feud, balcony, bedroom, tomb: the progress of events is so well known as to be clichéd, even when transplanted to religious, ethnic or national conflicts of the modern era. And that sense that for modern readers or viewers the play is always already known seems to have been true from the start, as the Prologue gives it all away in the first minute: 'a pair of star-crossed lovers take their life' (Prologue, 6).

In fact the play can be seen as self-conscious about this inscribed inevitability. On the one hand, *Romeo and Juliet* could not have ended otherwise: the feud means their love is 'death-marked' (Prologue, 9) from the start, portents and omens such as Romeo's dream anticipate the doomed outcome, and the story pre-exists the play in numerous forms. On the other hand, this tragic inevitability is set against its more flexible, unpredictable comedic opposite. *Romeo and Juliet* begins like a comedy: young people separated by unthinking parents, as in *A Midsummer Night's Dream* or *The Winter's Tale*, and it is striking that it is written in a period when Shakespeare's main dramatic output was comedies. It begins with conflict – the fight between the Capulet and Montague servants – and might have been expected to resolve into harmony (voicing a contemporary commonplace about genre, the playwright Thomas Heywood wrote that 'comedies begin in trouble and end in peace; tragedies begin in calms and end in tempest'). And things go wrong because of terrible coincidence: the Friar's letter to Romeo cannot be delivered because of plague restrictions; Juliet awakes only seconds after – and in many productions just as – Romeo dies. The play misses being a comedy by a whisker. The death of Mercutio, itself an unintended fumble, may be an early indication of just how intransigent this *liebestod* (love-death) plot is: Shakespeare's decidedly comic addition to his source material cannot withstand its relentless movement towards self-destruct.

This momentum contributes to the play's careful structure and symmetry. The dual focus suggested by its title is emphasised in the Prologue's 'Two households, both alike in dignity' (Prologue, 1). From this opening rhyming sonnet, Shakespeare incorporates a diversity of language, from the weird inventiveness of Mercutio's Queen Mab reverie, 'begot of nothing but vain fantasy' (1.4.98), to the inspired bawdy of the Nurse's rambling prose, and the formal sonnet the young lovers complete as their first exchange (1.5.92–105); the menacing prose exchanges of encounters between the two families are emphasised by their juxtaposition with the lyric intensity of love poetry; Tybalt's vaunting tragic idiom is matched by Mercutio's punning. Language is also a theme in a play concerned with the fatal consequences of names. Juliet's 'what's in a name?' (2.2.43) marks her naivety: names are all-important in the play, which turns, fatally, on their inescapability. The language of *Romeo and Juliet* includes both formal verse and colloquial prose, and thus marks a development of the rhetorical artifice of Shakespeare's early plays and points towards the muscular lyricism and emotional immediacy of the mature playwright. Images of light and of fire suggest the 'violent delights' (2.6.9) that, quite literally, burn themselves out.

Most often in Shakespeare we do not know the age of the characters: it is not important. In *Romeo and Juliet* much is made of Juliet's age: 13. This is not because early marriage was more common in the sixteenth century: Shakespeare's audiences would have expected couples typically to be in their mid twenties at the time of marriage. Rather, it brings out the youthful naivety of the protagonists. At times Juliet's speeches give her the maturity of a much older woman, and at others she is a child, whose measure for excitement is the impatience of having 'new robes / And may not wear them' (3.2.30–1). Romeo's erstwhile love Rosaline, never seen in the play, seems to exist solely to point up his adolescent fickleness: he may feel deeply, but not necessarily for long. Friar Lawrence's counsel 'love moderately' (2.6.14) is ignored by this helter-skelter play, in which Capulet's changing schedule for Juliet's marriage to Paris is an index of the way time seems to speed up during its course. *Romeo and Juliet* gives us two very young protagonists whose immature passions are fanned by a pointless feud which keeps them apart, and whose entire courtship and marriage can be measured in hours. It is not their appearance in this play but subsequent literary and popular culture which has, like the statues promised by their grieving families, lifted them into icons of romantic love.

The Sonnets and A Lover's Complaint

Mysterious, highly wrought poetry of desire

Synopsis

First published as a sequence in 1609, with 'A Lover's Complaint', Shakespeare's sonnets comprise 154 poems: 126 sonnets traditionally read as being addressed to a young man, then 127–52 read as being addressed to a dark-complexioned mistress, with a final pair, 153–4, on Cupid. 'A Lover's Complaint' is a narrative poem of 329 lines in the genre of 'complaint', depicting an abandoned woman lamenting her seduction.

Context and composition

It is clear that some of Shakespeare's sonnets were circulating in manuscript at the end of the sixteenth century, and two, 138 and 144, were published as the opening poems in the volume *A Passionate Pilgrim* (1599), which contains a majority of poems by other writers, many unattributed.

Sonnets had entered the English tradition in the first half of the sixteenth century via Sir Thomas Wyatt and Henry Howard, the Earl of Surrey, who produced translations of the fourteenth-century Italian poet Petrarch. Petrarch's sonnets, dedicated to Laura, depicted the speaker's unrequited love for a distant and unattainable woman (it is a matter of debate, although ultimately irrelevant, whether Laura ever existed) and set the tone for the sonnet's ongoing poetics of impossibility. The sonnet is a fourteen-line poem, and, whereas for Petrarch this was divided into an eight-line section (the octave) and a six-line (sestet), often rhymed a-b-b-a-c-d-d-c e-f-g-e-f-g, in English, the form developed into three four-line sections (quatrains) and a final couplet, often rhymed a-b-a-b c-d-c-d e-f-e-f g-g (sometimes called the Shakespearean sonnet). The couplet form gave the English sonnet an epigrammatic quality of final summary, sometimes pointedly inadequate to the complexity of the themes raised, or at other times the couplet was used to redirect the poem with a new conceit. Following Philip Sidney's *Astrophil and Stella*, first published in 1591 but circulated earlier in manuscript, sonnet writing became extremely fashionable, and the thousands of sonnets written in the Elizabethan period variously riff on Petrarchan themes of unrequited desire, and on Petrarchan tropes of paradox to express high emotional states. Being both like and unlike the Petrarchan model seems to have been the goal, as elsewhere in the Renaissance culture of imitation. When Shakespeare famously begins sonnet 130 'My mistress' eyes are nothing like the sun', the implicit target is the cliché of Petrarchan comparison.

Themes and interpretations

Many readings of Shakespeare's sonnets have been so compelled by their depiction of various figures that the 'Plot and Characters' section chosen for the plays in this volume might not be inappropriate. A synopsis would include the **Poet**, the **Fair Youth** whom the poet urges to marry and beget an heir, and who he also suggests will be made immortal by his own poetry. Later, the **poet's mistress**, the **rival poet**, and the **Dark Lady** make an appearance, not to mention the mysterious and unidentified **Mr W. H.** to whom the poems are dedicated. In fact it is misleading, however tempting, to try to make the poems into a coherent dramatic narrative. There is, for example, no evidence that the addressee of the first group of sonnets is a single person, and since many of the sonnets do not give a pronoun for the addressee, the sex of that person or persons is ambiguous. It is even more problematic to try, as generations of readers have, to convincingly link these representations to real people in Shakespeare's circle. The deeply confessional turn that poetry took in the twentieth century in the writing of Sylvia Plath or John Berryman would have been unthinkable in the early modern period, where poetry's purpose was more public, more rhetorical and more intellectual. The extent to which the sonnets are referential – in that they draw on a world of relationships and feelings outside of themselves – and the extent to which they are self-referential – creating their own verbal world without external reference – is one of the dominant critical questions. William Wordsworth's assertion that 'with this key / Shakespeare unlocked his heart' was countered by Robert Browning: 'If so, the less Shakespeare he!' If at times the poems seem to tease us with biographical references – to 'Will' (135–6) or 'Hathaway' (the maiden name of Shakespeare's wife, 145), at others it is their manipulation of the sonnet form or the pressure they put on a repeated word or concept which seems most prominent.

Shakespeare's changes to the traditional structure are striking. He is the only Elizabethan sonneteer besides Richard Barnfield to insistently address an intense relationship between two men. In place of the traditional sonnet mode of trying to persuade the unreachable woman by suggesting she should reproduce her beauty in children, Shakespeare addresses the call to procreation to a young man. This may explain their belated publication history: printed in 1609 they are at the tail end of the vogue, but may have spoken more directly to the homosocial world of the Jacobean court than to the gender politics of the Elizabethan, where the queen presented herself the sole and self-appointed object of unrequited courtly love. The sexuality of these sonnets addressed to 'the master-mistress of my passion' (20) is provocative, and has prompted excited biographical speculations (by Oscar Wilde, among others), but we should be wary of reading our own categories into the fluid world of Renaissance personal identity, as well as of assuming that the poems speak in the voice of the poet.

But one prominent theme of the sonnets must have had particular resonance for the writer of plays which, by their nature, are ephemeral happenings, rather than lasting objects. Again and again the sonnets stress that poetry is what will last, beyond love, beyond beauty, beyond 'devouring time' (19): 'Not marble nor the gilded monuments / Of princes shall outlive this powerful rhyme' (55). That the sonnets may ultimately be about themselves, and about transcendent poetry as the only bulwark against emotional mutability, resounds across the sequence. Poetry, not love for fair youth or for dark lady, is the real subject of these poems, and thus the thing they finally tell us is the one thing we already knew: they were written by a poet. Two of the most famous sonnets in the sequence are analysed in the 'Commentary' section below.

'A Lover's Complaint' has had relatively little critical attention compared with the sonnets, and many scholars have doubted its authorship, largely because they don't admire it. It is, however, a haunting poem with links to the depiction of madness in *The Two Noble Kinsmen*, *King Lear* and *Hamlet*. Its gender politics, in which the voice of the male intermediary who introduces the story falls away and the majority of the poem is spoken by the unnamed abandoned woman, complement and to some extent recuperate the sonnets' monologic masculinity and tendency to misogyny. For modern readers, though, her simultaneous shame at her seduction and appetite for more is unsettling: her listing of the man's beauty in the rhetorical device known as blazon recalls the voice of unrequited desire in the sonnets, and as a conclusion to the sonnet sequence, the lament both challenges and reinforces its power dynamics.

Commentary

Sonnet 18

Shall I compare thee to a summer's day?
Thou art more lovely and more temperate.
Rough winds do shake the darling buds of May,
And summer's lease hath all too short a date;
Sometime too hot the eye of heaven shines,
And often is his gold complexion dimmed;
And every fair from fair sometime declines,
By chance or nature's changing course untrimmed:
But thy eternal summer shall not fade,
Nor lose possession of that fair thou ow'st,
Nor shall Death brag thou wand'rest in his shade,
When in eternal lines to time thou grow'st.
      So long as men can breathe or eyes can see,
      So long lives this, and this gives life to thee.

The immediacy of this sonnet's opening question is memorable. Using the intimate form of the second person 'thou/thee', the poem never identifies its addressee, nor his/her sex. It moves from a comparison with nature to a redefinition of that comparison: 'thy eternal summer shall not fade', and eventually substitutes the 'eternal lines' of poetry in which the 'lovely' object is preserved. In identifying writing as the ultimate defence against the depredations of time, the poem echoes one of the sequence's abiding themes. The final couplet is triumphal: the poem will last as long as humanity itself, and 'this gives life to thee': that confident, teasing 'I' of the first line has been confirmed as the conqueror of the braggart Death. The initially perfect 'summer's day' can be upset by wind or heat, but even as these failings are acknowledged the poem is in process of becoming their flawless antidote. The object of admiration shifts: at the beginning of the poem it is the beloved 'thee', but by the end it is 'this', the sonnet itself.

Many of the sonnets, including this one, achieve their density of effect by putting individual words under interpretative pressure, or repeating them in contexts which animate new meanings. The word 'fair', repeated three times and sometimes employed as an adjective and sometimes a noun, is a typical example; the duplicated 'sometime' another. And the sonnets, as here, are criss-crossed internally, through their rhyme scheme but also through internal rhyme and echo: 'I/eye/eyes'; 'day/date/fade'; 'lease/lines/lives'. Clusters of words with particular associations also serve to unify the sonnet and send us back rereading: natural imagery here (summer, winds, buds) is interlaced with the legal language of ownership (lease, possession, ow'st). Against this recursive effect is a more headlong feeling produced by a large number of verbs, particularly in the prominent rhyme-word position (shines, declines, fade, grow'st, see). This verbal sense of activity and movement through time and space is a paradox when set against the thematic investment in preservation and stasis through poetry. The compelling torsion in the sonnet comes from this pull in different directions – the poem is drawn towards and back from beauty in nature and in art, is committed to change and to perpetuity, and is directed towards the writing subject and the beloved object.

Sonnet 116

Let me not to the marriage of true minds
Admit impediments; love is not love
Which alters when it alteration finds,
Or bends with the remover to remove.
O no, it is an ever-fixèd mark
That looks on tempests and is never shaken;
It is the star to every wand'ring bark,
Whose worth's unknown, although his heighth be taken.
Love's not Time's fool, though rosy lips and cheeks
Within his bending sickle's compass come;
Love alters not with his brief hours and weeks,
But bears it out even to the edge of doom.
     If this be error and upon me proved,
     I never writ, nor no man ever loved.

This well-known sonnet exemplifies many of the formal and thematic preoccupations of the sequence. In its form we can see three four-line quatrains, each ending with a full stop, followed by a couplet; in its theme the poem meditates on love and transience, triangulated with the power of poetry itself ('I never writ, nor no man ever loved').

In opening with a negative, the poem begins by characterising its object through what it is not: love does not alter, or bend. Even when the poem turns to more positive and concrete descriptions in its extended conceit of navigation and sea-voyaging (tempests, star, bark), these are shadowed with uncertainties: love is a star whose 'heighth' but not 'worth' can be measured. The imagery here is vast and awe-inspiring, anticipating, perhaps, the dread idea of 'the edge of doom' – presented as a positive sign of love's endurance but expressed in terms of horror. The mention of the sickle evokes the imagery of death or time as a reaper, with his human prey – 'lips and cheeks' – cast as flowers – 'rosy' – a recognisable symbol of earthly beauty and mortality. The 'hours and weeks' are disconnected units of human time – we might have expected 'hours and minutes' or 'days and weeks' – stressing their random brevity against the 'edge of doom'.

'Doom', the last word before the couplet heavily emphasised by fulfilling the rhyme established in 'come' (the rhyme makes their connection somehow inexorable), undercuts the poem's aspiration to establish love as durable in the face of time and change. As so often in Shakespeare's sonnets the final two lines twist or further complicate the position already set out. Here the speaker's assertions become tangled: having set out the proposal – love endures – and quashed the unheard counter-argument with the oratorical 'O no', the couplet allows for its undoing: 'If this be error'. Can a negative be 'on me proved'? Given that the poem's existence contradicts 'I never writ', is the charge of error discounted? The legalistic evasions of the final couplet stop short of affirming its central claim about love's resistance to change and decay, and open up a disconcerting void under the poem and its claims. The 'marriage of true minds' – a notable figure for intellectual, rather than physical or emotional union – sags open in this elusive and complex conditionality of the conclusion. The apparently celebratory opening line is compromised by the repeated negatives, revealing a sceptical undertow beneath the speaker's bravura attempt to define true love.

The Taming of the Shrew

Controversial battle-of-the-sexes comedy

Key Facts

Date: 1591–2
Length: 2,750 lines
Verse: 80% / Prose: 20%

Major characters' share of lines:

Petruchio	22%
Tranio	11%
Kate	8%
Hortensio	8%
Baptista	7%

Plot and characters

A frame story sees a trick played on a drunken tinker, **Christopher Sly**, to make him believe he is a sickly lord watching a play for his recuperation. That play introduces **Lucentio**, who comes to Padua and falls in love with **Bianca**. Her father **Baptista** will not let her marry any of her suitors, who include **Hortensio** and **Gremio,** until her shrewish older sister **Katherine** is married. Lucentio disguises himself as a schoolmaster to gain access to Bianca; his servant **Tranio** takes his place as Lucentio. **Petruchio** arrives, looking for a wife, and agrees to marry Katherine and to introduce Hortensio, disguised as a music teacher, to Baptista's household. The rival suitors agree to support his suit. Baptista offers a large dowry for Katherine and the match is agreed: Petruchio then meets Kate who is angry and disdainful of his suit but he tells her father she has agreed to marry him. Lucentio's suit (via Tranio) to Bianca is accepted by her father, on condition of gaining his own father **Vincentio**'s consent. Bianca's suitors vie for her attention. Petruchio's strange behaviour and demeanour at his wedding is reported: he takes Katherine to his country house, where he denies her food, abuses his servants **Grumio** and **Curtis**, and prevents her from sleeping. Hortensio gives up on Bianca to court a wealthy **Widow**. Tranio and Lucentio need to find a Vincentio to clinch the marriage to Bianca, and they present the **Pedant** to Baptista in the guise of Lucentio's father. The real Vincentio arrives, and is convinced that Tranio, wearing his master's clothes, must have murdered him. Newly married Lucentio and Bianca confess all to Vincentio. At a celebratory banquet Petruchio wagers that Katherine is the most obedient of the wives, and indeed, unlike Bianca or the Widow, she comes immediately at her husband's summons, delivers a long speech on wifely submission, and gains a bonus payment from a delighted Baptista.

Context and composition

The relation of the play as printed for the first time in 1623 to an earlier and similar play, *The Taming of a Shrew* (published 1594), is unclear. *A Shrew* completes the framing plot with a final scene in which Christopher Sly vows to go home and tame his own wife, and this scene is often incorporated in stage productions. Shakespeare wrote his play around 1591–2, so it is one of his earliest dramas, written around the time of the *Henry VI* plays and *Titus Andronicus*.
The story of Petruchio and Katherine draws on a boisterous tradition of unruly wives subdued by their husbands – and sometimes the other way around. The Lucentio–Bianca plot has a more literary source: it is drawn from George Gascoigne's comedy *Supposes* (1566), an English version of Ariosto's *I suppositi*.
Shakespeare's successor at the King's Men, John Fletcher, wrote an unofficial sequel to the play as *The Woman's Prize, or the Tamer Tamed* (1611) in which a widowed Petruchio now meets his match in a determined new wife.

Performances

This play, or its near namesake, was performed in 1594, and an edition of 1631 suggests it had performances at both the Globe and Blackfriars. The plot provided material for several popular rewritings in the seventeenth and eighteenth

centuries, including David Garrick's sentimental version *Catherine and Petruchio* (1754), which reassures us of Petruchio's genuine affection for his wife. Many twentieth-century productions attempted to ameliorate the uncomfortable spectacle of a wife subdued by her husband's violent treatment, either by having the couple fall in love despite their protestations (a version of the Beatrice and Benedick relationship in *Much Ado About Nothing*) or by maintaining signs of Katherine's independence in spite of her apparent capitulation in the final act. Elizabeth Taylor and Richard Burton's film performances (dir. Franco Zeffirelli, 1966) drew much energy from their passionate romance off screen, just as Cole Porter's musical *Kiss Me Kate* riffs on the tension between on- and off-screen relationships. A more recent high-school movie version of the play called *Ten Things I Hate About You* (1999) directed by Gil Lunger, and a BBC Shakespeare Retold adaptation featuring an abrasive female MP (2005) attest to the play's hospitality to modern updating. In the theatre, an all-female version directed by Phyllida Lloyd at the Globe in 2003 made the play's inscription of male posturing look comic; Gregory Doran, in an RSC production that played alongside

Fletcher's companion play, presented Katherine and Petruchio as mutually dependent oddballs, redeemed by a passionate love that enjoyed the erotic frisson of powerplay and submission (2003). Darker interpretations include Edward Hall's all-male company Propeller (2006), where Sly doubled as Petruchio, introducing his violent and cruel tyranny over Katherine. Charles Marowitz memorably rewrote the play as *The Shrew* (1973), a brutal, sexually violent fable.

Themes and interpretation

The Taming of the Shrew is a genuinely difficult play to describe, because its central premise can be represented in quite different ways, all of which have textual and theatrical sanction but which cannot be simultaneously true. Is this a play about the violent subjugation of Katherine, tortured and married off to a man before she has even met him and against her will, who ends by mouthing patriarchal platitudes, her spirit broken? Is this a play in which two refreshingly unorthodox characters meet and are each attracted to the other because of their shared eccentricity? Katherine: feisty and independent woman or fierce, damaged sociopath? Petruchio: bullying bounty-hunter or quirky individualist who wants a wife who knows her own mind? Is their relationship cracking with mutually exchanged sexual energy and puns or inflected only with the unequal power dynamic of a misogynistic society? Therapeutic or dangerous? That infamous final speech, in which Katherine offers to place her hand under her husband's foot in a gesture of complete submission: archly rehearsed pieties, delivered with sarcasm, a scripted and rehearsed double-act to extract money from the onlookers, or the abused wife's cowed complicity with her violent husband for fear of reprisal? By the standards of early modern sexual inequality, her manifesto of mutual obligation in marriage is a modern one, drawing on new Protestant ideas of so-called 'companionate marriage', in which the two partners have different but equally necessary roles, and that wives' duties to husbands are propped up by husbands' reciprocal obligations. But for modern readers and audiences it smacks of broken endorsement of dominant values.

The extent to which the play undermines its own principal narrative is also difficult to deduce, partly because of the textual confusion. The only early printing of Shakespeare's play is in his collected works of 1623: here the text, having begun by placing the whole Paduan story as an inset play performed for Christopher Sly's benefit, ends without returning to the frame story. Sly disappears from view. The purpose of the frame is unclear: does it underline the unreality of this taming plot by placing it as a fiction within a fiction (so we can say it is 'only' a play), or does it amplify that narrative by suggesting its parallels with the class inequalities that motivate the lord's initial trick on the unwitting tinker? Who's the true butt of the joke when Sly is introduced to his 'lady', the cross-dressed page Bartholomew, given that both the honeypot Bianca and the shrewish Katherine would have been played by young male actors? When, in *A Shrew*, Sly promises to go home and tame his wife, on the one hand his immediate application of the play-fiction to his own world seems chilling, but his evident drunkenness undercuts the menace of the threat, as if only a sozzled fool would interpret the play in the way he does. And even if Katherine is subdued, the thrust of the final scene suggests that other independent women take her place, as the newly married Bianca and the Widow robustly refuse to be bossed around by their husbands. Directors may adjudicate between these and other options, but the play itself has proved remarkably open to different tones and understandings of its central relationships.

Much of Petruchio's arsenal of taming devices is borrowed from falconry, where the bird must become accustomed to its handler through a process of sleep deprivation and the control of food. He also deploys, however, the manipulation of reality that is crucial to theatre. When Katherine agrees that the moon is the sun, or that an old man is a young woman, she agrees to enter a shared perception, at an angle to reality, just as spectators do in a theatre. Like us, she does not resist this interpretation of the world. Presenting the story, from the Sly Induction, as an inset play also suggests that here, in this early drama, Shakespeare is already self-consciously exploring issues of theatricality and of identity, of performance and authenticity, and of our willingness to enter into the deceits of theatre. The scene in which Vincentio knocks at the door and is greeted by 'himself', the Pedant acting as Vincentio, recalls the similar confusion of the twin Antipholuses in *The Comedy of Errors*: both scenes are funny, but they are also uncanny, in duplicating, dividing and misrecognising the self. It is these questions about and within the play that continue to hold our attention.

The Tempest

Magical, meditative late play

Plot and characters

A group of nobles – including **Alonso**, King of Naples, his son **Ferdinand**, and **Antonio**, Duke of Milan – are caught in a storm at sea and shipwrecked. On his island the magician **Prospero** tells his daughter **Miranda** that he has done this to bring his enemies into his power, and reveals that he is the usurped Duke of Milan, ousted by his brother and saved from death by a loyal councillor **Gonzalo**. He also introduces his sprite servant **Ariel** whom he controls through threats, and **Caliban**, son of the witch Sycorax, who curses him for his enslavement. An invisible Ariel makes Ferdinand believe his father is drowned. Ferdinand meets Miranda and they fall in love, observed by Prospero, who affects disapproval but has planned this outcome. Gonzalo tries to comfort Alonso, and as they sleep Antonio urges Alonso's brother **Sebastian** to kill him: Ariel foils the plot. Caliban encounters **Trinculo**, the ship's jester, and **Stephano**, the butler: they initially fear him but then tame him with drink, and Caliban swears drunken allegiance. He persuades them that Prospero must be killed so that they become rulers of the island. Ariel tricks the nobles by preparing a banquet for them which then magically disappears. Prospero prepares a wedding masque with **Iris**, **Juno** and **Ceres** to bless the couple's marriage, but breaks this off when he suddenly remembers the conspiracy against him. Ariel tricks Caliban, Trinculo and Stephano with a show of fine clothes and then hunts them through thorns and torment. He reports to Prospero, who is moved to pity by Ariel's description of the suffering of Gonzalo and Alonso. He vows to renounce his magical powers. Alonso and the nobles are brought to Prospero and recognise him as the Duke of Milan; Prospero expresses his forgiveness to the silent Antonio; the crew of the ship are revealed; Alonso is reunited with his son; Ariel is assured of his freedom; and Caliban repents his involvement in the conspiracy. The play ends with Prospero asking the audience to free him with their applause.

Context and composition

Among Shakespeare's final plays, *The Tempest* was probably written in 1611, since it draws on texts describing a spectacular shipwreck in Bermuda, only available in late 1610. The play thus depends on contemporary stories of travel and exploration, including Montaigne's essay 'Of the Cannibals', spliced with Ovid's *Metamorphoses*, from which Prospero's speech about giving up his magical powers is taken, but there is no major source for the play's narrative arc. We might see Shakespeare cannibalising his earlier themes – usurpation (*King Richard II*), fraternal rivalry (*As You Like It*), revenge (*Hamlet*) – and drawing them into a strangely compressed, oblique and lyrical play. *The Tempest*, even more than Shakespeare's other plays, has inspired countless retellings, symbolic interpretations and other artworks as a supplement to its own enigmatic simplicity. There are also similarities with other late plays: like *The Winter's Tale* it is preoccupied with a generation-old wrong and the reunion of parents and children; like *Pericles* it is strongly influenced by the sea and separation. Biographical readings of the play as Shakespeare's own farewell to the stage are attractive but probably misguided: Shakespeare continued to write plays in collaboration after *The Tempest*, and probably did not imagine himself in the tyrannical figure of Prospero. However, the play's commentary on theatre itself links it with other self-conscious plays and playmakers, such as *Hamlet* or the Duke in *Measure for Measure*.

Performances

We know that
The Tempest was
performed at court
in November 1611;
it was probably
also performed in
Blackfriars, where
some of the
elaborate stage
effects described in
the directions could
be spectacularly

realised: '*Thunder and Lightning. Enter Ariel (like a Harpy) claps his
wings upon the table, and with a quaint device the banquet vanishes*'
(3.3.53). The play was adapted during the eighteenth century to
develop its spectacle. On the modern stage it has tended to be a vehicle
either for a venerable classical actor or for a sympathetic Caliban
speaking to and for post-colonial sensibilities. Rupert Goold directed
a cruelly commanding Patrick Stewart in a polar setting (RSC, 2007);
Derek Jacobi's bitterness at his deposition shaped his performance for
Michael Grandage (Old Vic, 2002), in a production stressing his
magical omniscience. Jude Kelly (West Yorkshire Playhouse, 1999)
emphasised Prospero as colonial overlord, a reading latent in the
casting of a black actor, Geff Francis, by Michael Boyd (RSC, 2002).
Jonathan Miller cast Ariel and Caliban as black actors (Old Vic,
1988), but pessimistically suggested that the ending of the play merely
exchanged a white overlord for a black one (Ariel picked up
Prospero's broken staff in an ominous gesture of succession at the end
of the play). On film, Peter Greenaway's baroque *Prospero's Books*
(1991) stresses the esoteric knowledge in Prospero's library and casts
John Gielgud as the controlling magus playwright Prospero/
Shakespeare, writing the play's first word, 'Boatswain', in a
calligraphic hand. Derek Jarman's 1980 film stressed the dark
dynamic of Prospero's household and ended with a camp conga of

sailors to the strains of 'Stormy Weather'. In 2010 Julie Taymor cast Helen Mirren as a warm and witty 'Prospera' (Vanessa Redgrave had also played the role at the Globe in 2000).

Themes and interpretation

On the face of it, *The Tempest* is a rather simple story. Man, having lost dukedom long ago, now gets it back. After the high nautical realism of the opening shipwreck scene, there is little physical action: the play has a restricted cast and deliberately confined setting – the island – and claustrophobic time line – 'the time 'twixt six and now' (1.2.240). Shakespeare here experiments with the classical unities – the unity of time, place and action – which he so decisively discards almost everywhere else in his work. (*The Comedy of Errors* is his only other similarly structured play; the contemporaneous *The Winter's Tale*, with its dilated chronology, shows an opposite method of dealing with a similar structural problem.) The result is a concentrated but curiously decentred play whose most exciting events of palace machinations and the duke banished with his baby daughter are told, not shown. The central themes of power, authority and usurpation are shadowed rather than fully represented: hinted at by the disorder of the opening scene, or parodied in Caliban's doomed insurrection, or replayed as Ferdinand's desire and servitude mirror Caliban's. The play is overshadowed by the past: dramaturgically, in the long and difficult to stage scene of exposition; and psychologically, in Prospero's lexis of – possibly Catholic – guilt and penitence in his epilogue.

The play's simplicity means that it has been sustainedly read as symbol or allegory. One suggestive argument has taken its cue from Shakespeare's immediate sources, and seen a parable of colonial expansion into the Americas. Miranda's chastity seems to represent a kind of national sanctity; Prospero's enslavement of the island people with promises and threats recalls the activity of early colonialists who were both dependent on and contemptuous of native peoples; the language is of plantation and linguistic domination. In Caliban's lyrical moments and in his articulate anger, we see this colonial appropriation from the other point of view: if *The Tempest* is about the speculative enterprise of American colonisation in the early seventeenth century, it is not a propaganda piece for the Virginia Company. Some of the most provocative rewritings of the play have been in colonial contexts, such as Martinique-born Aimé Césaire's *Une Tempête* (1969), in which Caliban is a black revolutionary who wishes to strip himself of the oppressor's language. The 'brave new world' (5.1.183) is new only to an inexperienced young girl: here are no riches, only the fragile renewal of a broken old world, and the movement of the end of the play is westward ho, back home, 'where every third thought shall be my grave' (5.1.309).

When Prospero recognises Caliban with 'This thing of darkness I / Acknowledge mine' (5.1.273–4), one implication is that of possession and slavery. But another reading sees Caliban as part of Prospero (perhaps this is why the line break unexpectedly stresses 'I') – a psychoanalytic Id preoccupied with instinctual desires for food and sex which must be kept under control, just as Ariel, an intellectual, spiritual Superego, aspires to soar free of the physical body. It is Ariel who brings the testy and controlling Prospero away from thoughts of revenge and towards forgiveness: 'the rarer action / Is in virtue than in vengeance' (5.1.27–8). This clemency, however, is compromised by Antonio's response. Reading the play, it is easy to skip over the fact that the usurping brother makes no reply to Prospero's forgiveness; on stage this is a profound moment, which shapes the tone of the ending of the play. Is Antonio's silence the shamed repentance that cannot speak, or, as the poet W. H. Auden memorably elaborates in his sequence inspired by the play *The Sea and the Mirror*, the remorseless implacability of sin?

Throughout the play Prospero's magic is equated to, and demonstrated via, theatre. Like a playwright he arranges his characters in small scenes, and directs their actions through Ariel's intervention. He conjures the opening storm, and bewitches us by the power of theatrical, as well as magical, illusion. When he promises to abandon his magic, he does so in the language of theatre. If the language of theatre gives Prospero his power, it is also a source of weakness. In the end he must surrender to the audience: the themes of imprisonment, servitude and punishment from the play are, in its concluding lines, displaced into the relation between the artist and his audience.

Timon of Athens

Key Facts
Date: 1605–6
Length: 2,607 lines
Verse: 75% / Prose: 25%

Major characters' share of lines:	
Timon	34%
Apemantus	10%
Flavius	8%
Alcibiades	7%

Fable of misanthropy

Plot and characters

A party of petitioners gather at the house of **Timon**, a wealthy Athenian, including a **Poet, Painter, Jeweller, Merchant** and **Mercer**, in hope of his patronage. Timon is generous in welcoming all, including the soldier **Alcibiades** and the snarling philosopher **Apemantus**. He pays off **Ventidius'** debts and gives **Lucilius** money to enable him to marry. At a banquet Timon's generosity and the greedy self-interest of the guests are satirised by Apemantus, and a masque of Amazons is performed. Timon's steward **Flavius** knows that Timon's money is almost spent. **Caphis** is sent by a **Senator** to recover his money from Timon, and Timon's house is besieged by all his creditors. Timon sends to his friends **Lucius, Lucullus** and **Sempronius,** and to the recent heir Ventidius for a loan, sure that they will return his past generosity. All refuse. Timon, angry and bewildered, invites them to dinner where he serves them stones and water, berating them for their ingratitude and vowing misanthropy. Alcibiades falls out with the Senate after he pleads for one of his men who has killed another, and is banished: he vows to gather troops and revenge himself on Athens. Outside Athens the embittered Timon lives like a beast: the loyal Flavius follows him. Digging for roots Timon finds gold; he gives it to Alcibiades to fight Athens, and to his whores **Phrynia** and **Timandra**, to spread venereal diseases.

Apemantus points out that Timon's misanthropy is the inverse of his previous pride. Timon gives money to three thieves, who are converted by his radical message. The Poet and Painter return for more gold: Timon curses them. Two Senators plead with Timon to return to the city and lead the defence against Alcibiades, but Timon is indifferent to the fate of the Athenians and predicts his own death. A soldier finds an undecipherable gravestone; Alcibiades, victorious against the Athenian Senators, reads Timon's self-epitaph, mourns him and vows to enter Athens in peace.

Context and composition

The date of *Timon* is difficult to pin down but is usually pitched around 1605–6: it draws on William Painter's collection of prose moralities *Palace of Pleasure*, which Shakespeare also used for *All's Well that Ends Well*, and probably postdates a play called *Timon* acted around 1602. It is first printed in the collected edition of Shakespeare's plays in 1623, but studies of that book make it clear that *Timon* was a late substitution when it emerged that the rights for *Troilus and Cressida* were proving problematic: without this it might not have survived at all. It is now generally thought to be collaboratively written with Thomas Middleton – the only play Shakespeare co-wrote with the younger playwright, best known at this point for his satirical urban comedies. Stylistic analysis usually allocates 1.2, Act 3 and part of Act 4 to Middleton. Its sources include Plutarch's *Lives of the Noble Grecians and Romans* – Timon's epitaph is quoted almost directly from this source – connecting it to *Julius Caesar*, *Antony and Cleopatra* and *Coriolanus*. It has tended to be seen as emblematic rather than realist – a sharply depicted narrative of decline and invective, more akin to a fable than the more psychological tragedies such as *King Lear* (although the poet Coleridge dubbed it 'a *Lear* of ordinary life'.) Among Shakespeare's tragedies it is probably closest to *Coriolanus*; its satiric view of suffering allies it to *Titus Andronicus*; but it also retells the story of *The Merchant of Venice* from the point of view of an Antonio embittered by the actions of his false friends, and without the saving intelligence of a Portia.

Performances

There is no record of early performances, before an adapted version at the end of the seventeenth century, Thomas Shadwell's *The History of Timon of Athens, the Man-Hater*. The play's theatrical history ever since has been only sporadic. Musical versions or interpolations have been surprisingly popular: Nugent Monck's 1935 production had incidental music by a young Benjamin Britten, and for the 1963 Stratford Shakespeare Festival in Ontario Duke Ellington was the composer. This jazz score was revived by Greg Doran for an RSC production in 1999, in which Michael Pennington played an initially endearing, naive aristocrat turning towards sardonic disgust as a fascist Alcibiades takes over Athens. In 1991 David Suchet played Timon as a modern philanthropist in a post-Thatcherite London of conspicuous wealth and homeless people on the streets. He announced his patronage to television cameras by holding up his own commissioned portrait (dir. Trevor Nunn, Young Vic). Lucy Bailey's 2008 production at the Globe visualised the play's freeloaders as black-caped vultures on aerial wires, out for carrion, in a production widely reviewed as wittily topical amid the banking collapse; a modern-dress version directed by Barry Edelstein at the New York Public Theater in 2011 had the stagehands in overalls roll up the red carpet and impound the chandeliers as Timon's party lifestyle, with its sycophantic hangers-on, evaporated. No big-screen film exists, but Jonathan Miller's 1981 BBC television version was well received for its evocative palette of black, white and gold and a thin, self-consuming Jonathan Pryce in the title role.

Themes and interpretation

We tend to assume that Shakespeare's plays have been perennially popular, but in most cases plays have gone in and out of fashion (more out than in, in the case of *Timon*). But this play, like others in the canon, has spoken more loudly to certain eras than others: the modernist artist Wyndham Lewis, for example, drew a portfolio of angular representations of the play, finding that its unsentimental and stylised architecture seemed to resonate with the aesthetic preoccupations of the early twentieth century. Modernism's understanding and valorising of the fragmentary and the unfinished – because of its brevity and a number of inconsistent details, *Timon* has long been thought to be an incomplete play – was able to begin to re-evaluate this least liked of all of Shakespeare's works, but that work of critical and theatrical recuperation is itself unfinished.

It is appropriate, perhaps, that this play should be shunned: it is a play about rejection, when Timon turns against the society of Athens and the Senate turns against Alcibiades, and also about the question of what we value and whether it can have a cash equivalent. No wonder that one of its most noted advocates was Karl Marx, who understood in Timon's scornful description of the gold he finds when searching for roots to eat that money – exchange-value rather than use-value – was the 'alienation of human capacity'. Pointless conspicuous consumption, such as the 'four milk-white horses, trapped in silver' (1.2.173) sent by Lucius – is seen in the play's opening act as a cynical version of gift exchange: altruism and generosity are fig leaves for deeply manipulative manoeuvres in a financial game of escalating value, speculating to accumulate. In its depiction of the poet promising to shape Timon's reputation, the play's opening gets to the heart of the patronage system in which Shakespeare and Middleton both operated. Both poetic publication, such as Shakespeare's *Venus and Adonis* and *The Rape of Lucrece*, dedicated to the patronage of the Earl of Southampton, and the *Timon* theatre company itself, under the patronage of the King, were part of a complex economy of patronage in which protection, money and praise circulated. One of the many ironies of this satirical play is that it can anatomise this system even as it is implicated within it.

From his discussion of the play, Marx saw money as 'the universal whore', drawing his imagery from the misogynistic intervention of Alcibiades' courtesans whom Timon pays to spread disease. Otherwise there are no women in this play of homosocial bonding and estrangement. *Timon* is a drama uniquely devoid of familial or romantic attachments, or of affective relations not distorted by capital: Lucilius can only marry if he has money; Ventidius' family is significant only in bequeathing him a large fortune. Only Flavius, the loyal steward, demonstrates something approaching selflessness: in following Timon into his misanthropic exile he becomes a version of the Fool in *King Lear*.

Key to the play's off-key invocation of the tragic form is its treatment of Timon's death. For most tragic heroes, this is a moment of pathos and of a still focus: think of Hamlet's long death speech in Horatio's arms, for instance, or the affecting tableau that ends *King Lear*, or Othello's rhetorically controlled renunciation of life. Not so for Timon, who anticipates his death by writing a misanthropic epitaph on his own 'wretched corse' which curses 'you wicked caitiffs left' and identifies him as one who 'all living men did hate' (5.4.70–2). The bitter comfortlessness of this inscription is hollowly underlined as Alcibiades reads it out in the play's final lines: his unconvincing tears on Timon's death have already been sardonically pre-empted by Timon himself. Alcibiades' march on the Athens which has banished him forms the martial, active counterpart to Timon's inward railing: his revenge on his enemies is to fight them, whereas Timon's is to curse them. Timon's actual death is off stage, in a dramatic frustration of tragic expectations. His final words are his existentialist discussion with the Senators: 'graves only be men's works, and death their gain' (5.2.212). It is a bleak ending to a harsh play that has no truck with the transcendent values we like to attribute to tragedy.

Titus Andronicus

Key Facts

Date: 1593–4
Length: 2,708 lines
Verse: 98% / Prose: 2%

Major characters' share of lines:	
Titus	28%
Aaron	14%
Marcus	12%
Tamora	10%
Saturninus	8%

Violent tragedy drawing on Ovidian myth
to depict the decline of the Roman empire

Plot and characters

Brothers **Saturninus** and **Bassianus** marshal their rival
supporters for their claims to be emperor of Rome, but **Marcus
Andronicus**, the tribune, offers the crown to his brother **Titus** who
has returned from a triumphant military campaign. Titus rejects the
offer, and nominates the older Saturninus, who then asks for Titus'
daughter, **Lavinia**, for his wife. She is already promised to
Bassianus, but Titus hands her to the new emperor. As she escapes
with Bassianus, Titus kills his own son **Mutius** who tries to help
them. Among Titus' prisoners, **Tamora**, Queen of the Goths, pleads
with the Romans for the life of her son **Alarbus**, but Titus sacrifices
him. Saturninus takes Tamora for his queen. Urged by Tamora's
lover, **Aaron** the Moor, her two sons, **Chiron** and **Demetrius**, kill
Bassianus and rape Lavinia, cutting off her hands and tongue so
that she cannot reveal the names of her attackers. Titus' sons
Quintus and **Martius** are captured and Titus is tricked by Aaron
into chopping off his own hand for their release: instead he is
presented with their heads and responds with horrible hysterical
laughter. Lavinia reveals what has happened to her by drawing
with a stick in the sand and pointing to a schoolbook of Ovid's
Metamorphoses owned by **Young Lucius**. Her brother **Lucius**

leaves Rome to seek help from the Goths and returns with an army. Driven mad by his suffering, Titus plans revenge. Tamora gives birth to Aaron's son, prompting Aaron to protect the baby. Later Tamora disguises herself as Revenge accompanied by her sons and visits Titus to persuade Lucius into a trap, but wily Titus does not let on that he sees through the device, and agrees to invite Lucius to a banquet. Lucius arrests an unrepentant Aaron who is sentenced to death. Aided by Lavinia, Titus kills Chiron and Demetrius, and serves their bodies in a pie to their unwitting mother, then kills Tamora and Lavinia. Saturninus kills Titus, then is killed by Lucius who becomes the new emperor.

Context and composition

Opinions vary about whether *Titus Andronicus* is one of Shakespeare's earliest plays, possibly collaboratively written with George Peele around 1590–1, or whether it was sole-authored closer to its date of publication. First published in 1594 as *The Most Lamentable Roman Tragedy of Titus Andronicus*, the play is set in ancient Rome during the fourth century BC but has no historical basis. It is related thematically to Shakespeare's other Roman plays but it does not share their reliance on North's translation of Plutarch. Instead of an historical source, Shakespeare here makes self-conscious use of a literary one, Ovid's *Metamorphoses*, a popular narrative poem of mythical shape-changing tales. Ovid is both the source for the rapists within the play – they decide to cut off Lavinia's hands to prevent her taking Philomel's route of embroidering the name of her attacker – and the means by which the crime is revealed, the only time Shakespeare has his source as a physical prop in the play.

As a revenge play it draws on the Elizabethan best-seller *The Spanish Tragedy* by Thomas Kyd – some critics have seen in its excesses an attempt to out-Kyd Kyd – and its themes anticipate the later play *Hamlet*; its dependence on Ovid links it to the narrative poem *The Rape of Lucrece*.

Performances

A sixteenth-century drawing showing Tamora begging for Titus' mercy seems to be the earliest depiction of a Shakespeare play in performance: what is most striking is the solid blackness of Aaron's skin colour, and the mixture of costumes from Roman to Elizabethan. In 1596 a French tutor wrote home having seen it, saying that the spectacle ('la monstre') was preferable to the story ('le sujet'), and, indeed, the play's unflinching violence has meant a very intermittent stage presence. In the twentieth century it was recuperated, first in the heavily stylised production with Laurence Olivier and Vivien Leigh directed by Peter Brook at Stratford in 1955, which cut the more absurd aspects and rendered Lavinia's injuries as disturbingly beautiful streamers of red fabric. In 1987 Deborah Warner took the opposite tactic at the RSC, playing up the grotesque and tonal dissonances and depicting violence with startling realism. Warner's Titus, Brian Cox, described their play as a 'tightrope between comedy and tragedy', and above all, 'ludicrous'. Julie Taymor's bold film *Titus* (1999), with Anthony Hopkins in the title role, emphasises the play's aesthetic of excess, and develops the role of Young Lucius as a witness to, and perhaps ultimate inheritor of, the play's savagery.

Themes and interpretation

For centuries, critics were so disgusted by the perceived savagery and meaningless brutality of *Titus Andronicus* that they comforted themselves that it could not have been by Shakespeare. More recent critics, however, have returned to *Titus* and found in it a triumphantly modern, campily excessive, darkly ironic representation of unpalatable truths about human violence, suffering and inherent barbarism – one which detonates those pious accounts of tragedy as ennobling and cathartic.

Titus challenges assumptions about tragedy in other ways, too. It is undoubtedly a tragedy of serial sensation rather than a tragedy of introspection. The long opening scene incorporates both solemn ritual and merciless sacrifice, honour to the dead and a seeming disrespect for human life. The horror and barbarity which lie just below the surface of Rome's civilised rites is exposed. As in Shakespeare's other Roman plays, it is the nature of Rome itself which is under particular scrutiny. When Tamora expresses herself 'incorporate in Rome' (1.1.462), the boundaries which mark out Rome have been irreparably broached. Later in the play, Titus remarks that 'Rome is but a wilderness of tigers' (3.1.54), demonstrating how the civilisation once synonymous with Rome has been contaminated by the intrusion of the Gothic outsider. In the final lines Lucius decrees that the body of Tamora, 'that ravenous tiger', should be 'throw[n] forth to beasts and birds to prey' (5.3.194, 197), representing a final attempt to rid the state of this pollutant and to re-establish the boundaries of Roman civilisation, but Tamora may be only a scapegoat. Rome's civilised glories seem part of a bygone age (Taymor cleverly films scenes in the ruined Colosseum): it is both corrupted and corrupt. Lucius is emperor because the Goths have put him there: Rome cannot save itself. The play's concern with broached boundaries and blurred distinctions has its emblem in the baby born to Tamora and Aaron, a symbol of miscegenation and one whose fate is unclear at its conclusion.

This is also a tragedy without a tragic hero. We do not get the soliloquies we might expect to bond us with the agonies of the central protagonist: Titus, defined by public duty, remains an unreachable public figure throughout, never taking the audience into his confidence. It is part of the play's moral disequilibrium that its noblest soliloquiser is Aaron. Titus' revenge is unspeakably executed in a bloody charade at least equal in depravity to the acts performed by Tamora and her crew. While his behaviour can be seen as the insanely excessive but humanly explicable response to intolerable injuries, he is, even at the play's opening, a morally equivocal character. One of the play's most unsettling features is the studied absence of any character with whom the audience can readily identify or sympathise. It could be argued that the figure who most nearly fills this role is Lavinia, but while her symbolic weight in the play is considerable, her characterisation is minimal. Even before speech is taken from her, she rarely speaks. She is a pawn in a male world, the object of male personal and political rivalries in the opening scene. Later she is an object through which Tamora's wickedness and vengefulness can be expressed, and the play makes an uncomfortable spectacle of her mutilated body over which her father and uncle speechify with incongruous rhetorical control. The play's allusions to legend establish her more as a type than an individual, and it is with reference to a classical type that Titus gains the dubious authority to kill her. Her death can be interpreted in many ways: sometimes it is assumed that this is a mercy killing sealing a bond between broken father and broken daughter, but sometimes a stage Lavinia tries heartbreakingly to escape this final betrayal. And how this act is to be interpreted is more complex still, if, as the language of Marcus and Lucius in speaking of the ruined state of Rome suggests, she is to be seen less as a woman than as a symbol of the mutilated body politic, a destroyed female personification of a once great civilisation, a kind of vandalised statue.

The play's language parodically emphasises its physical dismemberments, punning gruesomely on body parts while their literal counterparts are disturbingly materialised. Titus' own horrid laughter approaches something central to the play: the brutalising effects of violence and the use of black humour as a shocking distancing function. Wordplay and puns disturbingly mock any impulse towards empathy. Embracing this as crucial to the play's dynamic has been easier for contemporary audiences brought up on the coolly ironic violence of film-makers such as Quentin Tarantino. Now, the only possible audience response is, like Titus' 'ha ha ha' (3.1.263), fundamentally unsettling laughter at this bleak, nihilistic, ultimately modern play.

Troilus and Cressida

Key Facts
Date: 1602
Length: 3,592 lines
Verse: 70% / Prose: 30%

Major characters' share of lines:	
Troilus	15%
Ulysses	14%
Pandarus	11%
Cressida	8%
Thersites	8%

Satirical and anti-heroic love story amid an inglorious and protracted war

Plot and characters

Seven years into the war between the Greeks and Trojans following Paris' abduction of Helen from her husband **Menelaus**, the Greek army is unable to break the siege of Troy. In Troy, **Troilus** is impatient with **Pandarus** who is supposed to be helping him to woo **Cressida**. Pandarus tells her of Troilus' suit, and although she returns his love, she will not show it. She watches the Trojan soldiers march past: **Aeneas, Antenor, Hector, Paris, Helenus** and Troilus. The Greeks – **Agamemnon, Ulysses, Nestor, Diomedes** and Menelaus – discuss tactics, and Ulysses blames the arrogant **Achilles** for disrupting morale. Aeneas brings a message from Hector challenging a Grecian to combat: mindful of morale, the Greek commanders send **Ajax** rather than their best fighter, Achilles. **Thersites** rails at Ajax: Achilles and **Patroclus**, later identified as Achilles' lover, look on. **Priam** and his sons Hector, Troilus, Helenus and Paris discuss Helen: against Hector, Troilus argues she should be retained, but his sister **Cassandra** prophesies the destruction of Troy unless Helen is returned. The Greek commanders flatter Ajax about the duel, and Ulysses lectures Achilles about his conduct. Troilus and Cressida finally meet, choreographed by Pandarus who makes them vow their fidelity before taking them to bed. **Calchas,** Cressida's father, has defected to the Greeks and persuades Agamemnon to exchange her for Antenor, a Trojan prisoner: Diomedes is sent for her. Aeneas tells Troilus that the lovers must be parted, and the pair exchange tokens and tears as farewell. The Greek lords treat her disrespectfully. Hector will not fight Ajax because they are cousins: Achilles vows to take up the fight. Ulysses takes Troilus to Calchas' tent, where, unseen, they watch Cressida unwillingly giving one of Troilus' tokens to Diomedes. Troilus vows to kill him. **Andromache** tries to persuade her husband Hector not to fight, but the two armies go into battle. Patroclus is killed and this prompts Achilles to join the fighting; he is beaten by Hector in the duel; Paris and Menelaus fight; Achilles' Myrmidons surround and kill Hector, dragging his body round the battlefield from Achilles' horse. Troilus and his brothers vow vengeance. Pandarus delivers a scabrous epilogue, bequeathing his diseases to the audience.

Context and composition

The play was probably written around 1602 and first printed in 1609. It draws extensively on Chaucer's poem *Troilus and Criseyde* and Robert Henryson's *The Testament of Cresseid*, as well as on George Chapman's translation of Homer (1598) and on Ovid's *Metamorphoses*. Whereas the preface to the 1609 edition describes it as a comedy, it is placed in the First Folio of 1623 between the histories and tragedies, and has no place on the catalogue table of contents, perhaps because permission to print it was late in coming. Titled as a 'tragedy', it does not end with the death of its eponymous characters (unlike, say, *Romeo and Juliet* or *Antony and Cleopatra*), and critics have been divided about its generic status. It has often been considered alongside other so-called 'problem plays': generically uncertain, ethically evasive dramas from the early seventeenth century, including *Measure for Measure* and *All's Well that Ends Well*. Its prevalent images of disease also link it to passages of *Hamlet*: in both plays, this is connected to the outbreaks of plague that haunted early modern London.

Performances

The two distinct states of the 1609 quarto text assert, contradictorily, that the play was acted 'by the King's Majesty's servants at the Globe' *and* that it comes in to print 'never staled with  the stage, never clapper-clawed with the palms of the vulgar'. No evidence exists to resolve this uncertainty about the play's early stage history. Dryden reworked it for Restoration audiences, but the play's cynical tone means that it has had trouble establishing itself in the repertoire. In fact, it was only in the anti-heroic and cynical second half of the twentieth century, and particularly in the wake of the Vietnam War, that the play found its voice. Andrew Hilton updated the setting to the First World War (Tobacco Factory, Bristol, 2003); the Trojans were Irish and the Greeks English in Dominic Dromgoole's seedy vision (Oxford Stage Company, 2000), introduced by the distinctly unheroic Ulysses in greying underpants and smoking a roll-up. Michael Boyd (RSC, 1998) presented Thersites, as one reviewer put it, 'as a filthy cross between a war photographer and a bowler-hatted music-hall clown', bringing out the play's queasy black comedy. Juliet Stevenson as Cressida (dir. Howard Davies, RSC, 1985) recovered the role from the stereotype of promiscuity, discovering real affection in her relationship with Troilus. An austere ensemble production by Terry Hands (Theatr Clwyd, 2005) topically presented a political system justifying itself with a morally dubious war. Declan Donnellan's Cheek by Jowl production (2008) doubled Helen and Cassandra and Paris and Menelaus.

Themes and interpretation

It's a grubby play. Washed-up military hero Achilles sulks in his tent instead of going into battle; the Trojan princes debate whether Paris' stolen bride Helen is worth all this trouble; the Greek commanders cynically moralise about order amid the pointless chaos of their protracted siege. 'Nothing but lechery' (5.2.83), as the railing satirist Thersites puts it, and at the play's end Pandarus implicates the drama itself in that seedy economy, complaining that bawds' clients are ungrateful as soon as they have got what they wanted: 'why should our endeavour be so desired and the performance so loathed?' (5.11.37–8). Performance is here both sexual and theatrical. No wonder we are left not with the traditional request of the epilogue for clemency and applause, but with a different sort of clap, venereal disease: 'I'll sweat and seek about for eases. / And at that time bequeath you my diseases' (5.11.53–4). We have been inescapably sullied by our dalliance in this soiled world.

Shakespeare's take, then, on the Trojan wars, is decidedly anti-heroic. Both the love plot he took from Chaucer and the story of battle from Chapman's translation of Homer are deflated and presented as pragmatic rather than honourable. Even the play's allocation of time undermines the proto-romantic thrust of its title: the eponymous couple occupies relatively little of the stage and action. Its main soliloquiser is not one of the noble princes or warriors of Homeric epic, but the satirical commentator Thersites, who speaks the majority of his lines, as an acid chorus, to the audience. The inglorious death of Hector structures the play's tragic plot, and yet it is not a tragedy, and Troilus' powerfully voyeuristic jealousy over Cressida's behaviour with Diomedes distracts from the narrative of Hector's downfall. Hector is fatally attacked by the Myrmidons while he is arming himself with the fancy armour of a Greek warrior he has just killed: he seems here the epitome of those proud 'princes orgulous' (Prologue, 2) identified by the Prologue in the play's opening words. Both the play and its pre-existing story tighten around the characters and close down their sphere of action. Within the static, claustrophobic context of the siege of Troy, all the protagonists seem to have their room for autonomous action circumscribed: they are trapped by the history that has already been written, as well as by the machinations of others that place both the war and life itself into stalemate. When Pandarus makes the newly met lovers swear an oath before dispatching them off to bed with salacious relish, he makes them vow on versions of their own stereotypes which are already known: 'let all constant men be Troiluses, all false women Cressids, and all brokers-between panders' (3.2.181–2). Even at the moment they meet, that is to say, they are already ironically the fictionalised characters of myth and legend, in one of Shakespeare's most interesting tricks of narrative time in the play.

In this trio it is Cressida whose conduct has traditionally attracted most blame. Whereas previously in Shakespeare's plays male jealousy about female constancy has been misplaced (see *Merry Wives* or *Much Ado About Nothing*), here Troilus oversees, voyeuristically, his lover pass on her affections with his love token. But from the start, Cressida's presentation has been off key. Her opening remark 'will you walk in, my lord?' (3.2.52) has often seemed suggestive of unseemly wantonness, and, in the first part of the play at least, she speaks assertively and wittily. Her soliloquy at the end of her first scene seems to try to reassure the audience about her intentions, but after this point she is opaque and distant: like Troilus in the Greek camp, we watch her performing certain actions without access to her motivation or feelings. In part her role is to stand in for the terrifying sexuality of Helen, which is blamed for the long war: when she arrives with the Greeks, Cressida's treatment replays in miniature the masculine bravado and the objectification of women at the heart of the conflict, and in a Greek camp preoccupied by homosocial, and on occasion, homosexual, bonds. In the end we may feel that Cressida has little choice – and it is telling that we never hear the contents of the letter she sends to Troilus. She remains rather an object of violent male desire and projection. Elsewhere the play's treatment of women is scant: Andromache, wife of Hector, who appeals to him before his fatal fight, seems merely to demonstrate the irrelevance of the domestic sphere in this tale of male bonding and aggression, and to nod towards a less romantic view of ultimate coupledom than that of Troilus for Cressida.

Twelfth Night, or What You Will

Key Facts

Date: 1601

Length: 2,579 lines

Verse: 40% / Prose: 60%

Major characters' share of lines:	
Toby Belch	13%
Viola	13%
Olivia	12%
Feste	12%
Malvolio	11%
Orsino	9%

Bittersweet romantic comedy of tricks and mistaken identities

Plot and characters

Orsino is lovesick with unrequited affection for **Olivia**. Shipwrecked in Illyria and believing **Sebastian**, her twin drowned, **Viola** dresses as a male page, Cesario, to enter Orsino's household, and she quickly forms a warm intimacy with her master which she alone is able to recognise as romantic love. In fact Sebastian is not drowned, and has been saved by his devoted friend **Antonio**, who, despite personal danger, has accompanied him to Illyria. Orsino sends Cesario as a messenger to Olivia, who is in mourning and has not responded to his advances. Olivia is intrigued by this new approach, and finds herself fascinated in a couple of flirtatious interviews with Cesario. Cesario realises when Olivia sends her a ring that she has inadvertently seduced her master's object of desire. Meanwhile, an enmity between **Malvolio**, Olivia's self-righteous steward, and **Feste**, her witty fool, is exacerbated when Malvolio disbands a riotous gathering of Feste, Olivia's disreputable uncle **Sir Toby Belch** and **Sir Andrew Aguecheek**, a hanger-on who is in love with Olivia himself. A plot is hatched with Olivia's waiting-woman **Maria** to trick Malvolio into believing Olivia is in love with him, and an enigmatic forged letter is planted to deceive him. Malvolio takes the bait, and dresses in outrageous yellow cross-garters as instructed, leading Olivia to assume he has gone mad. Imprisoned in darkness for his apparent madness, Malvolio is further plagued by Feste disguised as a clergyman, Sir Topas. Toby eggs Aguecheek on to fight Olivia's new suitor, Cesario – but the cross-dressed woman and cowardly knight are equally ill-suited to duelling. In fact Sebastian, mistaken for Cesario, fights Aguecheek, and is then swept, bewildered, to the altar by Olivia to be married. In a long final scene, Viola's true identity is revealed when she is reunited with her twin Sebastian, Olivia realises her mistake, and Orsino agrees to marry Viola. The forged letter is exposed as a trick, and Malvolio is returned, vowing revenge on his tormentors. Toby and Maria are to marry. Feste ends the proceedings with a song epilogue.

Composition and context

The play was probably written in 1601 and thus comes at the end of Shakespeare's period of writing romantic comedies. It has obvious affinities with earlier comedies – the twins confused plot of *Comedy of Errors*, cross-dressing in *The Two Gentlemen of Verona* and *As You Like It*, another devoted Antonio as in *The Merchant of Venice* – as well as some darker elements which may nod forwards: a preoccupation with madness, as in the contemporaneous *Hamlet*; a fool sharing some lines with his counterpart in *King Lear*; and a suggestion, in the literal and metaphorical deaths on the margins of the plot, of adjacent tragedy.

The sources are Plautus' *Menaechmi* (like *Errors*), the Italian intrigue play *Gl'ingannati*, probably via prose versions or as adapted in Barnabe Riche's *Farewell to Military Profession* (1581). The play is constructed to divide between a relatively large number of medium-sized parts, with Viola, Olivia, Feste, Sir Toby and Malvolio given broadly equal stage time. *Twelfth Night* is first published in the First Folio in 1623.

Performances

The prominence of music in the play suggests that Feste's part was written with the particular gifts of the sardonic, cleverly comic actor Robert Armin in mind. Evidence from an early performance,

at Middle Temple for Candlemas in February 1602, makes clear that the Malvolio plot was always popular. The law student John Manningham described the gulling of the steward as 'a good practice': for him it superseded the other plot elements such as cross-dressing and twins, which he does not mention. This role has tended to attract star actors, from Henry Irving in the nineteenth century to Laurence Olivier and Patrick Stewart in the twentieth and twenty-first. Often Malvolio's costuming bears out the specific suggestions of Puritanism in his part, strongly contrasting with the absurd assumed cross-garters. Viola's role became an alluring 'breeches' part with the advent of professional actresses at the Restoration.

If *Twelfth Night* used to be regarded as the ultimate light comedy – Dr Johnson described it as 'light and easy', and for William Hazlitt it was 'perhaps too good-natured for comedy' – more recent productions have tended rather to emphasise its darker elements. Peter Gill's RSC production of 1974 made prominent use of a picture of Narcissus to symbolise the self-absorbed quality of almost all the play's characters. Steven Pimlott at Sheffield's Crucible in 1987 opened playing a complete, eight-minute version of the *liebestod* from *Tristan and Isolde*, simultaneously suggesting Orsino's self-indulgence *and* the potentially tragic consequences of passion;

Edward Hall's all-male company, Propeller, found 'powerful alternating currents of morbidity and vitality', according to one reviewer of their 1996 production. Illyria, the play's dreamworld, has been variously represented as a hot, holiday romance island, a world locked in a wintery stasis, as an echo of historic half-timbered Stratford-upon-Avon, or as the Orientalist fantasy of its real counterpart, Yugoslavia, poised between East and West. Film versions include the 1990 recording of a Kenneth Branagh-directed stage production, with Frances Barber as Viola and Richard Briers as Malvolio, and Trevor Nunn's wistful 1996 version, set in the late Victorian era and emphasising the play's sea imagery through location shooting, in particular a memorable underwater shot in a prologue describing the shipwreck.

Themes and interpretations

The play's title, including its teasing subtitle 'or, What You Will', encapsulates both its sexually suggestive playfulness and its impulses towards melancholy. Although the festival of Twelfth Night (6 January) is not explicitly mentioned (Samuel Pepys noted peevishly in his diary after a performance on 6 January 1663 that it was 'not relating at all to the name or the day'), and the attractive suggestion that it was first performed on this date in 1601 has not been substantiated, an appropriate mood of carnival reversal operates. Early modern festive culture temporarily sanctioned the transgression of boundaries, with male and female roles and social hierarchies upended, as in the play's cross-dressing and its depiction of master–servant relationships. Sir Toby Belch seems to be the play's irrepressible Lord of Misrule or master of festivities, and his dedication to over-indulgence gives his quarrel with Malvolio an emblematic quality some critics have seen as the mythic battle between the principles of Carnival and Lent, as in Breughel's famous sixteenth-century painting. But crucial to the idea of 'Twelfth Night' is the end of festivity, the return of normal life, and a normal winter of 'wind and rain' (5.1.362), giving the darkness of Malvolio's imprisonment a distinctly uncomic terror. Almost in the centre of the play a clock strikes, and Olivia recognises 'The clock upbraids me with the waste of time' (3.1.115); the sense of haste as the play speeds up towards its ending with the tacit recognition that the world of comedy does not last forever. As Feste puts it, 'Youth's a stuff will not endure' (2.3.46).

'What you will' is a phrase susceptible to many interpretations. Sometimes it has the quality of 'anything goes', in response to the various forms of homosexual and heterosexual desire in the play, encompassing male and female same-sex eroticism in the encounter of Viola and Olivia and of Cesario and Orsino, and a strong male friendship between Sebastian and Antonio which is often understood as romantic. It can also register the self-determination of the characters willing themselves into new identities: Viola as Cesario, Malvolio as Count, Olivia as veiled cloistress, Orsino as Actaeon, turned into a hart and killed by a cruel goddess. It can carry a suggestion of responsibility, making us acknowledge our culpability in the excessive cruelty meted out to Malvolio. It is striking that Malvolio is the play's scapegoat, and this may tell us something about early modern attitudes to social hierarchy: there is no punishment in Illyria, only reward, for a woman dressing as a man, but when a servant aspires to become master, the torture is sustained. Feste's refusal to let this joke drop is an example of a tendency to excess shared by almost everyone in the play, from Orsino's extravagant love-melancholy at its opening to Olivia's rapid passion for Cesario.

At the end of the play two couples are formed from the erotic triangle of Orsino–Viola–Olivia: Sebastian becomes the fantasy fulfilment of the play's ambivalent sexuality. While critics have felt that the concluding marriages cannot fully compensate for the vehemence of Olivia's desire for Cesario or for the erotic intimacy between Orsino and his page Cesario – after all, these homoerotic scenes give us the play's only courtships – in the end the real male–female union is not marital but filial. The image of Sebastian and Viola, twins reunited as in *Comedy of Errors*, is the play's ultimate narrative conclusion, a private and Platonic reconciliation freighted, perhaps, with the playwright's own buried wish for the return of his dead twin son Hamnet. Only Sebastian can give Viola her name, which is spoken for the first time in their meeting in Act 5:

at a performance without prior knowledge or a programme, she would have been anonymous until this point. Their reunion effectively excludes all the other characters, with the loyal Antonio and the vengeful Malvolio potentially problematic features of the final scene.

The Two Gentlemen of Verona

Key Facts
Date: 1590
Length: 2,298 lines
Verse: 80% / Prose: 20%

Major characters' share of lines:	
Proteus	20%
Valentine	17%
Julia	14%
Speed	9%
Lance	9%
Duke	9%

Early comedy about sexual rivalry

Plot and characters

Valentine, accompanied by his servant **Speed**, sets out for Milan, leaving his bosom friend **Proteus**, who wants to stay in Verona to be near his beloved **Julia**. Julia's maid **Lucetta** brings her a letter from Proteus, but Julia is ambivalent about the suit, tearing the letter up and then attempting to reassemble it. She writes back to Proteus, but as he is reading it, his father **Antonio** decides to send him to the Milanese court. In Milan, Valentine has fallen rapidly in love with **Silvia**. Proteus and Julia are parted but exchange rings and vows of fidelity. Proteus' comic servant **Lance** recalls his own teary farewell to his family, to an unmoved dog **Crab**. Silvia's father the **Duke** favours **Turio** as her suitor. When Proteus arrives in Milan and is introduced to Silvia, he too falls in love with her, and decides to reveal his rival Valentine's intention to elope with her to her father. The Duke finds that Valentine has the rope ladder to spirit Silvia from her chamber, and banishes him. Meanwhile, Julia ignores Lucetta's misgivings and prepares to follow Proteus in male disguise. Proteus agrees to persuade Silvia of Turio's attractions, hoping to win her for himself, and Lance tells Speed about a milkmaid he has fallen for. In the forest, Valentine and Speed are ambushed by outlaws. Having impressed them, Valentine becomes their leader. The disguised Julia ('Sebastian') sees Proteus attempt to woo Silvia after Turio has left; Silvia decides to follow Valentine with the help of her friend Sir **Eglamour**. After a contretemps with Lance, Proteus employs 'Sebastian' as a messenger to send the ring given to him by Julia to Silvia. Silvia refuses, and pities Julia, not knowing the identity of the messenger. She and Eglamour flee to the forest, and are followed by Julia, Turio and Proteus. Proteus rescues Silvia from the outlaws, but she continues to reject his suit, which he presses more and more aggressively, unaware that Valentine is watching. Valentine intervenes to rescue Silvia, Proteus is repentant, and Valentine agrees that he can have Silvia after all. Julia faints and her identity is discovered; Proteus relinquishes Silvia and is reunited with Julia. The outlaws bring the captive Duke and Turio, who withdraws his claim to Silvia. Her father consents to the marriage with Valentine, and pardons all the outlaws.

Context and composition

Two Gentlemen is one of Shakespeare's earliest plays, perhaps dating from around 1590. While it shares some of the interest in same-sex friendships challenged by opposite-sex romance that animates *The Merchant of Venice* or *Much Ado About Nothing*, it is closer to Shakespeare's late play *Two Noble Kinsmen* and to the courtly comedies of John Lyly during the 1580s than it is to Shakespeare's later comedies. In particular, Lyly's popular prose story *Euphues* (1578), the story of inseparable friends parted by a woman, seems to be influential, and the darkness of tone and abruptness of resolution in Shakespeare's play may reflect his difficulties in transforming Lyly's own ending, in which the woman is ultimately sacrificed to preserve the friendship. Shakespeare also draws on a Spanish prose romance by Jorge de Montemayor, on Ovid's *Metamorphoses*, Sir Thomas Eliot's *The Book of the Governor* and on Arthur Brooke's poem, used extensively for *Romeo and Juliet*, *Romeus and Juliet*: the theatrically popular scenes of Lance and his dog Crab seem to be Shakespearean inventions.

Performances

There are no early records of performance, but it is often assumed that the Lord Chamberlain's Men's chief comic actor, Will Kemp, took the role of Lance. The play has the smallest cast of any of Shakespeare's plays (fourteen

named roles). Scenes from it, particularly of Lance and Crab, are prominent in *Shakespeare in Love* (dir. John Madden, 1998), and may indeed capture its early popularity: Lance and Crab continue to be the highlights of the play for most modern reviewers. It has not, however, had an unbroken history on the stage since then, and has had relatively few successful revivals in modern times. Productions have tended to stress the youth of the protagonists to make some sort of sense of their abrupt changes of behaviour: Ian Richardson as a short Proteus in Robin Phillips' 1970 version suggested adolescent spite as his main motivation. Rachel Kavanaugh set her outdoor production in 2003 in the Regency period; Ian Talbot envisaged the lovers as shallow bright young things in a busy Edwardian setting (1987), and this context also shaped David Thacker's RSC 1991 musical production with Cole Porter and George Gershwin countering some of the improbabilities of the febrile plot: one reviewer noted the deft depiction of the lovers as 'a generation lounging insouciantly between two world wars'. A provocatively modern take on the play's inscription of male friendship was offered by Stuart Draper (Greenwich Playhouse, 2004), who began the play with Valentine and Proteus embracing passionately under a tree and reciting Christopher Marlowe's 'Come live with me and be my love'.

Themes and interpretation

As with other of Shakespeare's early plays, *The Two Gentlemen of Verona* has suffered from the assumption that it is immature or slight. In fact it may be more appropriate to see the play as being *about* immaturity rather than itself immature: in presenting the swiftness of falling in love, the Boy's Own adventure of outlaws in the wood, and the changeability of tempers, the play seems to anatomise the strengths and the follies of youth. It presents itself as a journey towards maturation, in which its characters negotiate their relationships with parents (Proteus and his father Antonio, Silvia and the Duke, even Lance's description of his leave-taking of his family, zanily illustrated by his two shoes), and their progress towards romantic partnerships: a kind of rite-of-passage play, focused on the formation of adult males. While we tend now to think of romantic comedy as a genre particularly appealing to women, it is clear that the play, and all the others like it, was originally written with a male audience in mind. Its two eponymous gentlemen are types rather than people: their names suggest as much, with Valentine, the patron saint of lovers, as the constant lover who is rewarded, and Proteus, his name suggesting mutability and shape-shifting, the fickle one. Fickleness, however, proves more interesting than constancy: while Valentine has been idealised as the play's chivalric hero (in, for example, the pre-Raphaelite painter Holman Hunt's painting of 1851), it is Proteus' soliloquies and his sense of personal crisis that provide the play's sense of moral development, drawn from the play's heavily didactic sources.

Desire drives the play: from Proteus' changing and ultimately violent passions, to Julia's resilient and resourceful quest, and from Lance's blazon for his milkmaid love and Turio's attempts to woo Silvia with music and poetry. Desire feeds on lack and on rejection: Silvia's refusal to accept him inflames Proteus to rape; Julia sets out on her disguised journey to Milan immediately after we have seen

Proteus disavow her having met Silvia. And desire is quickly redirected or deflated. Interrupted by Valentine, the priapic Proteus subsides, even though, strangely, his friend rewards his disloyalty by offering him Silvia. Troublingly, in the play's twisted comic conclusion the two friends seem more alike than different, with both Proteus' attempted rape and Valentine's renunciation of his love resulting from a view of Silvia as owned property rather than autonomous person.

In part these shifts result from the idealisation of women: Silvia is like the mistress in a sonnet sequence or troubadour song, distant and perfect, as the song 'Who is Silvia? What is she?' (4.2.37) suggests. Julia is more active in asserting herself and her desires, but she, too, is constrained by male expectations of female behaviour. Only when dressed as Sebastian does Proteus see her as competent and useful, but, like Viola in *Twelfth Night*, Julia finds herself undertaking the role of go-between in her own betrayal. Part of Lance and Speed's role is to puncture the inflated tendency towards courtly love idiom and to bring out its self-regarding absurdity. Crab, in particular, is a comically unresponsive auditor. The scene in which Lance discusses Crab's misbehaviour stealing capon legs and 'pissing a while but all the chamber smelt him' (4.4.16–17), is well placed to undermine the courtly pretensions of the end of the previous scene, 'Sir Eglamour: Good morrow, gentle lady. Silvia: Good morrow, kind Sir Eglamour' (4.3.47–8). Crab's carnality also parodically anticipates Julia's meeting on Proteus' behalf with Silvia. Here, as elsewhere, the play is active in juxtaposing tones and plot lines to ironic effect.

The Two Noble Kinsmen

Key Facts

Date: 1613–14

Length: 3,169 lines

Verse: 95% / Prose: 5%

Major characters' share of lines:	
Palamon	18%
Arcite	16%
Emilia	11%
Theseus	10%
Jailer's Daughter	10%

Late collaborative tragi-comedy of love and death

Plot and characters

In procession to their wedding, **Theseus** and **Hippolyta** are interrupted by three **Queens** whose husbands have died fighting the wicked king Creon of Thebes and who have been denied burial. Hippolyta and her sister **Emilia** agree that the wedding should be postponed until Creon is defeated, and Theseus agrees. In Thebes, cousins **Palamon** and **Arcite**, Creon's nephews, prepare for battle. Having fought nobly but unsuccessfully, they are wounded and taken back to Athens as prisoners; the Queens are able to hold their funeral ceremonies. In the prison, a **Wooer** attempts to persuade the **Jailer** to give his **Daughter**'s hand. As Palamon and Arcite vow their eternal friendship, they both see Emilia and each falls instantly in love. They quarrel. Theseus releases Arcite and banishes him back to Thebes, but Arcite remains in disguise to be near Emilia; he wins a wrestling match and is made Emilia's master of horse by **Pirithous**. The Jailer's Daughter, in love with Palamon, arranges his escape, and follows him into the woods. **Gerald** the schoolmaster rehearses a troupe of morris dancers, and recruits the Jailer's Daughter to perform their dance before Theseus and his party. When Palamon and Arcite meet they agree that they must settle their rivalry through a duel, but Theseus' arrival interrupts this: he initially sentences them to death but is persuaded by Hippolyta and Emilia – who is unable to choose between her two lovers – to let the combat go ahead. Theseus sets a date three months hence, with the loser to be immediately executed. The Wooer tells the Jailer how he has found his Daughter roaming mad in the woods; she enters, raving. A **Doctor** suggests that the Wooer pretend to be Palamon to cure her, and so he takes her away to bed. At the combat, Palamon and Arcite, each accompanied by three **Knights**, pray to Venus and Mars respectively; Emilia prays to Diana, but cannot bear to watch the combat. After a close fight, Arcite wins; Palamon leaves his money to the Jailer for the Daughter's dowry. Just as he is about to be executed, Pirithous gives the news that Arcite has been thrown from his horse, and, as he dies Arcite bestows Emilia on Palamon.

Context and composition

Like *Henry VIII* and – probably – the lost *Cardenio*, *The Two Noble Kinsmen* was collaboratively written with John Fletcher, in around 1613–14. It was not included in the First Folio of Shakespeare's works, and was first published in 1634 and advertised under both playwrights' names, 'written by the memorable worthies of their time' (Shakespeare had died in 1616; Fletcher in 1625). Scholars who have seen collaborative writing as a process of division have identified the beginning and end of the play – the Theseus narrative and the establishment and conclusion of the rivalry between Palamon and Arcite – as distinctively Shakespearean, and the middle as attributable to Fletcher, but it may be more appropriate to see the whole play as a joint effort. The play's source is the opening story in *The Canterbury Tales*, 'The Knight's Tale' by Chaucer, as the prologue declares: the subplot of the Jailer's Daughter is invented, and recalls Ophelia's madness in *Hamlet*. The treatment of Theseus' interrupted wedding recalls *A Midsummer Night's Dream*; the conscious medieval source the use of Gower in *Pericles*; the play's stylistic variety at times echoes the earlier romantic comedies such as *The Two Gentlemen of Verona*, and at others the spectacle and prophetic quality of the late romances such as *The Winter's Tale*. Our tendency to focus on the Shakespeareanness of the play can lead to us ignoring its strong connections with Fletcher's work, particularly his tragedy *Valentinian* or *The Faithful Shepherdess*, his pastoral tragi-comedy, which defined the term for contemporary readers in its introduction.

Performances

The first edition of the play states that it was performed at Blackfriars, the King's Men's indoor theatre, and its reliance on the visual elements and on music allies it with the repertoire of that location.

Although the play was reworked, like so many, in the Restoration period – a time at which Fletcher's own dramatic stock was probably highest – it may be one of the least familiar plays in the contemporary theatre, and the one that theatregoers are most likely to come to in genuine uncertainty about how its plot will be resolved. Barry Kyle's landmark production at the Swan Theatre in Stratford in 1986 made sense of the play's ritualised scenes of love and honour with a Japanese-inspired set, and in its conclusion memorably juxtaposed a maddened Imogen Stubbs (Jailer's Daughter) with the poised mourning of Amanda Harris as Emilia. This stress on the play's female characters has been a feature of its recent stage history and of critical interest. Tim Carroll's 2000 production at the Globe was dominated by an image of chivalry, a tower mounted with a horse's head, which was lowered and raised to indicate the play's changing mood. A darker side to the play's homosocial rivalry was suggested by the all-male Cherub Theatre (1979), with its bitter tone and fetish costumes.

Themes and interpretation

With two writers, two heroes and (at least) two genres, it is not surprising that the doubled vision of *The Two Noble Kinsmen* has divided critics. Like Emilia faced with two pictures, or Palamon and Arcite consecrating their labours to two altars and two goddesses, the play's duplication now seems less, as earlier accounts tended to feel, the inevitable fractured result of co-authorship and instead a chosen technique for exploring the new genre of tragi-comedy. *The Two Noble Kinsmen* looks back to Shakespeare's earlier romantic comedies and stretches retrospection further to the medievalism of its Chaucerian source and the classicism of that plot, while still being a fashionable example of romance for Blackfriars audiences. There is a tone of yearning throughout, and in particular for a past uncontaminated by adult concerns. The play develops the theme seen, for example, in *Much Ado About Nothing* or *The Merchant of Venice* – that same-sex friendships are violently disrupted by heterosexual marriage – and amplifies it. This is revealed not only in the intimacy of Palamon and Arcite, who acclaim their friendship in prison seconds before they both spot Emilia, the cause of their fatal rift, but also in Emilia's own report of her girlhood soulmate Flavinia, which proves 'the true love 'tween maid and maid may be / More than in sex dividual' (1.3.181–2). Emilia's own refusal or inability to choose between her two suitors, like the fact that Theseus and Hippolyta's courtship has already happened by the time the play begins, means that there is not a central, parted romantic couple whose union is the focus of the play, and, as the play's title suggests, that narrative space is tragically filled by Palamon and Arcite. Emilia's final acceptance of Palamon after the sudden death of Arcite is hardly the conclusion to a high love affair: 'thou wert a right good man, and while I live, / This day I give to tears' (5.4.96–7). Likewise, Arcite's deathbed transference of Emilia to his rival friend suggests that women are tokens of affection between men rather than desirable in their own right: Arcite's abrupt 'take her. I die' (5.4.93) is more important as a symbol of male reconciliation than of romantic marriage. Similarly, the unrequited love which drives the Jailer's Daughter into madness can never be healed, and the doctor's prescription that the unnamed Wooer have sex with her in the name of Palamon rather suggests instead the therapeutic interchangeability of suitors as an antidote to tragic singularity. There is some connection here with the play's own switch of allegiances and its flirtation with different genres, and the Prologue's opening line makes the equivalence clear: 'New plays and maidenheads are near akin' (Prologue, 1).

The Two Noble Kinsmen is structured around static display, often indicated by lengthy descriptive stage directions. The interrupted wedding procession at the opening, in which the three queens intervene like a mourning chorus, is an indicative example of the play's stagecraft, perhaps drawing, like other of Shakespeare's late plays, on the formal aesthetic of James' favoured court masques. Set pieces like the dance of the countrymen, including a 'baboon', or the careful choreography before the altar of Venus where '*music is heard, doves are seen to flutter. They fall again on their faces, then on their knees*' give the energy of the lunatic Jailer's Daughter a particular dramatic power. In recent accounts of the play she has seemed one of its most interesting features. But the play seems to make it clear that this is less a drama of psychological protagonists and more a stylised visual pageant of feeling, particularly the irrational currents of sexual longing, externalised into action and props. Killed by his horse, a traditional symbol of passion, Arcite can be seen, like the Daughter, as a casualty of his own desire. The Epilogue invites approval from audience members who have 'loved a young handsome wench', noting ''tis strange if none be here': the play's valedictory address to the homosocial world of the Jacobean indoor theatres is the last piece in its complicated depiction of the intersection of sex, friendship and desire.

Venus and Adonis

Erotic narrative poem in which the goddess
Venus chases the reluctant youth Adonis

Synopsis

Adonis is out hunting when he is accosted by Venus, who pulls him
from his horse and, despite his protests, kisses him vehemently.
Adonis is unmoved by her actions or her rhetorical seduction, but
when, after some hours, he attempts to escape Venus his horse goes in
pursuit of a mare, leaving him stranded. Venus continues her
attempts at persuasion; Adonis is unmoved, but when Venus faints
he attempts to revive her with kisses. Finally he is able to leave, saying
he cannot meet her the next day because he will be out hunting boar.
The next day Venus encounters the bloodied boar, and finds that
Adonis has been killed by it. As she apostrophises his beautiful
corpse, it transforms into a purple flower, which she vows to cherish.
She returns to Cyprus to mourn her love.

Context and composition

Written and first printed in 1593, *Venus and Adonis* was a huge
popular success. It was widely reprinted and cited approvingly in
early modern culture. It forms part of the fashionable contemporary
genre of epyllion (miniature epic) – poems on erotic subjects inspired
by Ovid's *Metamorphoses* intended for a clever, satirical young male
readership, which also included Christopher Marlowe's *Hero and
Leander* and Thomas Lodge's *Scilla's Metamorphosis*. A student play
at Cambridge in 1598 cites the poem frequently, and elsewhere it is
mentioned by moralists and other writers.

Shakespeare dedicated these 'unpolished lines' to the Earl of
Southampton, Henry Wriothesley, calling the poem 'the first heir of
my invention' and promising 'some graver labour' (presumably the

tragic poem *The Rape of Lucrece*, dedicated to Southampton when it was published the following year) should it prove a success. As for the later poem, the source is Ovid: Shakespeare consulted both the original Latin and the influential translation by Arthur Golding (1567). Not only does he expand the story exponentially – taking almost 1,200 lines to treat a narrative given only 75 by Ovid, but he also significantly changes its focus. Only Shakespeare's Adonis is the unwilling adolescent object of Venus' desire: in Ovid, Venus' passion, caused by Cupid in error, is reciprocated by her young lover. The comedy of this unrequited passion is therefore Shakespearean. The poem's closest cousin is its dark obverse, *The Rape of Lucrece*, where erotic pursuit is distinctly uncomic, but in the theatre it may be that another powerfully erotic heroine, Cleopatra, draws on some of the energy of Venus (Enobarbus in *Antony and Cleopatra* describes the Egyptian queen as 'o'er-picturing...Venus' [2.2.120]).

The poem consists of 199 stanzas of six lines, each of which rhymes a-b-a-b-c-c.

Themes and interpretation

It is clear that *Venus and Adonis* is a poem written by a playwright – and by a comic playwright who enjoys dialogue, soliloquy and innuendo. Venus and Adonis squabble and fail to communicate like dramatic characters. Rhetoric is one of the great dilatory pleasures of the poem, as words and figures proliferate to consume time just like erotic dalliance. Tropes of contradiction and paradox are particularly active in capturing the simultaneity of erotic desire and disdain. Venus and Adonis' encounter is set against a rural world which is so far from the urban audience for whom it was intended and so realistically naturally detailed that some critics have felt this is the work in which the young Warwickshire writer is closest to his country roots. On the other hand, the setting in the poem is, as in melodrama, merely an amplification or externalisation of the febrile emotional states of its protagonists. What is sometimes called pathetic fallacy – the attribution of empathetic human emotions to nature – is a common device in the poem. As Adonis' corpse bleeds on the sward, 'no flower was nigh, no grass, herb, leaf, or weed, / But stole his blood, and seemed with him to bleed' (1055–6).

The section – invented by Shakespeare – in which Adonis' stallion chases lustily after a 'jennet' (female horse) is a good example. Eleven stanzas are spent on a description of Adonis' horse, and by the end of this rhetorical excursus the beast is as erotically overdetermined as its rider. A series of double entendre observations about 'his ears up-pricked' (271) and 'thick tail, broad buttock, tender hide' (298) make it clear that the horse, like his master, is an object of desire, even while it identifies the stallion's pursuit of the mare who is 'proud, as females are' (309) as a more orthodox courtship than that of Venus and her reluctant swain. Here it is Adonis who takes on the role of the unreachable love object traditionally allocated in amorous poetry to the woman (see 'The Sonnets' above). The libidinous horse, like the fruitful nature described in the wood, is a comic reproach to Adonis for his sulky pride, just as it draws on the metaphorical association of a ridden horse with man's passions. Dragged from his mount, Adonis is humorously passive – neither mastering his desires nor subject to them, but apparently indifferent. When Venus attempts to lure this young man who is more interested in hunting than in love goddesses, she exclaims: 'I'll be a park and thou shalt be my deer: / Feed where thou wilt, on mountain or in dale' (231–2). The landscape becomes the eroticised body: Adonis' fixation on hunting is both a version and a displacement of Venus' pursuit of him.

The darker side of this analogy between hunter and hunted becomes clear in Adonis' death. The boar's tusks have pierced Adonis in a grotesque parody of fatal sexual penetration: 'nuzzling in his flank, the loving swine / Sheathed unaware the tusk in his soft groin' (1115–16). Adonis' erotic passivity and Venus' transgressively active wooing have their physical embodiment, and Venus admits that it is her desire that is ultimately lethal: 'Had I been toothed like him, I must confess / With kissing him I should have killed him first' (1117–18).

In the poem's final stanzas the shape-shifting associated with Ovid re-emerges. 'A purple flower ... chequered with white' (1168) replaces the beloved body of Adonis – a flower that inevitably, Venus 'crops' (1175) so she can take it off to Paphos with her. The objectification of Adonis is complete.

The Winter's Tale

Key Facts

Date: 1609–10

Length: 3,369 lines

Verse: 75% / Prose: 25%

Major characters' share of lines:	
Leontes	20%
Paulina	10%
Camillo	9%
Autolycus	9%
Polixenes	8%

Late tragi-comedy of loss and resurrection

Plot and characters

Leontes, King of Sicilia, wants his wife **Hermione** to persuade his boyhood friend King **Polixenes** of Bohemia to extend his stay with them. He becomes jealous of their closeness, and wonders whether his son **Mamillius** is really his. He commands **Camillo** to murder Polixenes, but Camillo tells him to escape, and goes with him to Bohemia. Their flight is seen as an indication of their guilt, and Leontes pursues his mad jealousy, accusing Hermione of adultery and having her imprisoned pending a trial. He sends **Cleomenes** and **Dion** to Apollo's oracle at Delphos to determine her guilt. He ignores his noblemen who try to defend the Queen. In prison Hermione gives birth to a baby girl, and the redoubtable **Paulina** takes it to Leontes to soften his heart. Instead he threatens both with death, and, relenting, sends **Antigonus** to sea to abandon the child outside the kingdom. Cleomenes and Dion return from the oracle as Hermione is put on trial. She eloquently denies the accusations of adultery and treason, and the messengers from the oracle reveal that she is innocent. Leontes refuses to believe it, but when news comes that Mamillius has died, and Hermione faints, he repents his jealousy. Paulina informs him that Hermione has died, and he promises to mourn his dead wife and child in perpetuity. Antigonus arrives on the Bohemian coast, having heard Hermione's ghost in a dream telling him he will not see his wife Paulina again, and that the baby should be named **Perdita**. He leaves it and is chased away by a bear which kills and eats him. The baby is found by a **Shepherd** and his rustic son, **Clown**, and they take her away. The figure of Time indicates that sixteen years have passed and the scene has moved to Bohemia. Camillo and Polixenes disguise themselves on receiving news that Prince **Florizel** is in love with a shepherdess, and discover him pretending to be 'Doricles' at the sheep-shearing feast, where he promises to marry Perdita. The pedlar **Autolycus** tricks the Clown with a sob story and picks his pocket. **Mopsa** and **Dorcas** quarrel for the Clown's affections. There is much merriment and dancing, including a dance of twelve satyrs. Polixenes angrily reveals himself when Florizel makes to marry without consulting him, but despite his father's disapproval Florizel is adamant. Camillo persuades the couple to escape to Sicilia; changing clothes with Autolycus, Florizel takes Perdita to Leontes' court. When Polixenes and Camillo follow, Leontes agrees to help smooth the situation, but it is revealed that Perdita is Leontes' lost child. Under Paulina's direction they go to the chapel to see a statue of Hermione, which comes to life and is reunited with Leontes, who asks her pardon and that of Polixenes, and who joins Paulina and Camillo in marriage.

Context and composition

The play was probably composed in 1609–10, and is connected stylistically with *Pericles* and *Cymbeline*. It was first printed in 1623. *The Winter's Tale* takes as its source Robert Greene's prose romance *Pandosto, or the Triumph of Time* (1588); its most deliberate change is in the ending. Greene's Pandosto (Leontes) falls in love with his daughter before he realises they are related, and is so disgusted by his desires once this is revealed that he kills himself in shame; there is no return of Bellaria (Hermione); and the two locations have been switched to make Pandosto King of Bohemia. There is no equivalent of Autolycus nor of the sheep-shearing festive scenes. Giulio Romano, the sculptor of Hermione's statue, is a real artist although not a sculptor (he was infamous for some widely circulated pornographic images); the chapel/art gallery may have been inspired by James I's erection of memorial statues of Elizabeth I and his mother, Mary Stuart, in Westminster Abbey. The bear may have been inspired by the polar bears in Ben Jonson's *Masque of Oberon* (1610), or by the more general fascination with these animals after James was presented with bear cubs by explorers of the North American coast.

As a plot that draws in two generations and requires an infant's maturation to the threshold of marriage for its resolution, *The Winter's Tale* echoes *The Tempest* (but it has a very different way of encapsulating this long time scheme), just as Perdita's reunion with her father – described here rather than shown – recalls the moving scene at the end of *Pericles*. The pastoral sequence of Act 4 recalls *As You Like It*; jealous husbands appear in *Othello*, *The Merry Wives of Windsor* and *Cymbeline*: as here, in each case the jealousy is misplaced.

Performances

Unusually, we have an account of an early performance at the Globe in May 1611. Simon Forman, astrologer and doctor, was impressed by Autolycus

cozening the rustics and changing clothes with Florizel: he does not mention Hermione's statue or anything about the play's ending. The play was performed at court several times during the Stuart period, but during the eighteenth century only its pastoral scenes were popular. Recent productions have tended to stress the play's losses as well as its restoration. Edward Hall's 2005 Propeller production was haunted by Mamillius (Tam Williams also played Perdita), and the last image was of him, pyjama-clad, staring angrily at his father; David Farr's production (RSC, 2009) ended the Sicilia sequence with the unstoppable destruction of the tall bookcases on either side of the stage: the second half took place amid piles of reading matter worthless to prevent Leontes' madness; a chilling ending to the Maly Theatre of St Petersburg production directed by Declan Donnellan (1999) had the child Mamillius insinuate himself between his reunited parents as the ghost at the feast. No film exists except Jane Howell's BBC version (1980), although long extracts of and discussions about Greg Doran's 1999 production with Antony Sher are available on an RSC DVD.

Themes and interpretation

What does it signify about *The Winter's Tale* that its most famous line is – uniquely – a stage direction: '*exit, pursued by a bear*' (3.3.56)? In part, the line echoes because of its laconic combination of random absurdity and unemotional narration. But it is also a crucial hinge in the plot: the agent of the play's final death, that of Antigonus, also ushers in a new comic mode: it seems unlikely that the bear could possibly have been a real one, and a man in a bear suit is always funny rather than terrifying. The bear's pursuit joins a series of other handbrake turns as the play attempts to change its direction from intensely psychological tragedy towards redemptive comedy: like Time, who shifts us chronologically, the ship, shifting us geographically, and the Shepherd and his son, who shift us rhythmically from tragic verse into comic prose, the bear represents the play's movement between genres, as it grafts a comic second half on to an apparently powerfully complete tragedy.

In part the play goes through these generic contortions because its question – what happens after tragedy – is a genuinely new one for Shakespeare. Tragic heroes such as King Lear or Hamlet do not get a second chance: realising he, like Leontes (as he thinks) has killed his wife through jealousy, Othello prefers suicide over the more mundane protraction of lasting grief and guilt. For Leontes, however, there is redemption through suffering: his acknowledgement 'tears . . . / Shall be my recreation' (3.2.236–7) evokes both recreation as pastime and as the more substantive re-creation. The play moves from winter into the fertility rites of rustic Bohemia: Perdita, banished from Sicilia and crowned Queen of the Feast, seems a kind of Proserpine/Persephone, captured by Hades to spend half the year on earth and half in the underworld.

The Winter's Tale moves towards two conclusions. One is expected: the comic marriage, by which the union of the younger generation can heal the crack in the older. This plot suggests that the most significant emotional breach is that between Leontes and Polixenes, those 'twinned lambs that did frisk i'th'sun' (1.2.66): male friendship interrupted by women is a constant theme of Shakespeare's comedies, including, for example, *Much Ado About Nothing* or *The Two Noble Kinsmen*. It is, after all, initially unclear whether Leontes' jealousy most concerns his best friend whom he cannot persuade to extend his stay, or his wife, who can.

The second plot is a more unexpected one: the return of Hermione, counter to the story that Shakespeare inherited from his source in Robert Greene, and a plot which suggests that the rupture between husband and wife is the one the comedy must seek to heal. Although Paulina keeps a mystery about her statue, it seems clear that Hermione's return is not the result of magic, as Leontes fears, but of plotting: 'I . . . have preserved / Myself to see the issue' (5.3.127–8). It is almost the first time in Shakespeare's career that an important plot point has been kept from the usually knowing audience: nothing in the language of the play suggests to us that Paulina's report of Hermione's death is untrue, and the later appearance of Hermione as a ghost to Antigonus would seem to corroborate the fact. The ending of the play is thus loaded with two versions of comedy – romantic and recuperative. Paulina's stage management of the final scene leaves little space for the protagonists to articulate their feelings. Hermione only addresses her daughter, not her husband; Leontes busies himself more with Paulina's marriage than with his recovered family, and there is, of course, no explicit mention of Mamillius, the real sacrifice of Leontes' jealous rage, whom many recent theatre directors have brought back into the frame at the play's conclusion.

THE CONTEXT

Shakespeare's life

William Shakespeare was born in Stratford-upon-Avon, Warwickshire in April 1564: tradition has it that his birthday is 23 April, St George's Day, but the only detail we have is that he was baptised on 26 April 1564 in Holy Trinity Church in Stratford. Shakespeare's father, John, was a prominent citizen and a glover, living in Henley Street, Stratford. We know little of Shakespeare's early life: he almost certainly went to the town's grammar school, where he would have learned grammar and rhetoric, using textbooks including plays by Terence and Plautus, rhetorical treatises by Cicero and poetry by Ovid, which can be seen to influence his later writing. There is no evidence that Shakespeare attended university.

In November 1582, aged 18, he married Anne Hathaway, daughter of a local farmer. It is likely that she was already pregnant – as were many Elizabethan brides, partly due to different customs about betrothal and marriage – because their first child, Susanna, was baptised in May 1583. Twins, Hamnet and Judith, were born in 1585. (Hamnet died in 1596.)

We do not know what Shakespeare was doing for most of the 1580s: he turns up on the London literary and theatrical scene in a snide remark by the dramatist Robert Greene, who called him an 'upstart crow' in a 1592 publication. The so-called 'lost years' of Shakespeare's life have been inventively filled by biographical speculation: for those who maintain Shakespeare was a Catholic, for example, this is the period during which he served as schoolmaster to a northern recusant family; for those who enjoy romantic stories he left Warwickshire to avoid prosecution for poaching deer in Charlecote Park; for others he is picked up to supply a providential gap in a touring theatre company. Like many other ambitious young men of the period, he moves to the rapidly expanding metropolis to pursue his career, leaving the family behind in Stratford.

Shakespeare's early plays in London included *Henry VI*, *The Two Gentlemen of Verona* and *The Taming of the Shrew*. His first works in print – and the works for which he was probably most famous during his lifetime – were poetry rather than plays: the fashionable Ovidian *Venus and Adonis* (1593) and *The Rape of Lucrece* (1594), both dedicated to the young courtier the Earl of Southampton. In 1594 he joined a new company under the patronage of the Lord Chamberlain as sharer and resident playwright, and from then on he wrote exclusively for the company. He also worked as an actor in his own plays and those of other writers, including Ben Jonson's *Every Man in his Humour* (1598); he is listed at the top of the list of the King's Men printed in the First Folio of his works.

Both Shakespeare and the company prospered: Shakespeare bought property in Stratford and his father was granted a coat-of-arms which he inherited at John Shakespeare's death in 1601. His name was increasingly used to sell his – and sometimes other people's – plays, and is noted as 'among our best' for comedy and tragedy in a book by Francis Meres in 1598. The company built a new, state-of-the-art theatre on London's Bankside, the Globe, in 1599, were given the patronage of James I on his accession to the English throne in 1603 and became the King's Men, and acquired a new indoor theatre, Blackfriars, in 1609. Broadly speaking, Shakespeare wrote comedies and English history plays in the 1590s, and turned towards tragedy and the newly fashionable genre of tragi-comedy in the first decade of the seventeenth century. The dates of his works, many of them conjectural, are listed in the Chronology.

At the end of his career Shakespeare collaborated with his successor with the King's Men, John Fletcher. He seems to have largely retired from the theatre in around 1611, to live in Stratford, although in 1613 he bought property in London's Blackfriars by the theatre and his last collaborations with Fletcher date from 1613–14. He died on 23 April 1616 and was buried in Holy Trinity Church. The painted funerary monument, which can still be seen in the church today, must have been erected shortly afterwards.

We know very little about Shakespeare the private man, either from personal documents or from the works themselves, although this has not stopped people trying to deduce what he might have been like. Even the likeness of the familiar balding portrait at the front of his posthumous collected dramatic works, the First Folio of 1623, has been contested. Shakespeare's works are not biographical in any obvious sense: he writes in a form – drama – in which different perspectives and characters must have equal claims on our attention; he writes in an age which would be bewildered by the confessional turn in modern writing; and he writes commercially for a public theatre with an insatiable appetite for new plays. Claims that he retained the old religion of Roman Catholicism, or that he was gay, or that he was politically conservative, or whatever, tend to reveal more about the priorities of the speaker than the subject: Shakespeare's stock is so high that to recruit him to your ideological team is a real coup.

Chronology

For the plays, the dates are given in the form of date of putative performance and date of first publication. The poems are given their publication date.

1590; 1623	*The Two Gentlemen of Verona*
1590–1; 1594	*King Henry VI Part 2* [first published as *The First Part of the Contention of the Two Famous Houses of York and Lancaster*]
1591–2; 1595	*King Henry VI Part 3* [first published as *The True Tragedy of Richard Duke of York*]
1591–2; 1623	*The Taming of the Shrew*
1592; 1623	*King Henry VI Part 1* [? with Thomas Nashe]
1592–3; 1598	*King Richard III*
1593	*Venus and Adonis*
1593–4; 1594	*Titus Andronicus* [? with George Peele]
1594	*The Rape of Lucrece*
1594; 1623	*The Comedy of Errors*
1595; 1597	*King Richard II*

1595–6; 1597	*Romeo and Juliet*
1595–6; 1600	*A Midsummer Night's Dream*
1595–6; 1598	*Love's Labour's Lost*
1596; 1623	*King John*
1596–7; 1598	*King Henry IV Part 1*
1596–7; 1600	*The Merchant of Venice*
1597–8; 1602	*The Merry Wives of Windsor*
1597–8; 1600	*King Henry IV Part 2*
1598–9; 1600	*Much Ado About Nothing*
1599; 1623	*Julius Caesar*
1599; 1600	*King Henry V*
1599	*The Passionate Pilgrim* – including works by Richard Barnfield, Christopher Marlowe and others
1599–1600; 1623	*As You Like It*
1600; 1603	*Hamlet*
1601; 1623	*Twelfth Night, or What You Will*
1601	'The Phoenix and the Turtle', in Robert Chester's *Love's Martyr, or Rosalind's Complaint*
1602; 1609	*Troilus and Cressida*
1603–4; 1622	*Othello*
1604; 1623	*Measure for Measure*
1604–5; 1623	*All's Well that Ends Well*
1605–6; 1623	*Timon of Athens* [with Thomas Middleton]
1605–6, revised 1610; 1608, 1623	*King Lear*
1606; 1623	*Macbeth*
1606; 1623	*Antony and Cleopatra*
1607–8; 1609	*Pericles* [with George Wilkins]
1608; 1623	*Coriolanus*
1609	*The Sonnets* and 'A Lover's Complaint'
1609–10; 1623	*The Winter's Tale*
1610; 1623	*Cymbeline*
1611; 1623	*The Tempest*

1613; 1623	*King Henry VIII, or All is True* [with John Fletcher]
1613; lost and unpublished	*Cardenio* [with John Fletcher]
1613–14; 1634	*The Two Noble Kinsmen* [with John Fletcher]

The 'authorship question'

The suggestion that Shakespeare of Stratford was not the true author of the plays and poems attributed to him – the so-called 'authorship question' – has been intermittent since the nineteenth century. During his lifetime and after his death no one questioned that Shakespeare wrote the works. Although many different candidates, from Christopher Marlowe to Queen Elizabeth to Francis Bacon, have since been proposed as alternative authors, most sceptical investigations share a disbelief that a man who had such limited formal education, who apparently never travelled outside England, and who had no grand connections with the court could possibly have written plays drawing extensively on historical and classical sources, set in different countries and steeped in an understanding of politics and law. Faced with the biographical facts of Shakespeare's life it has seemed easier to correlate the man with the plays when a different man is identified: usually a nobleman whose social and intellectual access to learning is assured.

But while there *is* a real mystery about Shakespeare's authorship, the traditional authorship question tends to mislocate it. The issue is less how did Shakespeare know about Venice when he never went there (answer: he read about it) or how could Shakespeare understand squabbling nobles at court (answer: perhaps their jealousies and politicking were not all that different from the civic bureaucracy in which his father served in Stratford) but rather, how did the commercial theatre produce plays of such extraordinary linguistic and emotional complexity? How could anyone – of whatever social standing – write works that continue to generate new performances and critical insights? The mystery here is not solved by substituting any one author by another: perhaps, as Jonathan Bate has suggested in his *The Genius of Shakespeare* (1997), the invention of the concept of 'genius', with Shakespeare as its first exemplar, is a better attempt to explain the mystery than the substitution of another potential author in place of the one we have.

Shakespeare's theatre

Purpose-built theatres were an Elizabethan invention. The opening in 1567 of the Red Lion, the first playhouse building, began a process which would transform the travelling mode of medieval drama into a fixed, commercially successful and artistically innovative London industry. As with any new technology, there were anxieties about this project: Puritan preachers claimed that the theatre inculcated immoral behaviour, the London authorities feared that large gatherings of theatregoers were a cover for criminality and disorder, and the office of the Master of the Revels, who authorised plays for performance and for publication, increased in power over the period. But when in 1599 the Lord Chamberlain's Men, and their resident playwright Shakespeare, called their new, state-of-the-art theatre on the south bank of the Thames 'the Globe', there was no mistaking their ambition.

Jaques' famous 'All the world's a stage' speech in *As You Like It* gestures to a serious contemporary equivalence between theatre and life. As Sir Walter Ralegh put it, life is a 'short comedy' with 'Heaven the judicious sharp spectator': 'only we die in earnest – that's no jest'; both Queen Elizabeth and James acknowledged the inherent theatricality of the role of the monarch; and describing an actor, John Webster admitted that 'all men have been of his occupation'. The conventional opposition is not, as we might expect, between acting and real life, but between the professional and the amateur in a histrionic world where all are performing. It recalls York's description of the difference between the crowd's reception of the disgraced King Richard and his challenger Bullingbrook: 'as in a theatre the eyes of men / After a well-graced actor leaves the stage / Are idly bent on him that enters next, / Thinking his prattle to be tedious' (5.2.23–6). Frequent self-conscious comments like this make clear that the theatre is rarely illusionistic in this period, and, rather, reflects explicitly on its own material form.

Theatre design

Theatre construction exaggerated this equivalence between onstage and offstage drama. Outdoor, amphitheatre-style playhouses such as the Globe or the Rose attracted large audiences to daytime performances. There was no special lighting – hence those scenes set at night, such as the opening of *Hamlet*, where repeated linguistic indicators of darkness have to do the work visual techniques would do in a modern theatre – and sightlines meant that audiences as well as actors were always conscious of being surrounded by people. Soliloquies were probably directed explicitly out towards the audience, particularly to those standing in the yard around the thrust stage, rather than being presented as inner musings, as in film or more realist theatrical forms. Thus Hamlet's famous 'To be or not to be' speech may have taken on more of the quality of a genuine interrogative dialogue with the audience rather than the internal psychological tussle of the speech as presented in, for example, Olivier's 1948 film.

Actors

Clowns and other figures who interacted directly with the audience were popular: Richard Tarlton was a celebrity, and we know from the earliest printed text of *Much Ado About Nothing* that Will Kemp, the comic actor, was so identified with the role of Dogberry that the speech prefixes sometimes actually indicate his, rather than the character's, name. The most prominent tragic actor was Richard Burbage, son of the theatrical impresario James Burbage: an elegy on his death in 1619 included Richard III, Hamlet, Lear and Othello among his Shakespearean roles. Shakespeare is unusual among contemporary playwrights in writing consistently for a known company of actors: probably numbering about fourteen or fifteen, swelled by casual extras, but with most playing more than one part in a particular play. Doubling was both a practical necessity and also a means of structuring a play: in *A Midsummer Night's Dream*, for instance, the likely doubling of the terrestrial rulers Theseus and Hippolyta with their fairy counterparts Oberon and Titania is suggestive about the parallels, as well as the contrasts, between their worlds, and other doubling possibilities (the Fool and Cordelia in *King Lear*, or the two Dukes in *As You Like It*, or the ghost in *Hamlet* with Claudius) also add to the interpretation of the characters and their roles in the play.

Female roles

All actors were male, with female roles usually played by younger performers – youths, rather than children. The common trope in comedies of female characters dressing as men – Viola in *Twelfth Night*, Julia in *Two Gentlemen*, Imogen in *Cymbeline* – shows that the ambiguous possibilities of a transvestite theatre could be exploited for dramatic effect: Rosalind's epilogue at the end of *As You Like It* flirtatiously flits between a male speaking position – the actor – and a female – the character. Such titillating potential was one of the aspects of the theatre most troubling to its detractors: the theologian John Rainolds declared that 'the apparel of women is a great provocation of men to lust and lechery', and his fellow preacher Stephen Gosson likened the counterfeit female to 'the wreathings and windings of a snake'. Serious roles for women characters, however, such as Cleopatra, or Lady Macbeth, or Constance in *King John*, show that the prospect of men playing women's parts was not essentially comic, and that Shakespeare was confident in their ability to perform convincingly. Visiting the Venetian theatre early in the seventeenth century, the Jacobean traveller Thomas Coryate was pleasantly surprised that the women actors there were quite competent: 'they performed it with as good a grace, gesture and whatsoever convenient for a player as ever I saw any masculine actor'. His phrasing shows an untroubled acceptance of male superiority in all spheres, including female performance.

Props and scenery

One of the clichés about the early modern theatre is the idea of the bare stage, unadorned by props or scenery. That there was little or no large-scale scenery is true, and, rather than being a disadvantage this would have enabled a fluid and rapid transition between scenes in early modern performances. Small props – daggers, crowns, purses, gloves – are the most common currency of Shakespeare's stagecraft, but large props are sometimes necessary: tables for banquets, the bed at the end of *Othello*, for example, or the scaling ladders for the siege in *King Henry V*. Costumes, too, were an increasingly large expense: accounts do not exist for the Chamberlain's Men, but their rivals, the Admiral's Men under the management of Philip Henslowe, spent more on stage clothing than on scripts during the 1590s. New stage technology, and an aesthetic of elaboration derived from the court masques of James' circle, meant increasingly sophisticated special effects, such as the lowering of Jupiter from above the stage in *Cymbeline*. It may be that use of the indoor theatre of Blackfriars from 1609 encouraged these developments, although there is evidence that Shakespeare's late plays were performed both here and at the Globe. Indoor staging did mean that act breaks were observed, interrupting the continuous staging practices of the amphitheatre playhouses, because candles needed to be trimmed.

Audiences

One difference between Blackfriars and the Globe was cost, and therefore, audience. A penny gained entrance to the Globe theatre, with higher prices charged for seating in the covered galleries around the open yard, whereas the minimum entry to Blackfriars was sixpence. By way of comparison, a penny would buy two pints of beer. It is estimated that in the mid 1590s around 15,000 people would have attended theatre performances each week. The social range of audiences is difficult to demonstrate: it is assumed that Blackfriars had a more elite clientele than the Globe, and that a company like Shakespeare's, who were given the king's own patronage on his accession must, as the King's Men, have attracted some of the courtly audience for whom they also played at Whitehall. Blackfriars included the opportunity for gallants to sit on a stool on the stage for maximum visibility. Tourists, foreign ambassadors, citizens, city apprentices and students at the Inns of Court are all known to have attended the theatre in the period. There are relatively few references to women in the audience, and during the sixteenth century attendance at the theatre was linked with prostitution or sexual availability: contrary to popular myth, therefore, Queen Elizabeth would never have attended the public theatre. References from the second decade of the seventeenth century suggest that respectable women could attend the theatre by that time. Accounts of audience behaviour, largely derived from satirical literature or disapproving preachers, suggest high spirits and healthy disrespect were common collective responses to plays. We do not have any direct evidence for the reception of any of Shakespeare's plays, although the existence of a part 2 to the play first known only as *Henry IV* is testament to the popularity of his most abiding character, Falstaff. In a period hungry for new plays and in which the repertory system would give most scripts only single-figure performances over a period of a few weeks, audience demand was crucial to commercial success: it was a demand Shakespeare was adept at satisfying.

Shakespeare in print

Shakespeare's works have survived because they were printed. No manuscript exists of any of Shakespeare's works in his own handwriting or in any contemporary copy (although some scholars think he was responsible for writing a part of an unpublished manuscript play *The Book of Sir Thomas More*; see '*Shakespearean Apocrypha*' below). So it is impossible for us finally to determine exactly what Shakespeare wrote or how he revised it, or to know fully why and how some plays found their way into print, or to determine how far the texts we have register his own final thoughts, and how far they record intentional and accidental changes introduced by actors, scribes and printshop workers.

During his lifetime Shakespeare was probably best known for the two poems, based on Ovid, that he published in 1593 and 1594: *Venus and Adonis* and *The Rape of Lucrece*. *Venus and Adonis* went through fifteen editions by 1675; *Lucrece* eight editions: they are Shakespeare's best-sellers. Both poems were published by fellow Stratford migrant to London, the printer Richard Field – who has often been proposed as the source for some of Shakespeare's significant reading, since he also published Ovid, North's translation of Plutarch which was Shakespeare's source for his Roman plays, and Greene's *Pandosto*, the source for *The Winter's Tale*. Shakespeare probably wrote the poems while the theatres were closed because of the plague in 1592–3, and he dedicated them to Henry Wriothesley, the young Earl of Southampton. The date of Shakespeare's sonnets is more difficult to discern: there is a report of the circulation of Shakespeare's 'sugared sonnets among his private friends' in 1598, and two of the poems are printed in 1599 in the miscellany *The Passionate Pilgrim*. The collection is published in 1609, with a dedication apparently signed by the publisher Thomas Thorpe to 'Mr. W. H.', as 'the only begetter of these ensuing sonnets': there are many theories and speculations about the identity of this personage.

The publication of plays in this period is a different matter, not least because the rights to playscripts were held by acting companies rather than individual writers. The earliest play of Shakespeare's to be printed is *The First Part of the Contention* (later known as *King Henry VI Part 2*) in 1594; the most popular plays, by reprints, are *King Henry IV Part 1* (8 editions before 1640), *King King Richard III* (7) and *King Richard II* (6). The first play to be published with Shakespeare's name on the title page is *Love's Labour's Lost* in 1598; a flurry of books not now considered to be by Shakespeare suggest that they are, presumably for marketing purposes (e.g. *The London Prodigal*, 1605; *The Yorkshire Tragedy*, 1608). Seventeen of Shakespeare's plays were published during his lifetime, and one more, *Othello*, in 1622. These plays are all printed in quarto or octavo format – small, unbound single playbooks (the names signal that the paper is folded into four or eight respectively) of around forty pages, which probably retailed at sixpence.

In 1623 a posthumous collected edition of Shakespeare's plays was published, edited by two of his fellow actors with the King's Men, John Heminge and Henry Condell. This included the eighteen plays already printed and eighteen more: we would not have *Macbeth* or *The Tempest* or *Twelfth Night* were it not for this edition. It is known as the First Folio (there were second and third editions in 1632 and 1663/4), again signalling the paper size: a folio sheet is folded only once, and it was a luxury format associated with high-status literary works of history, theology and topography. Before Shakespeare only one vernacular playwright had published his works in this way: Ben Jonson, whose Folio in 1616 also included poetry and masques alongside verse and prose drama.

Amid the many controversies about Shakespeare's texts, two related issues are prominent. One is the question of how far Shakespeare intended that his plays be published. For some scholars, the market for printed plays in the period is so uncertain and the pressures of writing for theatrical performance so great that Shakespeare shows no interest in the print afterlife of his dramas and does not involve himself in the process of publication. Others have suggested that the length of some of Shakespeare's plays suggests that they cannot have been performed in full, and that therefore they represent extended versions for reflective reading.

The other question concerns those plays which exist in two or more distinct printed forms. How do we adjudicate between the claims to authority of, say the quarto text of *King Lear* published in 1608, and that included in the 1623 First Folio, when the two texts differ not only in their titles (called a 'history' and a 'tragedy') and their attribution of the final lines (to Albany and to Edgar respectively) but also in hundreds of minor and several major aspects? For many recent scholars the divergence between the two texts is evidence that Shakespeare revised his own play, systematically working through both verbal details and structural design: the logical result is that there is not one but two distinct *King Lears*. The same may well be true of *Hamlet*, where the earliest printed text (1603) has its most famous line in an unfamiliar place and an unfamiliar form: 'To be or not to be – ay, there's the point'. Censorship has often been suggested as a reason for differences in the early texts of *Richard II*. In the case of *King Henry V*, the quarto text may represent a version prepared for a particular theatrical occasion. Many of Shakespeare's plays that exist in both quarto and folio versions exhibit differences which may be variously due to authorial revision, theatrical exigency, the nature of the underlying printers' copy, or other factors in the transmission to print. For this reason, modern editions of Shakespeare are all slightly different, because their editors take a different view of the provenance and significance of these aspects of the early texts.

Shakespearean apocrypha

From relatively early in Shakespeare's writing career works not now believed to be his were attributed to him (the so-called Apocrypha). Sometimes this was explicit, as in *The Yorkshire Tragedy* which was printed with the designation 'Written by W. Shakespeare' (1608; it is now generally attributed to Middleton, although some scholars still believe Shakespeare had at least a hand in it). On other occasions the suggestion was implicit: *The Lamentable Tragedy of Locrine* was printed in 1595 as 'Newly set forth, overseen and corrected, by W. S.' (no other author has been firmly identified). Both these plays, plus *The London Prodigal*, *Sir John Oldcastle*, *The Puritan Widow* and *The History of Thomas Cromwell*, were added to the Shakespeare Folio (along with *Pericles*) in its third edition of 1663/4, but there has been little critical support for this post hoc attribution.

The cases of *Pericles* and *The Two Noble Kinsmen*, now known to be at least partly by Shakespeare, have made it difficult to hold the line that John Heminge and Henry Condell, two actors remembered in Shakespeare's will, were in the best position to know the extent of his canon, and that therefore everything was gathered together in the First Folio in 1623 – since neither of these plays was included. A number of plays have created speculative interest, although there is no external evidence to suggest that any of them is by Shakespeare.

Most interesting, perhaps, is a manuscript play which was probably never performed, '**The Book of Sir Thomas More**'. This play by various hands depicts Thomas More's role in calming a London riot against immigrants, and then his stoic refusal to submit to King Henry VIII's will despite the pressure put on him by his family. One section in particular, known by scholars as 'Hand D', is often attributed to Shakespeare. It gives More (who also appears, briefly, in Shakespeare and Fletcher's *King Henry VIII*) a rousing speech about tolerance which encourages the rioters to imagine themselves as refugees in an inhospitable land. Probably because this material was rather too topical in early modern London – the marks of the Master of the Revels, the Elizabethan censor, suggest this – the play was shelved, although it was evidently revised around four years after its first composition in 1600. The play has had a small number of recent revivals, and was performed in modern dress at the RSC in 2005, directed by Robert Delamere.

Perhaps the strongest case has been made for *Edward III*, anonymously published in 1596, a play about the eponymous king's wars against the Scots and the French and his wooing of the married Countess of Salisbury. The play was directed by Anthony Clark at the RSC in 2002 and has been edited for the New Cambridge Shakespeare by Giorgio Melchiori (1998). It has also been suggested that two anonymous history plays, *Thomas of Woodstock*, a sort of prequel to *Richard II*, and *Edmund Ironside*, should also be attributed to Shakespeare. One of the most controversial attributions has been not of a play but a poem, *A Funeral Elegy*, printed in 1612 as 'By W. S.', which was attributed to Shakespeare on the basis of computer-aided stylometry and therefore included in several collected editions of Shakespeare's plays during the 1990s. It is not now generally considered to be by Shakespeare – and even those who maintain it is don't think it is very good.

Shakespeare's language

Elizabethans often talked of going, not as now, to 'see' a play, but to 'hear' one. As the modern theatre director Richard Eyre has put it, 'the life of the plays is in the language, not alongside it, or underneath it. Feelings and thoughts are released at the moment of speech.' That language might be one of the most important aspects of the play-going experience – not merely a vehicle for plot or characterisation, but a thing in itself – can help us to get hold of the purpose of the density and richness of Shakespeare's dramatic language. Then, as now, Shakespeare's language must have seemed distant, estranged from the everyday, full of unfamiliar vocabulary or words used in ways or combinations that were puzzling or allusive. Then, as now, most people would have found paraphrasing every image or line of Shakespeare difficult, even while the overall sense or tone was clear. So we need to trust to enjoy Shakespeare's elaborate dramatic language rather in the ways we might enjoy music or other non-representational art forms, than only in the ways we might enjoy the sparser, more realist prose style of modern fiction or journalism.

Shakespeare has, of course, the capacity to write strikingly idiomatic or contemporary-seeming lines. The exchange from *Titus Andronicus* in which, seeing Tamora's newly delivered infant, Chiron accuses 'Thou hast undone our mother', to be met by Aaron's riposte 'Villain, I have done thy mother' (4.2.75–6) is simple and darkly comic. But the reply is pleasing in part because of its rhetorical structure, repeating the rhythm and form of the statement to redirect its angry charge. Rhetoric, the art of pleasing and persuasive language, was a crucial part of grammar school education, and Shakespeare would have learned this well.

At other times Shakespeare's language can be knotty and oblique. The opening scene of *Cymbeline* or the first speeches of the Duke in *Measure for Measure* are examples of forced word order and compressed syntax, but for dramatic effect. The Duke, for example, is explaining why he is abdicating his office in Vienna – but not really explaining: the language is intended to obfuscate. Although some Shakespearean words and phrases are obscure only to us and would have been comprehensible to their first hearers, for the most part, linguistic difficulty in Shakespeare is expressive of the character's pomposity, evasiveness or mental disturbance, or of the ineffability of what is being expressed – not of our stupidity.

Much of Shakespeare's dramatic work is in the form of iambic pentameter blank verse. Iambic pentameter means that each line has ten beats, with the dominant rhythm unstressed/stressed ('because' or 'today' are iambic words, with the stress on their second syllable). 'Blank' verse is unrhymed, although there is noticeable use of couplets in early plays such as *King Richard II* or *A Midsummer Night's Dream*, and the sense of conclusion in a rhyming couplet meant it was often used to close a scene. But the cantering da-dum da-dum rhythm quickly becomes monotonous, and Shakespeare often varies it. Like the beat in a jazz set, the variations draw attention to themselves. When Richard, Duke of Gloucester opens the play *King Richard III* with the famous line 'Now is the winter of our discontent' (1.1.1), part of the power of that arresting opening is the inverted iamb at the beginning, with the stress on the first syllable 'Now'.

Earlier plays tend to use the pentameter form in an explicit way, matching the syntactic unit to the metrical one and tending to end each line with a punctuation mark. Later plays make more use of the technique of enjambment – where the sense of the phrase runs over the line break and so no pause marks the end of the pentameter. But it would be wrong to see Shakespeare's career as a progression from more artificial forms of writing to a more naturalistic style: rhetorical patterning and poetic compression continue to be significant aspects of his craft across the two decades of his theatre work. Shakespeare also writes in prose – not only, as is sometimes asserted, for lower-status characters. Some of the most famously rhetorical speeches, such as Shylock's impassioned 'Hath not a Jew eyes' (3.1.46), are in prose, demonstrating that it can be as finely modulated and poetic as verse.

Shakespeare's vocabulary was extensive, although recent research suggests that it was not exceptional by modern standards, and that previous estimates of his coinage of new words may have been distorted by familiarity with his works over those of his contemporaries. However, what is noticeable is the range of his subject matter, from the specialist nautical vocabulary of the beginning of *The Tempest* to his mocking echo of fashionable neologisms (new words) in Hamlet's letter to Ophelia. The opening of the film *Shakespeare in Love* (dir. John Madden, 1998) shows a Shakespeare walking through a verbally hectic and inventive London soundscape, with a professional ear out for the language of preachers, street-sellers and brawlers, and it seems a likely scenario: the playwright's gift for capturing spoken cadences and his semantic attentiveness owe as much to the richness of contemporary language as to the rhetorical treatises of the grammar school curriculum.

Further reading

There is, of course, a huge literature on Shakespeare. This section is divided into general introductory studies and then some more specialised titles under different headings. Each of these titles in turn makes further suggestions.

Introductory books

Margreta de Grazia and **Stanley Wells** (eds.), *The New Cambridge Companion to Shakespeare* (Cambridge University Press, 2010)

David Scott Kastan (ed.), *A Companion to Shakespeare* (Oxford: Blackwell, 1999)

Laurie E. Maguire, *Studying Shakespeare: A Guide to the Plays* (Oxford: Blackwell, 2004)

Emma Smith, *The Cambridge Introduction to Shakespeare* (Cambridge University Press, 2007)

Shakespeare's biography

David Bevington, *Shakespeare and Biography* (Oxford University Press, 2010)

Katherine Duncan-Jones, *Shakespeare: An Ungentle Life* (London: Methuen, 2010)

James Shapiro, *1599: A Year in the life of William Shakespeare* (London: Faber & Faber, 2005)

Shakespeare's theatre

Andrew Gurr, *The Shakespearean Stage 1574–1642* (4th edn, Cambridge University Press, 2009)

Tanya Pollard, *Shakespeare's Theater: A Sourcebook* (Oxford: Blackwell, 2004)

Tiffany Stern, *Making Shakespeare: From Stage to Page* (London: Routledge, 2004)

Modern performance

Judith Buchanan, *Shakespeare on Film* (Harlow: Pearson Longman, 2005)

Barbara Hodgdon and W. B. Worthen (eds.), *A Companion to Shakespeare and Performance* (Oxford: Blackwell, 2005)

John O'Connor and Katharine Goodland, *A Directory of Shakespeare in Performance 1970–2005* (Basingstoke: Palgrave Macmillan, 2007)

Sarah Stanton and Stanley Wells (eds.), *The Cambridge Companion to Shakespeare on Stage* (Cambridge University Press, 2002)

Shakespeare in print

Eugene Giddens, *How to Read a Shakespearean Play Text* (Cambridge University Press, 2011)

David Scott Kastan, *Shakespeare and the Book* (Cambridge University Press, 2001)

Andrew Murphy, *Shakespeare in Print: A History and Chronology of Shakespeare Publishing* (Cambridge University Press, 2003)

Shakespeare Quartos Archive: www.quartos.org; Folio facsimile online http://internetshakespeare.uvic.ca/Library/facsimile/overview/book/F1.html

Shakespeare's language

David Crystal, *'Think on My Words': Exploring Shakespeare's Language* (Cambridge University Press, 2008)

Frank Kermode, *Shakespeare's Language* (Hamondsworth: Penguin, 2001)

Russ McDonald, *Shakespeare and the Arts of Language* (Oxford University Press, 2001)

Simon Palfrey, *Doing Shakespeare*, 2nd edn (London: Arden, 2011)

Shakespeare criticism

Marjorie Garber, *Profiling Shakespeare* (New York and London: Routledge, 2008)

Russ McDonald, *Shakespeare: An Anthology of Criticism and Theory 1945–2000* (Oxford: Blackwell, 2003)

Gary Taylor, *Reinventing Shakespeare: A Cultural History from the Restoration to the Present* (London: Viking, 1991)

Stanley Wells and Lena Cowen Orlin (eds.), *Shakespeare: An Oxford Guide* (Oxford University Press, 2003)

Index

Italic numbering references illustrations.

Index